Water and the Law. Water Management in the Statutory Legislation of Later Communal Italy (Thirteenth and Fourteenth Centuries)

ARCHAEOPRESS

Water and the Law

Water Management in the Statutory Legislation of Later Communal Italy (Thirteenth and Fourteenth Centuries)

Francesco Salvestrini

Archaeologies, histories, islands and borders in the Mediterranean 15

Archaeopress Archaeology

This book is part of the Italian PRIN (*Progetti di rilevante interesse nazionale* – projects of national interest) 2022 scheme, Prot. 2020S8K2Z3, "*Redde rationem*". *Order, calculation and reason in the societies of late Medieval Mediterranean Europe*. It has been supported by the Erasmus+ Call 2018 European project *University Network for Cultural Heritage – Integrated Protection, Management and Use* (UNINET), and the Department SAGAS (Storia, Archeologia, Geografia, Arte e Spettacolo) of the University of Florence.

In Loving Memory of my Mother

Archaeopress Publishing Ltd
Summertown Pavilion
18-24 Middle Way
Summertown
Oxford OX2 7LG
www.archaeopress.com

ISBN 978-1-80327-736-3
ISBN 978-1-80327-737-0 (e-Pdf)

Cover: Verona, Fontana 'Madonna Verona', 14th c. from reclaimed Roman materials.

This book is available direct from Archaeopress or from our website www.archaeopress.com

Limina/Limites

Archaeologies, histories, islands and borders in the Mediterranean (365–1556)

An Archaeopress International Series

Series Editors

The title, subtitle, and chronological span of the series require a few words of explanation. In the first place, the title 'Limina/ Limites' echoes the clear assonances between the root of two Latin words that respectively indicate 'thresholds' and 'boundaries' (and thus 'frontiers'), as well as that of the Greek word for 'harbour' (λιμήν), which, for an island – and, more broadly speaking, for any coastal city – is both a point of connectivity and a boundary of isolation.

Islands and boundaries/borders are two of the many possible keys through which we can study the post-Classical Mediterranean. Ever since the Mediterranean ceased to be a great Roman 'lake', that same Sea became an often-uncrossable boundary that both separated and protected the many worlds that developed in different ways and at a different pace along its extensive coast. At the same time, however, the Mediterranean continued to be a unifying element: it provided a shared identity to communities that were culturally and geographically distant; and it could still be crossed to reach other frontiers, and even beyond.

From this point of view, islands and borders, forming connecting lines and lines of separation, and offering unified identities but also socio-cultural diversities, can become spaces for reflection. As such, they are ideal for disciplines that seek to understand the past but also aim to make much more widely available the tools with which to interpret some of the basic needs of the contemporary world.

The subtitle – with all nouns in the plural – alludes to the need for a multiplicity of different approaches. Today, history and archaeology – especially in the Mediterranean – are understood as multiple disciplines – disciplines that search not so much for an a priori monolithic, specific definition, but rather for an exploration of the limits that must be overcome and the intersection points that need to be exploited.

The chronological span, 365–1556, providing a long-term vision, is essential for exploring in timedepth the multiple themes of study. AD 365, or, more precisely, the 21st of July 365, the day of the most violent tsunami documented in the literary sources, marks the moment at which, in the midst of transformation of the ancient world, the Mediterranean seems to reclaim its physical centrality. This was due to the devastating effects of this natural disaster and, above all, to its global visibility, as is evident from the many different witnesses describing the event, from both the eastern and the western shores of the Mediterranean. At the other end of the chronological span, January 16th, 1556, the day of the coronation of Philip II of

Spain, symbolically marks the date on which the Mediterranean enters contemporary historiography, as understood through the vision of the historian Fernand Braudel and his rewriting of the rules of historiographical analysis, pursuing directions that often cross paths with archaeology.

The Management Structure

Series Editors, who have conceived the series and who have the task of overseeing the production of the volumes, through mediation, selection and peer reviewing. Their interests and expertise span Late Antique to Medieval settlement, urbanism, trade, religion, economics, and society:

Associate Editors

Scientific Committee, which proposes themes, authors and texts for publication, and is formed by Khairieh Amr, Ignacio Arce, Thadeusz Baranowski, Fabrizio Benente, Dario Bernal Casasola, Andrzej Buko, Neil Christie, Giovanni Curatola, Nathaniel Cutajar, Elie Essa Kas Hanna, Mario Gallina, Juan José Larrea, Rossana Martorelli, Alessandra Molinari, Dominic Moreau, John Moreland, Etlveni Nallbani, Michele Nucciotti, Hamlet Petrosyan, Konstantinos Politis, Natalia Poulou, Stephan Schmid, Pier Giorgio Spanu, Giuliano Volpe and Chris Wickham.

The *Limina/Limites* series publishes peer-reviewed conference and workshop proceedings, as well as monographs and collective works that respond to a Mediterranean-wide, multi-facetted and long-term approach.

We look forward to your suggestions, proposals, and manuscripts, as well as general support for this important venture that will give fresh voice and impetus to Mediterranean studies from the Late Classical to the Late Medieval period.

All the volumes have a double-blind peer review.

Miguel Ángel Cau Ontiveros, Demetrios Michaelides, Philippe Pergola, Guido Vannini, Enrico Zanini

Limina/Limites

Archeologie, storie, isole e frontiere nel Mediterraneo (365–1556)

An Archaeopress International Series

Series Editors

Miguel Ángel Cau Ontiveros, Demetrios Michaelides, Philippe Pergola, Guido Vannini, Enrico Zanini

Titolo, sottotitolo e ambito cronologico di una serie editoriale richiedono qualche parola di spiegazione da parte dei curatori. Il titolo gioca evidentemente sull'assonanza della radice delle parole latine che indicano rispettivamente soglie e confini, dunque frontiere, con quella della parola greca che indica il porto, che per un'isola – e in senso lato per ogni città che si affacci sul mare – è al tempo stesso una soglia di connettività e un confine di isolamento.

Isole e frontiere sono due delle tante possibili chiavi di lettura per provare a studiare il Mediterraneo post-antico. Da quando cessa di essere un grande lago romano, il Mediterraneo diviene una frontiera spesso invalicabile, che separa e protegge reciprocamente i tanti mondi che si sviluppano con ritmi e forme diversi lungo le sue coste. Al tempo stesso però il Mediterraneo continua ad essere un elemento di unità: fornisce una identità condivisa a comunità culturalmente e geograficamente distanti; può essere attraversato per spingersi verso, e al di là di, altre frontiere.

Isole e frontiere, linee di connessione e linee di separazione, identità unitarie e molteplicità socioculturali divengono da questo punto di vista spazi di riflessione per discipline volte alla conoscenza del passato, ma che intendono mettere a disposizione della collettività strumenti per interpretare alcune esigenze fondamentali della contemporaneità, risolvendo, ad esempio, in termini di 'Archeologia Pubblica' spunti, risultati ed esiti delle ricerche proposte o almeno di alcune di esse, fra ricerca pura e ricerca applicata.

Il sottotitolo, tutto al plurale, allude alla necessità di una molteplicità di approcci diversi. Storia e archeologia – a maggior ragione nel Mediterraneo – sono discipline che appaiono oggi declinabili solo in forma plurale, alla ricerca non di una monolitica definizione disciplinare a priori, ma di un'esplorazione di limiti da superare e di punti di intersezione da sfruttare. Luogo di incontro tra le discipline non può che essere il territorio, inteso come prodotto della interazione tra culture e natura: unità minima di osservazione del fenomeno storico e unità minima di contestualizzazione delle tracce archeologiche.

Le date di riferimento (365–1556) – in un'ottica di 'lungo periodo' – sono sembrate ai curatori una possibile conseguenza logica delle premesse e possono quindi rendere più esplicito il progetto. Il 365 – per la precisione il 21 luglio del 365, giorno del più violento maremoto narrato dalle fonti letterarie – segna il momento in cui, nel bel mezzo della trasformazione del mondo antico, il Mediterraneo riconquista, quasi per metafora, la sua centralità fisica, fatta di onde e di venti, dando vita a un fenomeno epocale, per i suoi effetti disastrosi e soprattutto per la sua visibilità globale, come dimostrano i tanti testimoni diversi che dalle sponde orientali e occidentali descrivono lo stesso evento con lingue e voci differenti. Il 1556 – per la precisione il 16 gennaio 1556, giorno dell'incoronazione di Filippo II di Spagna – segna simbolicamente la data in cui il Mediterraneo entra nella storiografia contemporanea attraverso la grande lezione di Fernand Braudel, riscrivendo le regole del gioco storiografico in una direzione che ha molti punti di intersezione con l'archeologia.

Limina/Limites accoglie ormai atti di convegni e seminari, singole monografie e studi collettivi che, indipendentemente dalla loro origine disciplinare, si propongano come obiettivo l'integrazione di fonti e sistemi di dati diversi in funzione di una ricostruzione globale orientata alla lunga durata e alla dimensione spaziale mediterranea.

Tutti volumi sono sottoposti a una doppia peer review anonima.

Limina/Limites

Archéologies, histoires, îles et frontières de Méditerranée (365–1556)

Titre, sous-titre et arc chronologique d'une collection éditoriale ont besoin que leurs responsables s'en expliquent. Le titre joue à l'évidence autour de l'assonance des racines des mots latins qui indiquent à la fois des lieux de passages et des limites, donc des frontières, comme pour le mot grec qui indique le port, lequel représente, pour une île -et plus largement pour toute ville qui donne sur la mer- un lieu de connexion et à la fois une limite qui isole.

Iles et frontières sont deux des innombrables clés de lecture pour tenter d'ouvrir les portes de l'étude de la Méditerranée post antique. A partir du moment où elle cesse d'être un grand lac romain, la Méditerranée devient une frontière parfois insurmontable, qui sépare et protège réciproquement les nombreux mondes qui se développent à des rythmes et sous des formes différentes le long de ses côtes. Au même moment, la Méditerranée continue à être un élément d'unité : elle fournit une identité partagée par des communautés culturellement et géographiquement distantes ; elle peut être traversée pour aller vers, et au-delà, d'autres frontières.

Iles et frontières sont à la fois des lignes qui unissent et qui séparent, des identités unitaires et des multiplicités socio culturelles. Elles deviennent ainsi de vastes espaces de réflexion pour des disciplines tournées vers la connaissance du passé, mais qui entendent mettre à la disposition des collectivités des instruments pour interpréter certaines exigences fondamentales du monde contemporain, en résolvant, par exemple, en des termes d''Archéologie publique', des pistes, des résultats et des issues pour les recherches proposées, ou du moins pour une part d'entre elles, entre recherche pure et recherche appliquée.

Le sous-titre, entièrement au pluriel, est une allusion à la nécessité d'une multiplicité d'approches différentes. Histoire et archéologie – à plus forte raison en Méditerranée – sont les disciplines qui apparaissent devoir être aujourd'hui déclinées au pluriel, non pas à la recherche a priori d'une définition disciplinaire monolithique, mais qui doivent explorer les limites à dépasser et les points de rencontre à exploiter. Le lieu de rencontre entre les disciplines ne peut qu'être le territoire, entendu comme le produit de l'interaction ente cultures et nature, à savoir des unités minimales où contextualiser les traces archéologiques.

Les dates de référence se situent dans une optique de longue durée et se sont imposées comme l'une des conséquences logiques possibles de notre postulat de départ, pour rendre plus explicite encore notre projet. L'année 365 – et pour être plus précis, le 21 juillet 365, jour du raz-de-marée le plus violent qu'aient jamais rappelé les sources littéraires – marque le moment où, au beau milieu de la transformation du monde antique, la Méditerranée reconquiert, de manière quasiment métaphorique, sa centralité physique, faite de vagues déchaînées et de vents violents, pour donner vie à un phénomène qui marque cette époque par ses effets désastreux et surtout par la visibilité globale qu'il acquiert, comme le prouvent le grand nombre des témoins qui décrivent les dévastations de ce même phénomène, depuis les rives orientales et occidentales, en des langues et avec des voix différentes.

L'année 1556 – et pour être plus précis, le 16 janvier 1556, jour du couronnement de Philippe II d'Espagne – marque symboliquement la date retenue pour l'entrée de la Méditerranée dans l'historiographie moderne à travers la grande leçon de Fernand Braudel, en réécrivant les règles du jeu historiographique dans une direction qui a de nombreux points d'intersection avec l'archéologie.

Limina/Limites accueille désormais à la fois des actes de congrès et colloques, de séminaires, des monographies et des études collectives lesquelles, indépendamment de leur discipline d'origine, ont pour objectif l'intégration de sources et de systèmes, autour de données différentes, en fonction d'une reconstruction globale, orientée vers la longue durée et la dimension de l'espace méditerranéen.

Tous les volumes sont soumis à une double évaluation anonyme.

Contents

List of Figures

Introduction

A recent report by the World Meteorological Organization updated to January 2022 showed that around 11% of the world's population has no access to sufficiently safe sources of water. In addition, drought in some regions of Africa, Central Asia and the American continent is hastening the expansion of the desert belts and is causing serious difficulties in a growing number of countries, thereby contributing to migratory activity among so-called climate refugees, triggered elsewhere by ever more intense and frequent flood episodes.[1] Furthermore, sustainable use of water resources and the need to limit the damage caused by floods have long been problematic for the regions and societies of southern Europe. With their long, hot and mostly dry summers, intense rainfall in springtime and autumn, and sudden freezes in winter, Mediterranean coastal areas have all too often experienced issues related to the supply of water and sudden, excessive rainfall. Today, with the march of global warming and soil consumption, they are seeing an intensification of these well-known phenomena.[2]

As far as the Italian territory is concerned, the report of the Italian Institute for Environmental Protection and Research (ISPRA) issued in December 2021 revealed that more than 90% of municipalities across the entire country are affected by acute situations or hydrogeological instability. The report also levelled the criticism that more than eight million people live in areas defined as highly dangerous from this point of view.[3]

Efficient use of water has thus become a dramatically urgent requirement in this post-industrial age.[4] Nevertheless, an analysis of historical sources shows that this issue has a decidedly long history, suggesting that, leaving aside the gradual rise in temperatures, recent critical issues have mainly escalated, exacerbated, and made pervasive the impact of the phenomena that human groups have repeatedly and tragically had to contend with on account of their impact, great or small, on the ecosystem.[5]

Public opinion, environmental associations and government institutions often call for legislative intervention as a means to defend the environment and to protect populations from their own harmful actions. In other words, there appears to be an established idea that only when there is targeted, well-structured legislation is it possible, at least for planning purposes, to protect the natural and social environment. Conversely, critical situations are mostly blamed on what is often called a 'legislative void'. Verifying the validity of this thesis in the contemporary world is beyond the scope of this work.[6] The aim here is to investigate the reasons why this conviction has gradually taken hold, beginning more or less in the thirteenth and fourteenth centuries when, for the first time since the Roman era, Italy underwent a period of widespread rules-setting in which human use of environmental resources, particularly

1 Public.wmo.int/en/our-mandate/water (access October 2023).
2 Cassi and Tinacci Mossello (eds) forthcoming.
3 Triglia, Iadanza, Lastoria, Bussettini and Barbano 2021.
4 McNeill and Engelke 2016. See also Damiani 1994: 9-12; Mocarelli 2011: 83-84, 88-93.
5 Alexandre 1987; Miglio 1989: 63-64; Delort and Walter 2001: 162-171; Sabaté (ed.) 2007; Squatriti (ed.) 2007; Bebermeier, Hennig and Mutz (eds) 2008; Janku, Schenk and Mauelshagen (eds) 2012; Ballut and Fournier (ed.) 2013; Ito, Scaroni and Matsuda (eds) 2017; Ricci 2017; Prodi and Zaccaria 2019.
6 See Kidd *et al.* (eds) 2014; Gentilcore *et al.* (eds) 2023.

water, became subject to regulation. Indeed, by referring to that period we intend to verify the supposed effectiveness of legislation and to assess whether and to what extent it has been a useful means of ensuring access to and proper distribution of water for communities, and flood prevention.

In order to know the structures and the dynamics of the environment in the Middle Ages, scholars frequently refer to legislative texts, which are abundant and detailed on this subject. The usefulness of laws in historiographical investigations should not, however, be evaluated merely in terms of the extent to which rules aligned with or deviated from practice. Getting to know the norms of the past that were established to protect environmental resources can, in fact, be more useful for investigating the will of the ruling classes in this regard and discovering when the idea of a link between the law and protection of resources was first put forward. All the while, it is important to stress that the difficult balance between norms and their application should be traced back to medieval times, the first period from which, as we have said, a relatively large number of written records have come down to us.[7]

This work is part of a larger project pursued for several years now and related to the social impact of statutory legislation formulated in local settings in communal Italy. Specifically, it aims to highlight the intentionality of the ruling classes when it came to managing water resources and regulating piped water, from the perspective of the most recent historiographical considerations on the very meaning of the term 'water'. Indeed, for the legislative sources of the late Middle Ages, this was not considered in relation to its singular identity (that is, as one of the four elements of creation), but rather in a plural sense referring to its quality as clean and dirty, useful or harmful, inland – like rivers – or marine; and therefore water controlled by the public authorities (*aqua publica*), private property, or a resource available to all (*res communis omnium*).[8] In this regard, the book examines and compares the choices made by town and, to some extent, rural governments within the geographical area lying approximately between Rome and the Alps in the final centuries of the Middle Ages. The territory and the period chosen are, as we will see, relatively uniform in terms of their institutions and represent the most urbanised section of medieval Italy, with almost all the major cities of the time. These included: Milan, with a population of over 100,000 before the 1348 plague; Florence and Venice with about 100,000 inhabitants each; Genoa (over 50,000); Bologna, Siena and Verona (about 50,000); Brescia, Lucca, Pisa, Padua, Rome (35/40,000); Pavia, Parma, Perugia, L'Aquila, Ancona (20/30,000).[9] The areas under examination are also home to most of Italy's rivers and water resources, albeit with important internal differences which, we can already say, led to a suspicion on our part that a 'water frontier' existed between the north of the peninsula and the centre. In purely geographical terms, this would have been between continental Italy – the Po area, generically referred to as 'Lombardy' in the past, locked between the Alps and the Apennines – and peninsular Italy and the islands (*Tuscia*, Roman countryside, the kingdom of Naples, Sicily and Sardinia). The two macro-regions were distinct in terms of climate, production, economy and settlements.[10]

---

7 For some recent historiographical overviews concerning various European countries, see Caracciolo 1988; Cortonesi and Montanari (eds) 2001; Armiero and Barca 2004: 45-55; Schenk 2008; Hoffmann 2014; Nanni 2017; Canzian and Grillo 2019; Grillo 2022. On water management, Bevilacqua 2001: 41-46.

8 See Strang 2004; Linton 2010; Cazzola 2021; Fiorentini 2023: 141-142. On the polymorphism of water, Mastrelli 2008: 43-44. See also chapters 4 and 7 of this book.

9 Ginatempo and Sandri 1990: 100, 148, 224; Cherubini 2009: 45-46; Faini, Terenzi and Zorzi (eds) 2023.

10 Cfr. Traina 1992: 13-14; Andenna 1996; Garzella (ed.) 1998.

With these considerations in mind and as a preliminary matter, it is necessary to emphasise that this book is not about how water was used in the Italian Middle Ages, but rather that it examines the attitudes of legislators towards its use, particularly with regard to its supply and to flood prevention. In other words, the aim is to cast light on what, according to legislators in towns and cities and, to a lesser extent, in rural areas, needed to be regulated in water management.[11] On the other hand, the emphasis will not only be on what today's reader can deduce directly from legislative sources of the period, but also on what cannot be found in the records because legislators did not consider it important, even though other evidence confirms its significance for the environmental and social structures of the period.

The first chapter in this volume presents the statutes – the chief sources of law in communal Italy – and their potential to reveal information about the governance strategies of the ruling classes regarding water use and flood prevention. The next section (chapter 2) verifies one of the central hypotheses of the entire work, namely whether there was a 'water frontier' between central and northern Italy in that period. Two chapters (3 and 4) examine urban and rural laws and highlight the complex interrelations between them. Later sections look into the conflicts arising from access to the resource and attempts to resolve them through specific norms (chapter 5); the absolute and relative quality of water (chapter 6); hydraulic machines (chapter 7); waterways and timber rafting (chapter 8); laws aimed at preventing – albeit with profound contradictions – river floods and overflows (chapter 9); and finally, some of the religious and symbolic dynamics linked to the purifying and redemptive properties of water – a sacramental element invoked by legislators as a means for expiating guilt and, at the same time, punishing an offence.

I would like to thank those who have provided valuable information and advice, including: Duccio Balestracci, Federigo Bambi, Michele Campopiano, Dario Canzian, Paola Foschi, Maria Ginatempo, Paolo Nanni, Gerrit Schenk, Lorenzo Tanzini, Guido Vannini, and Gian Maria Varanini. The debt I owe Enrico Faini, my colleague at the University of Florence, regarding the discussion of 'sapiential' authorities and the value of water in the culture of communal Italy is truly immeasurable.

[11] See, in this regard, the considerations of Saragosa 2005: 13-20, 89-90; and Keller and Busch (eds) 1991.

I

Medieval Statutes and Water Management: The Italian Context

1. Why statutes?

It has been variously demonstrated that water management and the relationship between human settlements and inland waters (such as rivers, lakes, wetlands and streams) played a significant role in shaping the development of urban and rural communities in most parts of Medieval and *Ancien Régime* Europe.[1] From the late eleventh to the late fourteenth centuries, in the region usually recognised as 'communal Italy', that is, those areas approximately extending from Rome to the Alps,[2] urban and rural government authorities codified, *inter alia*, the use of water resources and flood management strategies into written legal instruments known as statutes (especially from the late twelfth century).[3]

The Latin term *statutum*, from the verb *statuere* ('to establish, determine') referred to a corpus of written municipal laws and regulations issued in large numbers by major and minor towns and enforced through legitimate coercive power.[4] *Statutum* indicated a municipality's own corpus of legislation: the fundamental law exercised at the local level (*ius proprium*), complementing the *ius commune* (an amalgam of inherited Roman law, the emerging canon of the Church, and feudal law),[5] and on which the current and deliberative community legislation, tied to 'constitutional' principles, firmly depended.[6] As long demonstrated in legal historiography and other fields, the statutes were 'open' texts that could contain reforms, derogations, additions and corrections made in the years following their promulgation. This aspect, moreover, did not affect their status as constitutional norms and did not equate them to the more changeable legislation of the current day.[7]

Before addressing the topic of regulatory water management, it should be noted that, at the time when most of the statutes became established and generalised, communal institutions had already existed for a long time and had evolved profoundly. In the northern areas of the peninsula, in particular, they had to some extent been overtaken, or at least been greatly transformed into oligarchic or seigniorial regimes.[8] The main organs of government, namely the municipal councils, had seen their actual political influence diminish somewhat, although

[1] Febvre 1935; Squatriti 1998; Magnusson 2001; Leguay 2002; Hoffmann 2005; Hoffmann 2014: 196-240; Ciriacono 2018b; Andermann and Schenk (eds) 2020. See also Teti (ed.) 2003.

[2] On the definition of this period as 'communal civilisation', see Hyde 1973: 94-123, 178-198; Maire Vigueur (ed.) 2000; Ascheri 2001; Menant 2005: 80-120; Chittolini 2007; Zorzi (ed.) 2008; Menzinger 2011; Zorzi 2011; Keller 2014; Ricciardelli and Fantoni (eds) 2020; Zorzi (ed.) 2020; Edigati and Tanzini (eds) 2022.

[3] See Balestracci 1992; Balestracci 1994.

[4] I use both the Latin plural *statuta* and the Anglicised term 'statutes' to refer to the legislative codes examined.

[5] See Calasso 1970[2]. An annotated anthology of translated texts is in Cavallar and Kirshner (eds) 2020. *Ius proprium* indicates a municipality's own corpus of statutes and legislation. See Canning 1996: 168-170.

[6] See Bartoli Langeli 1985; Ascheri 1991: 257-285; Chittolini and Willoweit (eds) 1991; Ascheri 1995; Pene Vidari 1999; Ascheri 2010; Zorzi 2010b; Zorzi (ed.) 2013; Loschiavo 2019.

[7] See Kirshner 2005: 322-323; Salvestrini 2019: 33-35.

[8] Pini 1981; Connell and Zorzi (eds) 2000; Zorzi (ed.) 2013; Gamberini and Lazzarini (eds) 2014.

they had retained most of the formal prerogatives of making and reforming laws.[9] Otherwise, the subject we have set out to address, which pertains to the governance of environmental resources, had not been transformed too greatly by the changing political regimes and the evolution of the institutional system, since the supply of water, the use of running water as motive power, irrigation systems and flood defences were issues that remained relatively constant over time.[10] From the point of view of environmental resources, the statutes continued to form the political and administrative agenda of the communes, regardless of the transformations to their internal organisation.

Furthermore, the municipal laws concerning these issues were, like many others, rooted in Roman law and the Justinian tradition,[11] which once again came to the fore (mid-twelfth century) after their 'rediscovery' by jurists and legal theorists mainly at the university of Bologna.[12] Jurists became particularly interested in exploring them from the second half of the fourteenth century onwards. Most prominent among these was Bartolus de Saxoferrato who, in his treatise traditionally known as *De fluminibus seu Tiberiadis* (1355), skilfully combined his Romanist knowledge with notions of Euclidean geometry, emphasising how this could prove useful for resolving de facto questions presented to the legislators.[13] This fact also contributed to the enduring, effective stability of water norms – particularly in relation to private law and despite the reformation of the statutes themselves[14] – and to their relatively uniform distribution in the regulatory collections of cities and smaller towns. It is precisely the persistence of the needs and conditions that led to the development of water management regulations and the administration of environmental resources that justifies, perhaps better than other areas of legislative intervention, the long-standing validity of government provisions helping to define the aforementioned 'communal' civilisation.[15]

Statutes gave similar answers to similar problems and did so in many different geographical contexts. They reflected both the specific physical, social, political and cultural characteristics of the local realities for which they constituted the basic law, and the shared legal culture expressed by professional legislators (*statutarii*).[16] In addition to common law literature, and much else besides, these texts presented what has been called 'living law', that is, the concrete interaction between the law and people.[17] They were issued in almost all the towns and cities in the regions considered in the following research, and present a fairly standard format. It should also be added that, for some smaller towns and villages, especially in the thirteenth century – a time when even statutes were still relatively few in number and often hybrid in structure[18] – these sources are not accompanied by others offering the same type

[9] Piergiovanni, 1989; Tanzini 2013; Tanzini 2014; Tanzini 2021b.
[10] For instance, Geltner 2019: 90-91 rightly writes, about Bologna, that after its entry in "its dispotic era [of the lord and papal legate Bertrand du Pouget, 1334] the city's basic administrative structure remained largely intact".
[11] Costa 1919; Astuti 1958: 348-350; Fiorentini 2003; Schiavon 2011; Bannon 2017.
[12] Brundage 2008: 126-162; Rosso 2018: 137.
[13] Cavallar 2010: 93-103.
[14] See Nico Ottaviani 2023.
[15] See Racine 1986; Prosperi (ed.) 1995; Malvolti and Pinto (eds) 2003; Salvestrini 2005; Sznura (ed.) 2010; Calzona and Lamberini (eds) 2010; Canzian and Simonetti (eds) 2012; Takada (ed.) 2020.
[16] Fried 1974; Keller 1988; Ortalli 1999; Chiappa Mauri 2003a: 237-240.
[17] Dani 2013: 57-61, 67-68; Dani 2020: 30; Cazzola 2021: 75-76.
[18] Odorici 1876; Keller and Busch (eds) 1991; Keller 1998; Tedesco 2023: 139.

of information.[19] For these reasons, statutes are perhaps the most fruitful kinds of texts for comparative analysis, on account of their size and structure.[20]

Since the 1950s, research on municipal statutes has no longer been the exclusive domain of legal historians. There has, in fact, been increasing interest in these types of regulatory records among medievalists specialising in a variety of subfields, including economic, cultural, environmental and religious history.[21] This analysis becomes self-explanatory when *statuta* of communal Italy are juxtaposed with similar legal documents from other European regions. For instance, the organised body of norms issued and codified in German-speaking areas had a less doctrinal foundation and an almost exclusively urban matrix (*Stadtrecht*).[22] Furthermore, it was consulted only in exceptional cases and, despite regulating and presiding over collective life, served as somewhat of a theoretical framework.[23] Apparently closer to Italian statutes were the laws of Flemish cities, whose main focus, however, was the regulation of production and trade activities.[24] In these territories even very important cities like Bruges and Ghent were strongly influenced by the authority of the prince, as were their local laws.[25] A decisive combination of urban legislation and provisions dictated by monarchs in parliaments also characterised the Kingdom of Castile (*Partidas*). Although the Crown of Aragon was subject to the much stronger 'bargaining power' of city law, especially in Barcelona and Valencia (*Furs*), city norms were never able to disregard the king's authority.[26] Generally speaking, only Italian municipalities and those of the twelfth- and thirteenth-century French Midi (*Royaume d'Arles*), which were closest to the models of 'Lombard' institutions[27] and part of the shaky political context of the Empire, were able to aspire to and, in some cases, achieve the status of *civitas sibi princeps* (self-governing city) and even obtained recognition to this effect from the imperial vicariate.[28] These cities were, in other words, true city states, entities which, in some cases, exercised full, de facto sovereignty at the local level.[29] Their statutes thus became the fundamental texts regulating the public and private lives of populations, at least until the second half of the fourteenth century.[30]

2. What statutes can say about water management

Despite the fact that the body of normative measures mirrors only part of the landscape of transformations occurring in late medieval Italy, municipal statutes have been taken as concrete evidence of the ambitions of the dominant classes who set the social and environmental agenda

[19] Salvestrini 2003.
[20] See Bonfiglio Dosio 1995.
[21] Toubert 1960; Fasoli 1976: 173; Genicot 1977: 45-55; Ascheri 1991: 257-285; Santarelli 1993; Salvestrini 2000; Salvestrini 2013a.
[22] Szabó 2001: 84-86, 90-91.
[23] Dilcher 2001; Blattmann 2001; Frank 2009.
[24] Blockmans 2001.
[25] Boone 2017; Boone and Haemers 2018: 108-109; Geltner 2019: 149; Hébert 2021.
[26] García Marsilla 2015.
[27] Balossino 2015.
[28] See De Matteis 1981: 42-43; Storti Storchi 1991: 322-324; Canning 1996: 168-170; Zorzi 2013b; Salvestrini 2023a: 22-30.
[29] See, in this regard, Ascheri 2023: 23-26.
[30] Capogrossi Colognesi and Gabba (eds) 2006; Ascheri 2013; Cammarosano 2021; Tanzini 2021a. Some remarks on the comparability of European statutes with legislative systems can be found in Broussais 2018.

for urban and rural spaces.[31] This is also true for water resources and water management.[32] Notwithstanding, since part of the legislation under discussion was written before cities and smaller centres had fully extended their dominion over the countryside, or after they had partially lost it to larger politically dominant cities and territorial lords, this study will not initially examine the already widely investigated subject of legislative and power dynamics between cities and rural areas.[33] Instead, we will try to understand the characteristics of water management legislation in both urban and rural contexts. If anything, we will highlight how choices made in country communities were sometimes later extended to the cities, regardless of the political hierarchies in place.[34]

It is not always clear from the statutory sources that all the norms regarding the use of environmental resources resulted from agreements, negotiations and bargaining between families and social partners, but it is possible to get a glimpse of this from an analysis of the historical-political and historical-territorial framework of the communities producing the texts.[35] Obviously not all government intervention in a territory was determined by statute. The slow move away from rigid constitutional norms – especially after the thirteenth century – and the gradual introduction of more current legislation consisting of resolutions (*deliberationes*, *provisiones*), meeting reports, public notices issued by local lords and so on, meant that political and administrative systems relied increasingly on the newer regulations to govern the management of water resources. However, unlike statutes, this type of source differs considerably from one place to the next and, as we have said, often no longer exists, especially in smaller centres. This makes comparison difficult. Statutes, on the other hand, were almost universally present and retained the original rationales of the planning documents local governments produced. They were on the receiving end of long-term investments, such as those for the construction of aqueducts, canals, water sources, fountains and other infrastructure. They also preserved the spirit of pre-communal local customs regarding the right to draw and exploit water.[36]

From the eleventh to the late thirteenth centuries, northern and central Italy underwent unprecedented, rapid and large-scale urbanisation. According to recent studies, despite the demographic crisis from the late thirteenth century onwards and the plague of 1348, which reduced the population by a third,[37] as many as 20/22% of inhabitants were urban-based during the second half of the fourteenth century: a considerable proportion when compared to other European areas of the time.[38]

Our investigation will bring to light the politics around the fresh supply of water and the conflicts of interest involved in the use of resources in the context of this extensively urbanised area. This is why the discussion will primarily be based on the statutes of urban communities and minor towns, without, however, neglecting examples of legal writings

---

[31] See Cherubini 1985; Rao 2015: 173-177; Geltner 2019: 36, 38-39.

[32] See Bocchi 1990; Keller 2001.

[33] See Grillo 2003; Cengarle, Chittolini and Varanini (eds) 2005; Milani 2009; Salvestrini 2009b; Franceschi and Taddei 2012; Salvestrini 2015b; Wickham 2015; Scharf (ed.) 2022.

[34] See Hoffmann 2007; Fiore 2012; Geltner 2019: 113-114.

[35] See, for example, Milner 2000.

[36] Piccinni 2002; Chiappa Mauri 2003b; Nico Ottaviani 2008: 68; Tanzini 2009; Geltner 2019: 36.

[37] Ziegler 1982^3: 40-62; Cohn 1992: 5-6; *La peste nera* 1994; Cohn 2002.

[38] Ginatempo and Sandri 1990; Chittolini 2010; Rawcliffe 2013: 1.

regarding castles and rural communities. We will refer to compendia of legislation produced both before and after the outbreak of the Black Death, noting that the event appears not to have left a significant mark on the way water use was governed. In this regard, it should be noted that this study follows on from the most recent analyses of natural phenomena and human use of environmental resources in different medieval regions. The concepts of *Great Geographical Divergence* (Europe compared to Asia or Africa), and *Little Divergence* (northern Europe compared to the Mediterranean)[39] have, in fact, become part of historiographical reconstruction and denote, from topological and chronological points of view, the different developmental processes which caused divergences on a global and continental scale. The fourteenth century, in particular, has been re-examined from this perspective, as a time in which responsive action, adaptability and local resilience were required in the face of disasters, famines and epidemics.[40] These were the key elements of the great transition,[41] or the different historical paths that preceded agricultural development in the early modern period and the Industrial Revolution.[42]

The aforementioned research led to a modification and integration of the concept of Medieval Climatic Anomaly or Medieval Warm Period, that is the time of warm climate in the North Atlantic region that lasted from c. 950 to c. 1250. Specific readings to this effect have been conducted by palaeoclimatologists, in particular on the Mediterranean area.[43] The new texts brought to light phenomena of accentuated 'climatic variability' (past global changes), precisely in the final centuries of the Middle Ages and outside of the traditional chronological scans linked to a rigid distinction between the Medieval Climate Optimum and the Little Ice Age of the modern era.[44] Similarly, the distinction between before and after the plague of 1348 is hardly appropriate. The impact of the event is not neglected, but undoubtedly relativised,[45] and, in particular, for the Lombardy area, as an example, almost completely denied in relation to the first epidemic wave.[46]

In this regard, we can note that perhaps other traumatic events that occurred during the period under examination caused a more notable impact on the dynamics of environmental and water management. The first among these and a recent object of focus for scholars[47] was the eruption of the Samalas volcano in Indonesia (1257-60), which had a negative impact on the global climate, in Italy most evidently from 1258 onwards.[48] We can also mention the low pressure vortex that hit the Ligurian sea, Central Europe and northern Italy in July 1342,[49] with exceptionally high water in Venice[50] and severe flooding in Germany, Austria, Hungary,

[39] Pomeranz 2000.
[40] Schenk (ed.) 2017; Rampp, Endress and Clemens (eds) 2020; Dijkman, van Onacker, Hannaford, de Keyzer, Curtis, van Bavel, and Soens (eds) 2020.
[41] Campbell 2016.
[42] Molinari 2016; Carocci 2018.
[43] Lüning, Schulte *et al.* 2019.
[44] See Luterbacher 2001; Mann, Zhang, Rutherford *et al.* 2009.
[45] Luongo 2019; Bailey 2021. For the impact on the Italian rural economy see Cortonesi 2022: 42-48.
[46] Grillo and Menant (eds) 2019.
[47] Grillo 2021a; Bufanio 2022a: 23-26; Bortoluzzi 2022: 82-84.
[48] Campbell 2017; Guillet, Corona, Stoffel *et. al.* 2017; Bauch 2020.
[49] Bauch 2019.
[50] Crouzet-Pavan 1999: 59-61.

Bohemia, Lombardy and Tuscany.[51] Albeit often indirectly, these circumstances influenced the political agenda of the municipal authorities and were reflected in the legislation they produced.

3. What statutes do not say about water management

A study of water and its uses in the Middle Ages would seem to require a look into the relationship between the sources used and the prevailing hygiene, medical and natural philosophical paradigm of Galenism, also called humoralism, which informed contemporary understanding of health and environmental hazards. These elements were undeniably fundamental to the considerations made by theorists. As demonstrated in Leguay's work on medieval France, in Bernat i Roca's on Mallorca in the fourteenth and fifteenth centuries, Rawcliffe's on England, and Coomans's on the Netherlands during the same period, some of the sanitation and 'hygiene' protections implemented for the general public did not start at the height of the modern era, but go back at least to the late Middle Ages and perhaps predate the 1348 plague.[52] This approach was followed for communal Italy particularly by Geltner who, in an exemplary study, investigated several cities and towns for which a wealth of records exists (Lucca, Bologna, Pinerolo), and also used the statutory texts from other areas of the Italian Peninsula for considerations of a more general nature.[53]

We will not delve too much into these topics in the pages that follow, as they are only indirectly reflected in the statutes relating to water management. It is my opinion, in fact, that the norms in the codes regulating waste water and sewage systems, clean drinking water, access for healthy or sick people and animals to springs and drinking troughs, and punishments for polluting rivers are more a response to a demand for harm reduction, protection of communal and private property and social order than all-out conscious planning of hygiene and sanitation conditions; at least not in the way we understand the terms today or the way they were construed by philosophers and physicians in the Middle Ages[54] or by some humanist intellectuals.[55] In fact, the articles of the statutes (*rubriche*) are not short of theoretical considerations, for example, on justice, joint liability, good governance, the need for reform, the origins of law or respect for authority,[56] but are lacking in general references – comparable to those found in texts like, to name one example, the hallowed classic *De architectura* by Leon Battista Alberti – to the protection of health through the provision of clean water.[57] In other

[51] Salvestrini 2017a: 60.

[52] Bernat i Roca 1998; Rawcliffe 2013: esp. 27, 41-45, and, about water, 188-210; Coomans 2019. See also Carriero 2014. An online bibliographical resource is Geltner and Coomans (eds) access October 2023.

[53] See Geltner 2019: esp. 2, 5-31, 34-67 (with special attention to statutes), and 100-112. On Bologna, see also Zaneri and Geltner 2020. In a different perspective, Zupko and Laures 1996: 114.

[54] See Nutton 1981; Federici Vescovini 1989; García-Ballester 1994; Grmek (ed.) 1997; Skinner 1997: 22-39. The following share my interpretation of municipal statutes: Mazzi 1978: 21-26; Zupko and Laures 1996; Morpurgo 2000: 13, 37-38; Chandelier 2013. For a comparison with the same legislation in other territories, see Petaros, Skorobonja, Culina, Bosnar, Frkovic, and Azman 2013.

[55] As shown in Lefebvre 1996. See also Naso 1982: 32-34; Park 1985; Leguay 1999: 48-50; Cavallo and Storey 2013 (with some texts from sixteenth to eighteenth centuries). A different interpretation of this topic is in Geltner 2019: 40, 52, 65-67.

[56] See Dondarini 2003; Tanzini 2001; Tanzini 2021c.

[57] "Need not stress here how important drains are in maintaining the sanitation of the city" (Alberti 1988: 4, 7: 67-68), mentioned in Geltner 2019: 41; see also 47-51, 65-67, 74, and 134-138. Considerations about the preservation of public health seem to emerge from the statute of the Podestà of Pistoia (1296) referred to by Geltner. However, I do not believe that the expression *Quoniam civile est et expedit pro salute hominum* has the precise meaning of public health as we understand it today, nor that it corresponded to the beliefs of physicians and theorists of the time [Zdekauer (ed.)

words, there is no explicit reference to 'hygiene' measures in the laws collected within the statutory *corpora*. Moreover, we must not forget what must have been the oldest 'sapiential' source in this regard for centuries, certainly known to notaries and jurists drafting statutes, as well as to the governing classes, namely the Gospel of Mark: *Nothing that goes into a person from outside can defile him, but the things that come out of a person are what defile him* (Mark 7:15–16). This passage, in my opinion, says a lot about the beliefs of Italian legislators on the inherent dangers of ingesting polluted water.[58]

The only evidence of any notion in the collective mind and, therefore, in the work of the statute drafters of the possible spread of diseases appears to have concerned the state of the air (often referred to in terms of *puza, fetor, fetidus, infectio aeris, malus odor, turpis putredo*),[59] and therefore miasma theory[60] – though in a very general sense and not to the extent of manifest and systematic recourse to 'advice' from 'experts'[61] – and conditions in which food could be sold at market (e.g. with the banning of the sale of animal meat that had not been properly butchered).[62] Norm sources reveal less concern over the risks related to the use of dirty or infected waters, whose discharge into rivers, canals and the sea was authorised with no thought for the fact that the same waters were used for fishing and bathing.[63] Moreover, those political treatises on good governance and the common good that touched on these issues did so by merging the search for bodily health with the pursuit of spiritual salvation and moral rigour, which were considered to be interrelated,[64] and had been since the beginning of the Christian era.[65] Moreover, it should not be overlooked that, although the general culture of the society and ruling classes of the communal age was in many respects broader than that of the earlier urban society, municipal institutions generally did not, with important exceptions, implement pervasive management of the school system, especially for the intermediate levels of education, perceived as essentially a private matter that concerned only the teachers and

1888, repr. 2002: t. III, b. III, 162: 150-151]. Another example cited by the author, the statutes of L'Aquila, which we will also refer to in this work, contains a sentence for those who threw *molza pelliczariorum* (tanning water) 'offending' their neighbours (*unde poxint vicini eorum, et alii transeuntes exinde, ex fetore predictorum offendi*), which, in my opinion, stems more from a desire to protect urban propriety and social peace than to consciously defend the public from the risk of disease [Clementi (ed.) 1977: rubr. 269, 271: 182].

58 "In epoca medievale [...] non si immaginava che l'acqua potesse essere un importante vettore di trasmissione di alcune malattie" (Mantelli and Temporelli 2007: 115).

59 *Neuno artefice possa o debba exercitare o fare infra li muri della cittade alcuna arte o alcuno lavorìo onde nasca puzo* [Bambi, Salvestrini and Tanzini (eds) 2023 *Gli Statuti della Repubblica fiorentina del 1355 in volgare*: t. II: *Statuto del Podestà*: b. IV. rubr. 110: 590].

60 See Fantoni 1990: 115; Vigarello 1996: 59-61, 69.

61 Hoffmann 2007: 309; Geltner 2019: 53-54, 58, 70-71, 74, 76, 79, 81, 88, 97-98; Canzian 2022a: 112. Commenting on a 1389 deliberative source from Lucca that speaks of *puza... che corrompe laire dela cita*, Geltner admits that "the prevention of disease and its spread is probably implicit here" (199, n. 25).

62 *Niuno ardisca di vendere nela città di Firençe carne d'alcuna bestia la quale di sua infermità overo per caso overo di fedita non usata sia morta*, with a clear equivalence between the animal's death from disease and its inappropriate slaughter, therefore regardless of the health status of the livestock [Bambi, Salvestrini and Tanzini (eds) 2023 *Statuti della Repubblica fiorentina del 1355 in volgare*, t. I: *Statuto del Capitano del Popolo*: b. I. rubr. 92: 186]. This is a very frequent area of legislative intervention, to which Geltner strangely does not devote attention.

63 See below in this text. In general: Biraben 1985.

64 See, for example, the political programme of Giovanni da Viterbo's *Liber de regimine civitatum* (mentioned in Geltner 2019: 5-6). See also Sorcinelli 1998: 25-27, 32-42; *La ricerca del benessere individuale e sociale* 2011; Rawcliffe 2013: 89-104 and 222-228 (water use); Smith 2018: 14-17.

65 See, for example, the opposition between 'good' and 'bad' water in Fulgentius of Ruspe (fifth/sexth centuries), Monceaux 1920: 335-339.

families of pupils.[66] There is, therefore, no evidence of widespread theoretical education in what we now identify as 'hygiene protection'.

Thus, we will limit ourselves to pointing out the existence of statutory articles on the pollution of water to show that large part of these requests did not generally come from medical treatises or from the *regimina sanitatis*,[67] which the statutes do not suggest were necessarily known to their drafters or notaries,[68] but from local customs rooted in empirical observations and/or ideas left behind by classical authors in the *ius commune* tradition.[69]

4. Typological and territorial delimitations

The selected corpus of statutes we will examine consists of 183 municipal texts, mainly from the thirteenth and fourteenth centuries.[70] Only a few are from the fifteenth, sixteenth or later, and have been included because they contain and summarise earlier laws. Given the difference in political organisation between the semi-independent cities of northern and central Italy and those administrations that were under the monarchical thumb of the Kingdom of Naples – considering the fact that it had no local dominant city and no institutional and legislative dialectic between cities and towns[71] – we have excluded municipalities in the South and we will refer to some of their legislative texts for comparison purposes only. With this in mind, we will also take in some of the codes of Sardinia. This island, in fact, despite poor levels of local urbanisation, was deeply influenced by the legislation of the cities of Pisa and Genoa, given the strong and prolonged political hegemony these two republics exerted over the four kingdoms (*giudicati*) and cities in the region.[72] This is, by the way, to demonstrate that territorial policy and water management decisions conceived in the heart of communal Italy could be extended to regions which, although politically dependent, were socially, economically and morphologically very different.[73]

Most of the selected *statuta* are written in Latin; only a few are in Italo-Romance or Catalan vernaculars.[74] The corpus mainly includes modern printed editions of medieval texts and some digitised manuscripts. Its numerous and easily accessible published sources have enabled the wide-ranging geographical and chronological scope of this study.[75] However, it is also important to evaluate the skew determined by a greater availability of published texts for some regions than for others. For example, fewer statutes will be examined for Lazio than for Lombardy, Veneto, Piedmont or Tuscany, because more statutes have been published and studied for the latter four regions.

---

66 Petti Balbi 1990: 32-33.

67 Nicoud 2007. On Islamic medicine, Martín-Bueno and Reklaityte 2008: 210-214.

68 On the culture of notaries in communal Italy, see Rosso 2018: 164-165; Salvestrini 2023c.

69 This topic can be extended from the statutes with territorial validity to those of guilds and other corporate institutions. See Doren 1940. 2: 127. See also Grossi 2000^2: 182-190.

70 95 from Northern Italy, 80 from the Centre, 6 from Sardinia, 1 from Sicily, and 1 from Dalmatian coast.

71 Abulafia 1977; Terenzi 2019; Terenzi 2022.

72 Pavoni 1992: 249-254; Polonio 2003: 157-158; Tangheroni (ed.) 2003. On the political organisation of medieval Sardinia, see Ortu 2019^2: 109-126.

73 See Bocchi 1995: 73-75; Gamberini 2021; Seche 2021; Borghero and Salvestrini 2023.

74 On this topic, see Salvestrini and Tanzini 2015; Tanzini 2021d; Salvestrini 2023a; Salvestrini forthcoming a; Salvestrini forthcoming b.

75 Fortunately, most Italian cities and towns have experienced the modern printed edition of their municipal statutes [see Chelazzi 1943-2022; Albini *et al.* (eds) 1998, 2009, 2017; Raveggi and Tanzini (eds) 2001].

Some of the statute norms exemplify interesting hydraulic engineering schemes to run water technologies, which we will look at, focusing particularly on the use of watermills and fulling machines for cloth. Many texts regulate the use of waterways, since rivers were the arteries of the local economy and the medium for long- and short-distance communications. For our discussion we will look at several river cities. Part of the presentation will focus on how municipal authorities tried to avert flooding and protect inhabited centres; following on from that, the book will conclude with an analysis of some of the unfavourable choices which, owing to the overwhelming impact of political and cultural forces, effectively frustrated all normative solutions aimed at preventing natural water disasters.[76]

It is my contention that law codes regulating water resources provide a multidimensional interpretative key to contextualising the complex interactions between political, social and environmental factors. Although the theme of water supply has already been the object of historiographical analysis, the approach has mostly been localised to individual cities and specific territories and, moreover, in isolation from each other.[77] Here I provide a comparative perspective by juxtaposing a broad range of law codes. The aim is for the selected statutory texts to cover a variety of cultural contexts and geographical areas: smaller towns and larger cities, central and northern regions of the peninsula, hilly and lowland locations. Many of the law codes examined here have never been studied before from a water management perspective. One interesting finding of this comparative study regards the use of similar terms to define the same concepts both in Latin and vernacular statutes written in cities and regions considerably distant from each other (for instance *navis*, *stillicidium*, *guaçatorio* and *steccaia*). This testifies to a widely shared, water-related, technical vocabulary and an active network of interconnected professional statute writers, despite cultural, geographical, and political differences.

[76] See Alberth 2000; Canning (ed.) 2004; Matheus, Piccinni, Pinto and Varanini (eds) 2010.
[77] Raggio 1995.

II

Verifying a Hypothesis

1. Environmental structures

By way of introduction, one other aspect should be emphasised. As we have said, through the lens of the water policies included, at least at planning level, in statutory provisions, I believe certain differences are apparent between the choices made by the governments of cities and smaller centres in northern Italy and the policies pursued in the centre of the peninsula; in other words, across the north-south divide of the Tuscan-Emilian and Tuscany-Romagna Apennines, regardless of whether located in hilly, flat, river or coastal areas.[1] We will try to show that these differences were based on heavier public intervention (by the towns' governing institutions and their normative texts) in the supply and distribution of water, and irrigation in areas of central Italy and Sardinia; whereas in the cities and smaller centres of the Po region there was more freedom for private parties to take action without having close connections with local administrative orientations and alignments.

This observation should also be linked – without giving in to excesses of environmental, geographical and climatic determinism[2] – to the greater availability of water in the north (continental Italy) than in the centre and south (peninsular Italy and Sardinia).[3] Indeed, the Po plain is a vast, integrated system with a central collector of water in the form of the Po River, almost 700 kilometres long, which receives more than 140 tributaries, each supplied by lakes and other basins located mainly on the Alpine arc (*Transpadana*) and, in the south, along the northern Apennines (*Cispadana*).[4] An important supply of water also comes from groundwater aquifers, such as the Bacchiglione and Livenza basins in the Veneto area.

Until the nineteenth century, the main stream maintained an average flow rate of around 400 metres per second, which made saltwater intrusion from the delta in the Adriatic Sea relatively limited, enabling extensive canal systems and irrigation of the countryside.[5] This abundance of water was particularly evident in medieval times and in the modern era. Indeed, even in the midst of the eighteenth century, the end section of the great waterway was similar to that of today's Rhine in Germany (about 2,700 cubic metres per second, whereas today it is no more than 1,350), the distance between the banks was significantly greater, and it had far more branches along its entire course.[6]

In the vast depression dug out by the Po, there is also a large section of low hills and high plains closer to the ranges and delimited by the belt of lowland springs known as *risorgive* (natural) and *fontanili* (human-made), which stretches from central Piedmont to the Po-

[1] On the liminal value of this mountain range, see Di Stefano 2012; Foschi (ed.) 2022; Panero and Pinto (eds) 2023.
[2] Acot 2004: xiv-xv, 99-130.
[3] See Day 1984: 683-686; Andreolli 2008: 449; Ciriacono 2020: 74-75.
[4] Strabo 1928: V. 4. c. 212.
[5] See Andenna 2018.
[6] Dell'Oro 2022: 241-243.

Veneto and Friuli area.[7] This belt is roughly 10 to 30 kilometres wide and formed along the line where permeable and impermeable soils meet. Along this stretch can be found all the points where water rises to the surface, due to overflow, causing the water table to emerge. The belt runs along the low Alps (upper line) and also, for a shorter section, along the Tuscan-Emilian Apennines (lower line). Both of these sections of territory appear drier where, in the area south of the subalpine line and north of the sub-Apennine line, water discharge caused by changes in the composition of river drift and by the gentler slope of the terrain, not to mention human intervention often dating far back in time, have scored the countryside with a dense network of long and short waterways.[8] These structures include the two largest canals in Lombardy. The first was the *Naviglio Grande*, which was excavated between 1177 and 1272. It was derived from the Ticino River and led to Milan, irrigating the western part of the region. The second was the Muzza Canal (twelfth and thirteenth centuries), which was derived from the river Adda and crossed the Lodigiano area. Branching from these two large canals were numerous irrigation ditches (*rogge*) that brought water to almost all localities in the plain.[9] The artificial canals were accompanied in medieval times by numerous pools, lowland lakes and marshes, the products of soil subsidence to the right and the left of the Po and along the Adriatic coastline. These areas opened up into sub-regions that were mostly amphibious, such as the river delta itself and the entire Ferrara and Ravenna territories, or were completely marsh-ridden, such as the large Venetian Lagoon and those of Marano and Grado in Friuli, or Lakes Comacchio and Volano in Romagna. Near the Adriatic coast, the valley bottoms were of two types: freshwater and saltwater.[10]

The situation with the water network south of the Tuscan-Emilian and Tuscany-Romagna Apennines is different. Here, in fact, the rivers are generally torrential (although with a much higher flow rate in the past),[11] and are relatively modest in length, given the narrowness of the Italian peninsula. The scarcity of heavy rainfall, except for short periods and sometimes with disastrous consequences, together with an almost total absence of glaciers on the Apennines to retain water during the coldest months and release it in the warm season, have led to difficult-to-resolve problems in Tuscany, Umbria, Marche and Abruzzo regarding the steadiness of run-off and the use of rivers as reserves of water and as waterways.[12] Moreover, the paucity of flat spaces (lower Valdarno between Florence and Pisa, Val di Chiana, middle Tiber valley and the Roman countryside, Tyrrhenian Maremma, Fucino depression in Abruzzo) has severely limited or prevented the formation of springs (*risorgive*), and therefore the accumulation and the slower release of water. This situation also applies to Sardinia.[13] In several regions of central and southern Italy, the supply and storage of water required special characteristics, including the incorporation of buildings and rocky underground structures into settlements, architectural designs and housing modules.[14]

---

[7] Ferrari and Uberti 1979; Fantoni 1990: 104-106; D'Angelis 2021: 69-70.

[8] Cazzola 2021: 19-33, 85-86.

[9] See Di Tullio 2012: 285-287; Roveda 2012: 260-271.

[10] Sassu 1985: 134-135; Bacchi 1988: 187; Pasquali 1995: 11-36, 95-103; Pasa 1999a: 53-54; Cracco Ruggini 2008: 97-100, 108-120; Vergani 2010: 508-509; Bertoncin, Pase and Quatrida 2014; Canzian 2014; Bassani, D'Acunto and Madricardo (eds) 2022; Campopiano forthcoming.

[11] Salvestrini 2005: 13-15.

[12] Rombai 1993: 55-93; Autorità di Bacino, website: http://www.adbarno.it/cont/testo.php?id=11 (access October 2023).

[13] Borghero and Salvestrini 2023.

[14] De Minicis 2020.

In conclusion, the two macro Italian areas we have highlighted differ, with a prevailing regime of concentration – accumulation of water resources in reservoirs and transport infrastructures – in the south, and a prevailing regime of dispersion – given the greater availability of natural resources – in the north.[15] A similar direction is proposed by Maire Vigueur, who draws a distinction between the cities of northern Italy rich mainly in wells, which intercepted water that was not too deep, and the hilly cities of central Italy with numerous fountains that benefited from aqueducts built in the 'Roman style'.[16] This reality, in Mocarelli's opinion, certainly contributed to the shaping of the economic divide between northern and southern Italy in modern and contemporary times.[17] Indirect proof of the situation described also comes from the use of artificial floods as a strategy of war. This was a recurring practice in the Po area up to at least the twelfth century, one which, in Tuscany and central Italy, was adopted rarely and with unsuccessful consequences in the fourteenth and fifteenth centuries.[18] In addition, the use of moats built for defensive purposes close to city walls played a significant strategic role in cities such as Florence, but never as important as it was for communal and Visconti Milan, for example.[19] South of the Apennines the only actual use of water in the military field was the transportation of supplies along rivers, as was the case in fourteenth-century Sardinia.[20] More generally, naval clashes on rivers were recurring forms of battle in northern Italy, but almost completely absent in the centre of the peninsula.[21]

2. A 'frontier' in the ecosystem and regulatory provisions

The situation described diverges from Wittfogel's famous 1957 theory[22] (taken up in the 1980s by Worster),[23] which was centred on the hypothesis of an existing relationship between the presence of irrigation systems and the emergence of centralised political authority. It postulated that, under certain conditions, large-scale irrigation systems lead to centralised coordination and administrative bureaucracies, which, in turn, result in greater political integration.[24] According to this interpretation, flood control in low-lying river valleys was a big incentive for 'state formation' as a way of coping with water scarcity.

As Glick has pointed out, this author's thesis appears valid, in reality, only under certain conditions that presuppose arid regions and large rivers which need to be regulated by strong centralised powers, such as Mesopotamia or Egypt.[25] And indeed, it is important to make all the necessary distinctions between the mostly Asian contexts presented by Wittfogel and the reality of late medieval Italy. Nevertheless, I believe that where there were well-established rules, as in the case of the communes, the centralising intervention of government authorities to organise the supply of water and carry out public works to regulate and facilitate its distribution seems to have been more common in upland areas of central Italy, where water

[15] See Saba 2013: 59.
[16] Maire Vigueur 2023: 226-229, 239.
[17] Mocarelli 2011: 89. Cazzola writes in this regard: "sotto un profilo generale, si può affermare che la creazione del paesaggio agrario italiano dal Medioevo all'età contemporanea è stata condizionata dall'acqua" (Cazzola 2021: 74).
[18] See Salvestrini 2005: 54; Piovan and Hodgson 2019: 105; Pagnoni 2022.
[19] Fantoni 1990: 75-83.
[20] Castellaccio 1990: 95-107.
[21] Settia 1998; Romanoni 2008; Romanoni 2023.
[22] Wittfogel 1957.
[23] Worster 1985.
[24] Discussions of Wittfogel's work are in Bichsel 2016, Campopiano 2017, and Cazzola 2021: 75.
[25] Glick 1970.

was scarce and had to be intercepted before its rapid descent into the valley. Meanwhile, in the flatlands, especially in the Po area, with their complex and extensive hydrographic networks where water flowed slowly but more abundantly along canals and riverbeds, there was more scope for private withdrawals and diversions, hence, for private initiative in the management of the resource. According to Chiappa Mauri, this is the reason why the statutes of important centres such as Cremona and Mantua appear singularly poor in terms of water management.[26]

In addition to this, I believe, the longer history of communal institutions in the towns and cities of central Italy than could be boasted by their northern counterparts meant that municipal magistrates had more time to manage the supply of water, the economic exploitation of rivers, and flood defences, at least until the fifteenth and sixteenth centuries, when the seigniorial regimes began to take over these sectors of social life and gradually removed the governance of water from the sphere of the statutes also in *Tuscia*, Umbria or Lazio.[27]

Obviously, the governing regimes had control over water everywhere, both north and south of the Apennines. This control was part of an *Öffentlichkeit* ('public sphere'), meaning shared space, as well as public/governmental domain.[28] This is clear from the fact that statutes governed the lives of individuals and, as Geltner has rightly pointed out, constantly invaded the 'private' sphere to protect the 'common' good.[29] Geltner's detailed work also highlights that cities and small communities everywhere introduced magistrates (often called *viarii* and in smaller centres *camparii*) who oversaw the use of water resources, among other sectors.[30]

However, although part of the wider agricultural economy, the public nature of water management in central Italy and the private enterprise seen in the Po region did not necessarily generate, as Wittfogel claims, authoritarian regimes similar to the hydraulic civilisations of Asia.[31] If anything, the German scholar's perspective, which places more emphasis on human activity than on geography, could apply to the area under examination, if we consider man's work moulding and modifying the environment, in an attempt to make up for the natural shortage of water, with aqueducts and artificial sources. This is done by drawing on traditions and cultural tendencies belonging to the community and by incorporating into the relatively standardised statutes model additional features that are specific to the local ecosystem and dependent on the availability of resources, and the convictions and demands expressed by the local community to which the rules apply.

The purpose of this book is not to re-assert the well-known fact that water management in central and northern Italy was a political action, just as it was in the British Isles, France, the various contexts of the Iberian peninsula[32] and, most of all, in the Netherlands – which has

[26] Chiappa Mauri 2003a: 240 writes in this regard: "si può affermare che tanto più il contado [lombardo] fosse ricco d'acqua e il rifornimento per gli usi primari agevole, tanto più rattrappite fossero le competenze che trovano espressione negli Statuti".
[27] Cutini Zazzerini 1990; Schenk 2017; Ricci 2017.
[28] On this concept, developed by Habermas for the modern age and extended historiographically to the medieval period, see Habermas 1965; Boucheron and Offenstadt 2011; Geltner 2019: 22-24, 35, 72.
[29] Geltner 2019: 41-47.
[30] On the office of *viarii*, Geltner 2019: 51-65; Cazzola 2021: 78.
[31] This is something the author himself admits underlining that Venice, the Po plain and Holland underwent important changes to their hydrogeological structure without developing government-run 'hydraulic systems' or forms of ownership comparable to those in the East (Wittfogel 1957: 88-90).
[32] Guillerme 1985; Glick 1996; Racine 1986; Delort and Walter 2001; Campopiano and Menant 2015: 301-307; Furió

in fact been compared with the Po valley[33] – where public and private actors squabbled and haggled over the management of a resource that would come to define the country's identity.[34] Our focus will be on the way the interplay of the choices made by a relatively effective public authority, certain traditions, and objective environmental conditions produced different or similar forms of water management interventions at local level. Only a large-scale comparison based on relatively uniform sources from a broad territorial context will shed light on any such interventions.

On the other hand, bearing in mind the differences between the various cities and regions of communal Italy, we will try to ascertain the extent to which the laws collected into statutes reflected specific environmental management programmes, irrespective of their actual implementation.[35] Rather than looking at the effects of the (bio)politics (to use a term coined by Foucault),[36] the focus will be on the programmes, meaning the planning, and therefore on the intentions of the local (bio)power, which is what is most clearly reflected in the legislative sources of *ius proprium*.

2015; Morgan 2017.

[33] Curtis and Campopiano 2013.

[34] Kaijser 2002; TeBrake 2002 (on the relationship between government choices and the conditioning of technological culture); van Dam 2010. See also van der Linden 1984: 667-668, and Mostert 2020, who show, however, that water only became a feature of the Dutch identity during modern and contemporary times.

[35] On the effective application of statutory law, see Geltner 2019: 38-39; Grillo 2021b.

[36] Foucault 1997^2: 73.

III

Legal Norms for Water Management: The Urban Context

1. Water supply

The communal statutory legislation shows that among the primary concerns of municipal governments were: the supply of water for domestic and work purposes (both inside and outside the built environment), well digging, building and protecting water reservoirs, opening and preserving mains and canals, and the management of sources of fresh water.[1]

A key goal of local administrations was to ensure the supply of water to both the urban and rural populations and, more precisely, to town dwellers and farmers settling in areas under the control of a privileged group of families.[2] The fourteenth-century statutes of Milan regulating roads and water stated the paramount necessity for a suitable natural flow of water from the Olona, one of the main rivers in the Lombard region, to power watermills and irrigate fields (*Como se debbe multiplicare l'aqua nel lecto de la Olona*). In the thirteenth century, Bologna, which is located in the Po valley on the northern edge of the Apennine mountains, enacted legislative norms whereby the superintendent of roads and waters (*praepositus stratis et aquis*) would take an oath to oversee the continuity of the water supply to the city. Similarly, the 1265 law of Reggio, the 1327 statute of Verona, the 1359 code of Forlì and the Paduan statute of 1362 (which upheld certain thirteenth-century rules) announced that one of the main responsibilities of the *podestà* (the commune's chief civic magistrate) was to supervise the running of the public rivers, canals and the network of sources of fresh water, and to coordinate their conservation.[3] Bergamo's 1353 statute stated that one of the civic authorities' responsibilities was to oversee the collection and distribution of water resources.[4] Similarly, Parma's municipal governing bodies were required to provide all townspeople with equal access to water.[5] The statute of this Emilian city required the *podestà* to appoint a *dugarolo*, that is, a worker in charge of water conduction, and a notary to record his activities, for each of the gates that opened in the city walls.[6]

In central Italy, the statutes of Rome's popular regime, which date to 1363, stated that the city's magistrates (*marescalli Curie Capitolii*) were required to take care of waterways and, in

[1] For a comparison with pre-industrial England and the court of Savoy, see Rawcliffe 2013: 180-188, and Pibiri (ed.) 2018: 69.

[2] See Guillerme 2015; Maire Vigueur 2023: 223.

[3] Frati (ed.) 1869 *Gli statuti di Bologna*, t. 1. rubr. I: 159-175; Rinaldi (ed.) 1913 *Statuto di Forlì*: b. I. rubr. 32: 69-70; Stella, Farina, and Balestreri (eds) 1992 *Gli statuti delle strade e delle acque del contado di Milano*: rubr. 69, 70: 78-79; Bianchi, Granuzzo, Mariani Canova and Varanini (eds) 1992 *Statuti di Verona*: t. I. b. I. rubr. 231. 232: 242; Pittarello (ed.) 2017 *Statuti di Padova*: b. I. rubr. 1. 3: 97, 108, 110; see also b. II. rubr. 21: 314; Cazzola 2020: 83.84; Simonetti 2022: 159-160; Campopiano 2023: 32.

[4] Forgiarini (ed.) 1996 *Lo statuto di Bergamo*: b. XV. rubr. 23: 310 (*De aqua habenda in fontibus in maiori habondancia quam haberi poterit*).

[5] *Qualiter aqua fontium de Marano debeat dividi, et inter quos* [Ronchini (ed.) 1857 *Statuta Communis Parmae*: rubr. IV: 378]. On Parma's statutes, see Racine 2001; Cazzola 2021: 83.

[6] Ronchini (ed.) 1857 *Statuta Communis Parmae*: rubr. I: 25.

particular, the Claudian Water (*Aqua Claudia*) and the ancient *Aqua Virgo* pipeline, one of the eleven ancient Roman aqueducts, restored during the late Middle Ages and still existing today (**Fig. 1 and 2**).[7]

A clear example of hydraulic engineering and of how rivers were used as a source of hydropower can be seen in the 1276 statute of Verona. It set out the canalisation of the river water bodies of *Fiumicello de Monte Aureo* and extension up to *Campomarcio*, close to the centre of the urban area. This code also decreed that only one master (*unus bonus magister solus*) should set up and be in charge of the water supply and distribution system consisting of a network of moats and pipelines.[8] Verona, whose patron saint, Zeno, is also recognised in liturgical calendars as the protector of freshwater fishermen, is unique among the cases examined in northern Italy. A lowland city close to the Alpine range, its late-medieval constitutional legislation mentions a case of direct intervention taken by the commune for the construction and management of major water supply infrastructure.[9]

In any case, the fact that magistrates had to resort to expert *inçigneriis*, real professionals capable of assisting them in the control of dykes, canals and other hydraulic infrastructures, is a recurrent prescription in the statutes of the Po Valley area during the transition from the thirteenth to the fourteenth centuries. The long heading to the section on the duties of the *podestà* in these matters contained in the Modenese statutes of 1327 demonstrates this.[10] Experts needed to be called in for this sphere of activity, since politicians did not consider themselves to be sufficiently qualified for the requirements they set out in law.

2. Towns and cities of the plains

During the Middle Ages, towns and cities built on level ground, mainly around the Po valley, had similar situations to that of modern-day Venice, in that they could count on a sufficient inflow of water to meet the needs of the local population.[11] These centres and their neighbouring areas were transected by a series of torrents and canals, which facilitated water collection, internal navigation, the use of water-driven machinery and waste disposal. This unusual landscape was the result of the gradual and significant transformation of a hydrogeological environment that was mostly surrounded by wetlands during the early medieval period. The initiative stemmed from the combined wills of lay and ecclesiastical landowners and rural communities.[12] Milan, for instance, had artificial canals, including the so-called *navigli*, built from the thirteenth century onwards at the behest of the ruling classes of the Commune and, later, by the Visconti and Sforza families.[13] Its waters were praised by

[7] Mendoza 2022 *Gli Statuti del Comune di Roma*: b. III. rubr. 131-137: 596-600. During the eighth century Pope Hadrian I had four ancient aqueducts restored at great expense to feed the *cantaro* in the quadriporticus of St. Peter's Basilica (Finch 1991; Ermini Pani 2008: 399-401; Carriero 2013: 49; De Francesco 2017: 57-58). See also Annoscia 2007: 104-105, 113, 161-165; Maire Vigueur 2023: 224.

[8] Sandri (ed.) 1959[2] *Gli statuti veronesi*: t. 1. b. IV. rubr. 173: 633-635; Bianchi, Granuzzo, Mariani Canova and Varanini (eds) 1992 *Statuti di Verona*: t. II. b. IV. rubr. 129: 598-599; t. II. b. V. rubr. 13: 633-634. See also Borelli (ed.) 1977; Saggioro and Varanini 2012; Brogiolo (ed.) 2017.

[9] See also Bianchi, Granuzzo, Mariani Canova and Varanini (eds) 1992 *Statuti di Verona*: t. I. b. I. rubr. 240: 245; Pasa 1999b: 63-67; Canzian 2019: 19.

[10] Campori 1864 *Statuta civitatis Mutine*: b. IV. rubr. 188. See also Cazzola 2021: 86-87.

[11] See Tosi Brandi 2007: 9-11.

[12] Bortolami 1988: 300; Chiappa Mauri 1990: 63-99; Cortonesi 1995: 22-24; Gardoni 2010: 151-160; Saggioro 2012; Campopiano 2013: 380-387; Maire Vigueur 2023: 253-254.

[13] Biscaro 1908; Maire Vigueur 2023: 256-259.

the poet Bonvesin de la Riva at the end of the thirteenth century.[14] On the strength of the imperial concession of rights over the river Oglio obtained in 1329, Cremona had built itself a branch canal, the *Naviglio Civico*, thanks to the actions of Azzone Visconti, lord of the city. The statute of 1339, promulgated four years after the local government had lost its communal autonomy to the lords of Milan, regulated the cleaning of the canals (*dugali*), which tended to become silted. This was to prevent floods and facilitate navigation.[15] Other cities, including Padua, Verona, Parma and Bologna, also featured waterway networks.[16] In particular, the then young communal institutions of Padua undertook major works in 1142 to divert the waters of the Brenta River, with the aim of opening a new river communication route in the direction of Venice. Later, between 1189 and 1201, they built a long hanging canal with landfill, which connected the city to the fortified town of Monselice, a kind of Paduan bridgehead on the Adige River, which became easy to reach by boat as a result of this construction.[17] On the other side of the Apennines, in Florence and Pisa, the river Arno formed a fluvial system made up of tributary streams and artificial trenches.[18]

In northern and central cities, drinking water was supplied from private and public wells and reservoirs. Less frequently, it came from aqueducts, some of which dated to the Roman period.[19] Law codes from early fourteenth-century Modena (Emilia region) established that water flowing from the Apennine hills to the south of the city in the Po valley was to be stored in the commune's cistern located alongside a public road, equidistant from the city's two main gates, ensuring easy access to it.[20] Thus, the norm confirmed the right established in *ius commune* to draw freely from public reservoirs (*ius aquae ductus*). Reservoirs were sometimes called *castella aquae* or *aquatoria*, and many had been in existence since ancient times.[21] Coeval normative legislation from Ravenna (Romagna region) stated that public wells had to be maintained and that the population living in the areas around the infrastructures was responsible for cleaning them in summer and for supplying *mezzine* (buckets used to collect water).[22] The Florence statutes of 1325 likewise required annual cleaning of public and private wells to ensure a sufficient supply of water suitable for human use.[23] The collection of legislation from the Tuscan hill town of Santa Maria a Monte, close to the Arno River valley in the Pisa area (1391) contains stipulations that such maintenance was to be carried out in August, when water basin levels were lower.[24] The 1250 municipal statute of Bologna prescribed that wells were to be fitted with a pulley and an iron chain for collecting water.[25] Pistoia, a city in the Tuscan lowlands with no large rivers nearby, but at the southern foothills of the Apennines, had to rely on aqueducts from nearby centres, such as Montale and Serravalle.[26]

[14] Fantoni 1990: 27-31; Boucheron 1994. See also Chiappa Mauri 1990: 132-162; Greci 1990: 439-441.
[15] *Statuta et ordinamenta comunis Cremonae*: 152: 205-206.
[16] Varanini 1988: 335; Pesci and Ugolini (eds) 1997; Zanotti 2000. See also Pini 1993: 15-38.
[17] Simonetti 2022: 160-168. See also Bortolami 2003; Canzian 2014: 225; Tognana 2019: 44-45.
[18] Redi 1991; Salvestrini 2005; Salvestrini 2009a; Salvestrini 2012.
[19] Salvestrini 2016.
[20] Vicini (ed.) 1929-32 *Respublica Mutinensis*: 143.
[21] Costa 1919: 54-55; Fiorentini 2003: 56-57; Capecchi 2012; Maire Vigueur 2023: 224-226. See the *aquatoria* mentioned in Caprioli (ed.) 2008 *Lo statuto della città di Rieti*: t. III. rubr. 32: 204-206; t. IV. rubr. 7. 47. 60: 291-292, 311-312, 317-319.
[22] Pasolini (ed.) 1868, repr. 1985 *Gli Statuti di Ravenna*: t. V. rubr. 74, 78: 119.
[23] Caggese (ed.) 1910. Pinto, Salvestrini and Zorzi (eds) 1999 *Statuti della Repubblica Fiorentina*: t. I: *Statuto del Capitano del Popolo*. b. IV. rubr. 9. 26. 27: 163, 174.
[24] Casini (ed.) 1963 *Statuto del Comune di Santa Maria a Monte*: rubr. 99: 133.
[25] Frati (ed.) 1869 *Gli statuti di Bologna*: t. 1. rubr. 9: 404.
[26] Zdekauer (ed.) 1888. Nelli and Pinto (eds) 2002 *Statutum Potestatis Comunis Pistorii*: b. I. rubr. 16: 21-22; b. I. rubr. 21: 23-25. See Berti and Landi (eds) 2019: 53-55.

The regulatory norms found in the municipal *Breve et ordinamenta Populi Pistorii* of 1284 stated that the network of urban trenches, conduits and canals (*viae circularum*) were to be supplied continuously with water from mountain streams.[27]

Normative regulations of the commune of Venice (the 1242 statutes survive in a manuscript datable to 1281) present an unusual scenario.[28] In the medieval city, water management was about urban metabolism of fresh water intake and the flushing of salt water canals.[29] The need for fresh water was met by numerous wells and rainwater cisterns located in *campi* and *campielli* (squares).[30] The supply system involved filtering rainwater through sand. The Serenissima ordered the digging of no fewer than 50 cisterns in 1325 alone.[31] At the time, water resource management was a strictly internal issue for the city authorities, as Venice did not have large extra-territorial dominions to administer. It was only with the acquisition of the *Terraferma* (Veneto region), from the early fifteenth century onwards, that the city provided itself with stable magistrates in charge of controlling the water supply. In particular, the *Savij a le Aque* derived their origin from a 1415 decree, whereby the *Consejo dei Diese*, the supreme criminal and police authority, ordered the establishment of a board of six magistrates, whose duties included overseeing the maintenance and defence of the lidos, the harbour inlets, and excavation of inland canals.[32] On the other hand, it was in fact water that ensured Venice's total independence. According to local jurists interpreting Roman law, the Venetian government had no higher authority precisely because the city was built on the waters of the sea and its shores (*litora*). Being by definition *res communes omnium*, the property of all men,[33] shores were prone to falling under the dominion of anyone who erected buildings there (it was not possible on *res publicae*, which did not belong to everyone, but to the organised community that was the 'state').[34] We should also remember that a new conception of property law had begun to gather pace from the twelfth century, whereby possession was no longer perceived as existing in its natural state, and thus the consequence of God's will, but rather only as the result of man's desire for appropriation.[35]

Nevertheless, the Venice government did not bother to promulgate official statutory measures on the subject of freshwaters. It is noteworthy that in the 1242 statutes the only reference to the topic is the ban on hindering the flow of water in canals.[36] It is safe to assume that the existence of non-statutory norms and a well-designed system of water tanks and wells –

[27] Zdekauer (ed.) 1891. Nelli and Pinto (eds) 2002 *Breve et ordinamenta Populi Pistorii*: II. b. I. rubr. 51: 23.

[28] See Salvestrini and Tanzini 2015: 278-279. On the previous Venetian regulations, Pitzorno 1913.

[29] Ravegnani 2020: 13-14.

[30] Rizzi 1982.

[31] See Crouzet Pavan 2019.

[32] See Besta 1899: 159, 161.

[33] According to the *summa divisio* of the jurist Marcianus accepted in the *Digesta*, *res* were divided as follows: 1) *res communes omnium*, belonging to everyone by natural law; 2) *res publica*, belonging to the Roman people; 3) *res universitatis* belonging to the community; 4) *res nullius* – such as wild animals – belonging to no one, among which, as we know from another fragment, Marcianus also included *res sacrae*, *religiosae* and *sanctae*; 5) *res privatae* belonging to private individuals (see *Instit.* 2.1.1; Dell'Oro 1962-63; Dani 2013: 31-32; Dani 2020: 40).

[34] *Circa aedificia quaero numquid sit licitum aedificare in mari sicut in litore? Et dico quod sic eadem ratione et ita Veneti faciunt, qui sunt fundati in mari et de iure gentium civitates in mari aedificatae sunt ipsorum qui aedificant [...] haec ratione Veneti praetendunt libertatem, quia non aedificaverunt in solo alicuius* (Baldo degli Ubaldi 1616: 45). See also Sini 2008 (access October 2023); Schiavon 2011: 126-129; Cangelosi 2021.

[35] Manselli 1974: 184-185; Grossi 2006: 32-36, 61-68.

[36] Cessi (ed.) 1938 Gli statuti veneziani di Jacopo Tiepolo: t. III. rubr. 60: 169-170.

from 1386 the *corporazione degli acquaroli* (the guild of water suppliers) made sure the city had enough water throughout the year – were such that no further code chapters were required.[37]

3. Hill towns

Unlike lowland cities, the fairly numerous inland hill towns that were not built alongside rivers had to develop, especially in central Italy, a range of different solutions to ensure a safe and reliable supply of water. This could only be achieved through a complex and expensive hydraulic system of canalisation to store and release water in a controlled manner via distribution basins and cisterns commonly located at the end of an aqueduct (*caput aquae*) and in the centre of the communities (*in platea Communis*).[38] The statute of Fucecchio, a hill town in Tuscan Valdarno, expressly stated that a stone fountain was to be built at the *cassero*, the oldest part of the town, and paid for by the municipality and the town residents.[39] Due to seasonal changes and in order to avoid the frequent floods, the 1342 Perugia statutes (promulgated in the year of the great rains that hit central and northern Italy) required the course of the Nestóre stream to be diverted and straightened to ensure sufficient quantities of running water during the summer and non-excessive amounts in autumn.[40] An earlier code of the same city from 1262 provides evidence of the care given to waterworks and the functionality of reservoirs of water and *canaligia* (a system of pipelines and conduits), which were managed by specially appointed *magistri*.[41]

Mainly in central Italy, city governments erected monumental fountains (*fonti* and *fontane*) in the middle of their squares in celebration of constituted power and local identity.[42] The construction of hydraulic infrastructures, primarily aqueducts and fountains, could play a similar role of symbolic representation to the erection of the cathedral, as has been observed for Orvieto.[43] It was above all the People's Regimes that, from the second half of the thirteenth century, initiated this kind of buildings, thanks to the fact that the ranks of this political faction included merchant entrepreneurs and other professionals capable of planning and managing important public works.[44] The idea was to incorporate beauty and aesthetics into the structures designed and built for important essentials (water supply). I fully agree with Maire Vigueur that almost all of the fountains from the communal period preserved today are part of the historical-artistic heritage of the hill towns located in central Italy.[45] Suffice it to say that most Umbrian towns acquired a monumental fountain in the short period between 1275 and 1285. The prevalence of medieval public fountains in this and neighbouring countries is a numerical fact that clearly emerges from the extensive and documented repertoire compiled by Visentin.[46] Only a few highland or valley floor towns in the Po Valley and pre-alpine area

[37] See Ciriacono 2018a; Maire Vigueur 2023: 229-231.
[38] Vannucchi 2009: 14; Bartoli Langeli and Merli 2013.
[39] Carmignani (ed.) 1989 *Statuti del Comune di Fucecchio*: b. III. rubr. 89: 135.
[40] Salem Elsheikh (ed.) 2000 *Statuto del Comune e del Popolo di Perugia*: t. II. b. IV. rubr. 28: 370.
[41] Nicolini (ed.) 1969 *Reformationes Comunis Perusii*: 13; Caprioli (ed.) 1996 *Statuto del Comune di Perugia*: rubr. 151-170: 169-180. On the Umbrian rivers, see Grohmann (ed.) 1990; Nico Ottaviani 2008: 55-67.
[42] On the meaning of the main squares and fountains, see Schulze 1994; Treggiari 2012: 224; Visentin 2016: 14-15.
[43] Riccetti 1992: 90-92; Riccetti 1994: 241-244.
[44] Merli 2000: 91-92, 113-121; Maire Vigueur 2023: 232-236.
[45] Maire Vigueur 2023: 240-252. This author introduces another distinction: that between monumental fountains built primarily for aesthetic and ornamental reasons and those made especially for practical motivations, a distinction which, however, I find less incisive. Utility and decorum, in fact, I believe, almost always proceeded at the same time.
[46] Visentin 2016: 373-377.

have significant examples of medieval fountains – primarily Brescia (the Statue-Fountain of the Bishop Maggi, 1309-17) and Belluno –, which, however, hardly ever achieve the structural articulation and decorative relief of the constructions in central Italy[47]

We therefore focus our attention on this part of the country. The statute of Arezzo, for instance, decreed in 1327 – the year the lord of the city, Bishop Tarlati, tried, though not without difficulty, to consolidate the political role of his family[48] – the construction of a public well just outside one of the town's gates, in the exact location of a source of fresh water (*cum ibi sit vena aquifera*), which was to have a *guaçatorio*, that is, a space to wash animals and carts.[49] Siena's situation was unique, owing to its topography. Being an inland hill town located in an area particularly poor in water, it faced challenging water supply problems, which were only partly resolved, during the thirteenth and fourteenth centuries, by a network of tunnels and underground conduits with settling tanks called *Bottini*.[50] The commune's *Costituto* of 1309-10 regulated the payment due to vendors who sold water in barrels on public streets and the city's squares, a clear indicator of the scarcity of clean water.[51] Masonry fountains built in the thirteenth and fourteenth centuries by the communal government played a major role in supplying the city with water and characterising the urban architectural aesthetic.[52] The aforementioned *Costituto* contains a specific norm to protect the strategic fountain of Pescaia (**Fig. 3**) located just outside the city walls. Also mentioned is the appointment of two officials to monitor pack animals and to ensure they had access to the fountain and could be watered safely (*sì che commodamente possano andare le bestie ad abeverare, et lavatoio et guaçatoio si facciano ine*).[53] The statutes of Siena devoted appositely written sections to the maintenance of all urban and suburban fountains (for instance *Fonte Branda* – **Fig. 4**, *Fonti di Follonica*, *Fonte di Porta Ovile*, *Fonte Nuova*, the suburban *Fonte Becci*),[54] and prompted the construction of private cisterns.[55] The early fourteenth-century code of the *Capitano del Popolo* contains interesting jargon and a set of technical terms regarding access to water. These include expressions such as *fontana guazzatoria*, *lavatoriae*, *pescines* to emphasise that specific fountains or sections of them could be used to draw either drinking water or water for washing objects and animals.[56]

Apart from the case of Cortona and its thirteenth-century fountain decorated with tiles depicting the Months of the year, now destroyed,[57] another upland town in central Italy which

[47] Visentin 2016: 37-46, 49-79, 81-325, 327-335.
[48] Licciardello 2015: 93-101.
[49] Camerani Marri (ed.) 1946 *Statuto di Arezzo*: b. I. rubr. 60: 41.
[50] Balestracci 1990: 19-20; Balestracci 2000; Balestracci 2003; Kucher 2005; Balestracci, Costantini and Vigni [2006]; Visentin 2016: 94-96; Maire Vigueur 2023: 237-238.
[51] *Come si porti l'aqua con li barili* [Salem Elsheikh (ed.) 2002 *Il Costituto del Comune di Siena volgarizzato*: t. 1. b. I. rubr. 235: 202].
[52] Bargagli Petrucci 1906; Balestracci and Piccinni 1977.
[53] Salem Elsheikh (ed.) 2002 *Il Costituto del Comune di Siena volgarizzato*: t. 2. b. III. 25: 12-13. It is worth noting the use, in this text too, of the term *guaçatoio*.
[54] Salem Elsheikh (ed.) 2002 *Il Costituto del Comune di Siena volgarizzato*: t. 2. b. III. rubr. 26: 13; t. 2. b. III. rubr. 96-110: 43-49; *D'acconciare la fonte da Montecchio*; *Di fare la fonte ne la contrada di Casciano*; *Di rivedere le fonti dintorno a la città di Siena* (*ivi*, t. 2. b. III. rubr. 27, 28, 111: 13-14, 50; see also rubr. 112-139: 50-62). On the fountains see Visentin 2016: 98-121.
[55] *De la pecunia la quale si die dare a coloro e' quali faranno ... citerne ne la città et borghi*; *De' consorti de le case e' quali volessero fare citerne* [Salem Elsheikh (ed.) 2002 *Il Costituto del Comune di Siena volgarizzato*: t. 2. b. III. rubr. 137, 138: 61].
[56] Ciampoli (ed.) 1984 *Il Capitano del Popolo a Siena*: b. I. 312; b. IV. 333, 387, 392-393, 398: 73, 117-119. These were common terminologies. The construction of a *guaçatore* annexed to an urban source was, for example, provided for in the Reggio Emilia statute of 1265 [Campanini and Vasina (eds) 1997 *I rubricari degli statuti comunali di Reggio Emilia*: 39].
[57] Visentin 2016: 275-283.

carefully planned water provision through monumental infrastructures was L'Aquila, an atypical commune co-administered by local authorities and monarchs in Naples.[58] The *Fontana della Riviera*, known today as *Fontana delle Novantanove cannelle* (**Fig. 5**), is a famous public fountain in the town that dates back to the thirteenth century.[59] In addition to being a manifestation of the efforts made by civic magistrates in the area of water resource management, it is also a landmark of the meticulous and strategic initiatives of the communal administration. The municipal statutes of 1313 proclaimed a series of regulations for the maintenance of the aqueducts which supplied water to the local community and for conveyance to the various city districts (*Quod conductus aque dividatur per Quarteria*).[60] Similarly, in Perugia, the main fountain (*Fontana Maggiore*), a masterpiece by Nicola and Giovanni Pisano (1277-78), was a major public work commissioned by the commune for the main square, significantly located at the end of a massive aqueduct that had required construction work lasting over twenty years (**Fig. 6**).[61] On the rim of the upper basin of this monument is a long inscription in Latin hexameters that emphasises the importance of the water supply for this city, and culminates with the following invocation: "May He who sits above the stars preserve the waters" (*cons[er] vet latices q[ui] sup[er] a[s]tra sedet*).[62] This monumental structure must be closely related to the dismembered fountain *a piè di piazza*, intended above all for everyday use, but no less ornate than the *Fontana Maggiore*.[63]

Also emblematic is the case of Massa Marittima (southern Tuscany), whose monumental fountain (1265) bears the rare pictorial decorative motif of trees laden with phalluses, symbolising fertility in a figurative context of possible Etruscan, or South Tyrolean and Ghibelline, origin (**Fig. 7 and 8**).[64] In the Sardinian city of Sassari, the *Fontana del Rosello* was 'monumentalised' at the beginning of the seventeenth century, but had already been strategically important three hundred years earlier (**Fig. 9**).[65] In San Gimignano (central Tuscany), one of the most populous and dynamic 'minor centres' of communal Italy, the public cistern was built in the middle of the market square in 1273, as the centrepiece of one of the largest collective spaces, second only to the area on which the mother church and the town hall were located (**Fig. 10 and 11**). Mentioned in the 1314 statutes, this construction was extended during those years, and the well above it became a monumental presence.[66] In a similar position to that of San Gimignano was the decorated cistern built between the thirteenth and fifteenth centuries in the centre of the market square, known as *Piazza della Sala*, in Pistoia. It is no coincidence that during the sixteenth century a stone lion representing the dominant authority of the municipality of Florence was placed above this structure, considered one of the most prominent in the city (**Fig. 12**).[67] The last structures we can mention are: the thirteenth-century three-arched *Fons*

---

[58] Terenzi 2016.
[59] Visentin 2016: 169-193
[60] Clementi (ed.) 1977. *Statuta Civitatis Aquile*, rubr. 280-284: 188-190; see also rubr. 93, 255, 286-290: 77-78, 175, 190-192; Bologna 1997; Berardi 2005: 155.
[61] Salem Elsheikh (ed.) 2000 *Statuto del Comune e del Popolo di Perugia*: t. IV. rubr. 1: 333-340; see Silvestrelli 1996: 83; Benvenuti 2009: 251-252; Bocchi 2009: 338-341; Gunzburg 2013; Visentin 2016: 233-260.
[62] See Bartoli Langeli and Zurli 1996; Bartoli Langeli and Marchioli 1996; Visentin 2016: 245, 260-265; Cavallucci 2019: 62; Maire Vigueur 2023: 249-252.
[63] Sperandio 2005; Visentin 2016: 305-325.
[64] Benvenuti 2009: 252; Visentin 2016: 151-167; Maire Vigueur 2023: 242-243. On the possible Ghibelline matrix of the decoration see Tigler 2005: 23; Hoch 2006.
[65] Cadinu 2015.
[66] See Brogi (ed.) 1995 *Gli albori del Comune di San Gimignano e lo statuto del 1314*: b. IV. rubr. 209: 247-248 (*De citernis faciendis*).
[67] See Perazzi, Millemaci and Taddei 2010.

Marosus in Genoa, now no longer existing, the fountain installed inside the Palazzo dei Consoli in Gubbio in the 1330s, and the fifteenth-century *Fonte Gaia* in Siena, sculpted by Iacopo della Quercia and located in *Piazza del Campo*, at the physical and political centre of the city.[68]

Monumental structures were erected primarily in urban communes.[69] Nevertheless, even in a small town like Stroncone (Terni), the large cistern built in the main square from 1395 was accompanied by a similar monumental fountain completed during the sixteenth century (**Fig. 13 and 14**).[70] Other interesting examples in this regard are the fountains in the Viterbo area, such as the *Fontana dell'Olmo* in San Martino al Cimino (thirteenth c.), the *Fontana di Porta Tiberina* in Vitorchiano (fourteenth c.), the *Fontana Vecchia* in Soriano al Cimino (fifteenth c.), and the *Fontana Nova* in Tarquinia (fourteenth c.). The fourteenth-century fountain in the Abruzzo village of Fontecchio, the lost Communal Fountain of Spoleto (ca. 1279), and the *Fontana di Piazza dei Priori* in Narni (TR, 1303) are clearly inspired by the Viterbo structures and Perugian masterpieces (**Fig. 15**).[71]

The town of San Gimignano had also a large public fountain near its outer walls, installed above several springs at the foot of the hill on which it stood (**Fig. 16 and 17**). It was a complex structure, built between 1232 and the end of the thirteenth century and based on the architecture of Sienese fountains, which could be reached via a specially built road.[72] It was designed so that water could be drawn on several levels: drinking water at the top; for watering animals below that; and a third level for washing clothes. Waste water was conveyed into nearby streams and partly collected in irrigation tanks.[73] According to the statutes of 1255 and 1314, a fountain, referred to as *di Docciola* supplied water for domestic use only.[74] Lastly, we know, again from the statutes, that the commune of San Gimignano planned and began construction of an aqueduct to carry water not only to the main centre, but also to other localities in the territory.[75]

The architectural model of Sienese *fonti* was also used for the fountains in the nearby hill communities of Poggibonsi (SI, *Fonte delle Fate*, **Fig. 18**), Piombino (LI, *Fonti di Marina*, thirteenth c.), Montieri (GR, *Fonti di Sopra* and *Fonti di Sotto*, thirteenth c.), Montalcino (SI, *Fonti Castellane*, thirteenth c.), and Volterra (PI, *Fonti di Docciola*, *Fonte di San Felice*, **Fig. 19 and 20**), built near natural springs (*vene*) and featuring arches and basins.[76] The thirteenth-century statutes of Volterra stipulated that the above-mentioned *di Docciola* fountain at Vallebuona, where the Roman theatre and an ancient spa complex stood, was to have a trough for pack animals (not separate from the one for humans), a *guacçatorium* and a wash basin with easy access for anyone carrying jars, barrels or other receptacles.[77]

[68] Silva (ed.) 1987 *Corpus inscriptionum*: 106-108; Grohmann 1996: 52, 56-58; Balestracci 2011: 25-27; Visentin 2016: 337-345, 364-365; Maire Vigueur 2023: 246-252.
[69] See Fiore 1992.
[70] *Statuto della terra di Stroncone* 1707: b. III. rubr. 19: 27.
[71] Visentin 2016: 44-45, 52-69, 71-73, 146-147, 269-270, 299-303, 347-351; Coppa 2017.
[72] Brogi (ed.) 1995 *Gli albori del Comune di San Gimignano e lo statuto del 1314*: b. V. rubr. 78: 290.
[73] Casali 1998: 24-25; Visentin 2016: 125-127.
[74] Diacciati and Tanzini (eds) 2016 *Lo statuto di San Gimignano del 1255*: b. III. rubr. 36: 99; Brogi (ed.) 1995 *Gli albori del Comune di San Gimignano e lo statuto del 1314*: b. IV. rubr. 234: 256-257.
[75] Brogi (ed.) 1995 *Gli albori del Comune di San Gimignano e lo statuto del 1314*: b. IV. rubr. 110: 216 (*De mictenda vena de Septefonti usque stratam Pisanam*).
[76] *La Fonte delle Fate a Poggibonsi* 1990; Visentin 2016: 45-46, 81-91, 96-98, 123-125, 127-132.
[77] Fiumi (ed.) 1951 *Statuti di Volterra*: b. II (1224): rubr. 230: 222-223; see also b. I (1210-22): rubr. 76: 37; b. II. rubr. 43: 128; Fiumi 2006²: 35, 255.

Very similar architecture is found in the eight-arched *Fonte di Scannebecco* in Todi (PG, thirteenth-century, **Fig. 21**), from the name of Scannabecco dei Fagnani da Bologna, *podestà* of the town, and the three-arched fountain known as *della Valle* in Gagliano Aterno, near L'Aquila, commissioned during the first half of the fourteenth century by Countess Isabella d'Acquaviva (**Fig. 22**). Of simpler but similar design are the ancient fountains located in Gubbio (PG, *Fonte al Corso*, 1293), in Atri (TE, *Fonte Canale*, fourteenth c.), in Arischia (AQ, *Fonte degli Archi*, fourteenth c.), in Scanno (AQ, *Fontana Sarracco*, fourteenth c.), in Pennapiedimonte (CH, thirteenth-fourteenth c.), and in Fermo (*Fonte Fallera*, 1309). Finally, a remarkable elegance and great uniformity, marked by the orderly succession of round arches opened in a massive masonry, characterise the fountains of the Marche: Fermo (*Fonte di Sfumico*, 1320), Macerata (*Fonte Maggiore*, 1326), Ripatransone (AP, *Fonti*, fourteenth c.).[78] Also worthy of note is the complex fountain of the *Fraterna* in Isernia, whose unique portico structure is the thirteenth century and modern result of the recomposition of numerous architectural elements, some of which certainly come from medieval buildings in the city (**Fig. 23**).[79]

The aforementioned Viterbo, a town in southern Tuscia less than 70 kilometres from Rome along the *Via Francigena*, installed an important aqueduct in the early thirteenth century, about 10 kilometres in length, at a place known as *Pietrare*, in turn originating from a Roman infrastructure, which supplied a large public fountain (*Fontana Grande* or *Fonte del Sepale*, **Fig. 24**).[80] This structure and other *aqueducti* or *alvei sub terra* that formed a widespread water network supplying around twelve fountains are mentioned in the 1251 statutes, which stipulated that they were to be maintained constantly (*De conductis aptandis et alveis, De aqua fluenda in abbeveratorio Sunçe, De purgatione fontis Sepalis*).[81] Known for its hot springs, Viterbo was the site of an important papal residence.[82] In 1268, the commune had an aqueduct built specially for this building by the *capitano del Popolo*, Viscount Gatti. This construction had one part suspended on arches and several sections of penstock displaying significant engineering and architectural work consistent with the most advanced principles of hydraulics widespread in the towns and cities of central Italy during the thirteenth and fourteenth centuries.[83]

Other examples that can be given, in fact, do not only concern the ancient territory of Tyrrhenian *Tuscia*. It emerges (from the 1296 statutes) that the water supply in the Umbrian city of Spoleto was centralised: the local code of norms mentions a caretaker for the main fountain and one for the aqueduct (which included the famous *Ponte delle torri*, **Fig. 25 and 26**), all appointed by the city government.[84] Spoleto's aqueduct bridge, perhaps installed on the foundations of a Roman building of which no trace remains, owes its complex and imposing structure to important works carried out by the commune and the papal legate Cardinal Egidio de Albornoz in the second half of the fourteenth century. Its structure is similar to that of the Sulmona aqueduct, again in central Italy (Abruzzi region), which dates back to 1256 and ends with the monumental *Fontana del Vecchio* (fifteenth c., **Fig. 27 and 28**). Built by King

[78] Visentin 2016: 134-146, 196.
[79] See Valente 1982; Merli 2000: 48; Visentin 2016: 217-231.
[80] Romagnoli 2020.
[81] Ciampi 1872 *Statuto di Viterbo del 1251*: b. I. rubr. 53, 55, 61: 467-468. See also b. IV. rubr. 184: 596. As Romagnoli 2020 notes, the fountains, often equipped with a drinking trough and a wash-house, were "il principale simbolo della ricchezza e del prestigio del Comune viterbese" (155).
[82] Mack 1992.
[83] Romalli 2006: 321-322; Visentin 2016: 49-52.
[84] Antonelli (ed.) 1962 *Statuti di Spoleto*: rubr. xi, xii: 12. See also Geltner 2019: 62-63; Maire Vigueur 2023: 236-237.

Manfred of Sicily and the local municipality, the Sulmona aqueduct was a suspended artificial canal that, as the local statute shows, conveyed running water from the distant river Gizio, which was also exploited for its motive force.[85] The new aqueduct, known as the Sanguinone aqueduct, restored between 1304 and 1306 to bring water to Assisi, was built over an existing Roman construction. This structure was flanked by another, the so-called conduit of Brother Elias, a derivation of the previous one built from 1228 onwards.[86] This second conduit had its *caput aquae* in the *Fontana dei Leoni*, originally located in an eminent position in the square in front of the upper church of the Basilica of Saint Francis. The city's 1319 statutes regulated how the fountain and its waters were to be protected.[87] Finally, one absolutely exceptional artefact, albeit from a later period, is the *Pozzo di San Patrizio* in Orvieto (**Fig. 29**), built in 1527 by the architect Antonio da San Gallo il Giovane at the behest of Pope Clement VII, to ensure the supply of water to that city in the event of a military siege. Although this is a Renaissance artefact, it was preceded by a well and fountain made by Venetian masters in the thirteenth century.[88]

In the Sardinian community of Villa di Chiesa, the drought-plagued principal town of the Sulcis mining district, there are records of several fountains built by the commune and the Aragonese royal authority, and an unusual relief on the public fountain in the oldest square (*Fontana di Piassa Vecchia*), which was the *caput aquae* of the aqueduct of *Bangiargia*.[89] If we compare the community's statute (1303-04, revised before 1338) with those from which it partly derives, the 1287 *Breve* of Pisa revised in 1313, we see that the Tuscan code made provision for important works for the construction of a public aqueduct to be used by the nearby subject community of Livorno and a similar construction to supply a new bath (*balneum*) in the Pisan district of Kinzica.[90] In this regard, however, it is worth emphasising, precisely in relation to the *Breve Pisano*, how the communes' planning did not always have rapid effects. The fact that the aforementioned 1287 rule was reported in the 1313 version of the statute suggests (beyond the formal conservatism typical of these texts), that the work in question had not yet been realised.

4. Water magistrates

As we have said, the important construction works, which would become symbols for the cities where they stood, often involved a highly centralised administration. The Pisan statutes of 1287 and later reforms decreed the election of a non-resident overseer of canals and aqueducts and, from 1337, the holder of the position would be known as the *operarius generalis*. Assisted by several collaborators, this officer was responsible for the upkeep of roads, streams and ditches.[91] A similar magistrate, possibly a descendant of the Roman *curator aquae*,[92] was described in the Ferrara's law (1287),[93] in the statutes of Montepulciano, another Tuscan town

[85] Mattiocco 2001 *Capitula civitatis Sulmonis*: 30, 102, 130. See Di Benedetto 1995. On the relationship between Roman and medieval aqueduct bridges, see Benoît 2006: 79-82.
[86] Merli 2000: 59; Barbanera and Stefanucci 2015: 12, 25-27, 46-47.
[87] Cenci 1974-76: 16; Barbanera and Stefanucci 2015: 53-60.
[88] Tigler 2005; Visentin 2016: 285-297.
[89] Ravani (ed.) 2011: b. I. rubr. 74: 87. See Bocchi 1995: 94.
[90] Bonaini (ed.) 1870 *Breve Pisani Communis*: t. IV. rubr. 23. 26: 411, 413; Ghignoli 1998 *I Brevi del Comune e del Popolo di Pisa*: t. IV. rubr. 26: 439.
[91] Ghignoli 1998 *I Brevi del Comune e del Popolo di Pisa*: b. I. rubr. 4: 476-477.
[92] Fusco 2011-13: 58-62.
[93] Montorsi (ed.) 1955 *Statuta Ferrariae*: b. II. rubr. 7.

(in this case inland);[94] in the code of Cremona (1339),[95] in the eighth book of the *bonacolsiani* statutes of Mantua (1303, *iudex ... super aggeribus et laboreriis*),[96] and in the norms of the Pistoia territory communes of Buggiano (1378, *officiales fontium*) and Uzzano (1339, *operarii super muris, fontibus, viis et aliis*).[97] This code tasked a notary of 'damages given' (*damnorum datorum*) with the supervision of bridges, roads, fountains and canals. The Veronese statute reform of 1276 attests to the existence of a magistracy called the *Judex fossatorum*, and of an office in charge of supervising water courses (*officium dugalium*). These figures and institutions were completely reorganised and their duties extended in the city statute promulgated by Cangrande della Scala in 1327.[98] During this period, numerous legal codes in the towns of the lower Po Valley (statutes of Modena, Polesine di Rovigo and Lendinara) provided for the appointment of *arginerii* (embankment care staff), also known as *cavarzerani* or *cavarzellani*. These operators worked under the supervision of officials in charge of distributing among the inhabitants of the countryside the burdens of hydraulic defence and land drainage used by both the rural areas and the cities.[99] Finally, the *iudex stratarum et aquarum civitatis Mediolani et ducatus*, mentioned for the first time in 1385, had extensive jurisdiction over the city and territory of the major Lombard centre.[100]

At the end of the thirteenth century, immediately after the completion of the city's aqueduct and the *Fontana Maggiore*, the commune of Perugia established officers to protect these monuments.[101] The statutes of the Florentine Republic of 1355 placed the maintenance of bridges and embankments under the direct responsibility of the *Capitano del Popolo*.[102] The statutes of Pescia, in northern Tuscany (1339), provided for the election of guards similar to *camparii* to oversee the use and maintenance of the *Rio dell'Asino*, a tributary of the Pescia River, and the surrounding wooded areas.[103] In Rieti, in Rome's hinterland, a similar *notarius viarum* was responsible for overseeing the river's path (*viam torrentis*).[104] We find a comparable situation in the Umbrian city of Orvieto, whose statutes from the early fourteenth century (a period when the city's ancient aqueduct was in a critical condition)[105] prescribed a custodian for each source within the plan of the settlement.[106] These administration decisions went hand in hand with what could be defined as a monopoly for the distribution of water that was held by the commune. An emblematic example is found in the 1279 statute of Perugia, which issued a ban against women selling water (*aquatragole*), not long after the construction of a public fountain and a well (*putei de platea communis*).[107] At Villa di Chiesa, in the event of drought, anyone was allowed to draw water from public and private fountains without paying a fee; a demonstration of a greater interest in the needs of individuals being guaranteed by the

---

[94] Morandi (ed.) 1966 *Statuto del Comune di Montepulciano*: b. I. rubr. 9: 10-11.
[95] *Statuta et ordinamenta comunis Cremonae*: 153, 155: 205-208. See also Cazzola 2021: 79-80.
[96] D'Arco 1872: b. VIII. rubr. 5: 220-221.
[97] See Vannucchi 2009: 13.
[98] Castagnetti 1977: 81, 88-89.
[99] Rovigo. Accademia dei Concordi. Biblioteca. Ms. Silv. 480. *Statuta totius Policinij*. 1440: rubr. 295-353. See also Cazzola 2021: 87, 91-93, 95. See also the next chapter.
[100] Fantoni 1990: 119, 121-125, 131.
[101] Silvestrelli 1996: 90.
[102] Bambi, Salvestrini and Tanzini (eds) 2023 *Gli Statuti della Repubblica fiorentina del 1355 in volgare*: t. I: *Statuto del Capitano del Popolo*: b. III. rubr. 19: 473.
[103] Onori (ed.) 2000 *Lo statuto di Pescia*: b. IV. rubr. 39. 41: 233, 235.
[104] Caprioli (ed.) 2008 *Lo statuto della città di Rieti*: b. IV. rubr. 28 and 33: 301, 303-304.
[105] Riccetti 1994: 246-248.
[106] Andreani (1986-87) Un frammento di statuto del comune di Orvieto; Geltner 2019: 56, 192. note 59.
[107] Caprioli, S. (ed.) 1996. *Statuto del Comune di Perugia*: rubr. 430: 392-393.

town authorities.[108] An entirely similar rule, although with no apparent distinction between periods of drought and periods of normal water availability, are found in the fifteenth-century statute of the rural community of Montisi, near Montalcino, in the Sienese countryside.[109]

Of course, officers with similar duties were also a feature of towns in northern Italy, where, apart from the frequent excavation and maintenance of rivers and canals and the construction of bridges, there was usually less need for expensive major hydraulic infrastructure during the thirteenth and fourteenth centuries, especially in smaller municipalities.[110] The detailed legislation of Bergamo is a case in point. Nestled at the foothills of the Alps in Lombardy, this city could rely on numerous good quality sources of fresh water previously praised by local poet Mosè del Brolo in the twelfth century, and had an aqueduct since at least the previous century, accompanied by a modest fountain with very simple architectural forms (*Fonte Antescolis*, thirteenth c.).[111] In spite of this, the municipal statute of 1353 declared a certain number of regulations, mostly in the fifteenth section of the code, to control and protect the communal water supply.[112] Ferrara is an important city located close to the Po valley and the Adriatic Sea. Its communal magistracies, which came under the authority of Marquis Obizzo d'Este, allowed, in the city's 1287 statutes, for the trade of drinking water in jars and placed it under regulatory control. It is worth noting that water and wine sellers were required to charge the same fee for the same quantity of either product (*quatuor ferrarinos de anphora*).[113]

5. A comparison of northern and central Italy

Undoubtedly, in the normative tradition embodied in municipal statutes, water management was connected to the exercise of communal sovereignty, while, almost everywhere, the right of use was related to the right of citizenship.[114] Shared throughout 'communal' Italy was the principle whereby proper law (*ius proprium*) was invoked to supplement and modify the *ius aquandi* of the Roman law tradition by introducing local customs and norms.[115] Given these general principles, it should, however, be emphasised that the statutes written in the communities of central Italy and the Po valley area bring to light a different state of affairs.[116] For example, fourteenth-century law codes from Milan regulating roads and water (1346 and 1396) demonstrate a certain flexibility around waterworks. These documents encourage private initiative and state that everybody is allowed to build channel conduits to bring water to their homes, as long as it does not hinder or damage the urban passageways.[117] Only in the case of the *Naviglio Grande* or *Ticinello*, the main navigable artery, were restrictions imposed.

---

[108] Ravani (ed.) 2011 *Il Breve di Villa di Chiesa*: b. IV. rubr. 88: 212-213.

[109] Ciampoli and Gatti (eds) 1994 *Lo Statuto di Montisi*. rubr. 153: 98. See Dani 2003: 288-289, 291.

[110] See the statute of Omegna (late fourteenth c.), north of lake Orta in Piedmont [De Regibus (ed.) 1946: *Statuto di Omegna*: rubr. 1: 2]; Toubert 1960: 418; Vergani 2010: 507-508.

[111] Gorni 1970: 442, 445; Capellini 1990: 149; Visentin 2016: 148-149.

[112] Forgiarini (ed.) 1996 *Lo statuto di Bergamo*: b. XV. rubr. 4-24: 302-311. It is worth noting that law codes from Lombardy use the term *guazatorius*, which is also attested in Tuscany (20: 309).

[113] Montorsi (ed.) 1955 *Statuta Ferrariae*: b. II. rubr. 332: 176.

[114] See Casalini 2014: 309-359; Dani 2020: 42-43.

[115] See Moscati 1997: 327; Conte 2002: 21-28.

[116] See the Bolognese case introduced by Albertani 2007: 21-24.

[117] Milano, Biblioteca Ambrosiana, ms. B.19: *Statuta Civitatis Mediolanensis de anno MCCCXCVI*: P. inf. c. cap. 241; Besta and Barni (eds) 1949 *Liber consuetudinum Mediolani*: b. XVIII. XIX. rubr. 1-2: 107; Fantoni 1990: 43, 47; Stella, Farina, and Balestreri (eds) 1992 *Gli statuti delle strade e delle acque del contado di Milano*: rubr. 7-11, 30: 57-58, 65-66.

Although not prohibited, the drawing of water was subject to stricter controls here and required a formal public concession.[118]

The 1390 statute of Lodi also allowed any citizen to freely derive water from non-navigable lakes and rivers.[119] The 1393 Pavia statute only invited those who wished to impose levies to share the costs of the relevant conduit by creating consortia among owners.[120] Comparable provisions appear in the statutes of Verona (1327),[121] and in the law of the Veneto municipality of Marano Vicentino (1429), located in a flatland area abounding with natural waterways and artificial canals, some of which date back to Roman times. The text of Marano allowed anyone to direct water along the road leading from Marano to Vicenza, with the simultaneous right to build private elevated conduits enabling the transportation of water without impeding the passage of men and vehicles along the road itself.[122] Similarly, the 1305 statute of the Piedmontese commune of Savigliano allowed anyone to draw water from rivers and springs to water their fields, to draw it from the commune's ditches running alongside the roads in communal territory and have the right to run independent conduits through public and private land.[123] The 1255 statute of Parma allowed town dwellers to bring water in from the city's systems of canals, tunnels and pipes built to convey water, in order to clean entrance halls and private spaces and for similar domestic usage.[124] The 1323 normative legislation of Piacenza granted the local community permission to transfer water from powering waterwheels in canals (*rivos macinatorios*), confining its intervention to resolving the inevitable disputes and settling them by arbitration.[125] The statute of Quarona in Valsesia (Vercelli, 1384) provided for the existence and maintenance of a number of canals (*riane*) derived from the Cavaglia stream, a tributary of the Sesia River, destined to irrigate the most fertile meadows and pastures at the bottom of the valley. From these canals it was possible to freely derive water for irrigation. However, water could not be taken outside of these pipelines, not so much because there was a scarcity of the resource, but because the local authorities wanted to carefully control how much water was actually taken and by whom.[126] Articles of law in the codes of other subalpine communities went in the same direction, such as the statute of Orzinuovi (1341–87), in the Brescia plain, which only allowed the inhabitants of the community to derive water from the river Oglio. These men, moreover, could freely form associations for the construction of pipelines, sharing the costs among private individuals (*si aliquis vicinus fecerit aliquod aquaductum, canalle vel pontem ... primo solveret sibi partem contingentem de dictis laborariis*).[127]

Therefore, these regulations show a desire to control the efficiency of the water supply and the functioning of the waterways, but they also show that the relative abundance of water meant that the public and private sectors shared the burden and benefit of conveying and

[118] Milano, Biblioteca Ambrosiana, ms. B.19: *Statuta Civitatis Mediolanensis de anno MCCCXCVI*: P. inf. c. cap. 328.
[119] *Laudensium Statuta* 1390: rubr. 677 (*De aquis derivandis*): 7. See Cazzola 2021: 76-77.
[120] *Statuta civilia Civitatis Papiae* 1393: rubr. 133: 8.
[121] *De pena cavantis in fossatis alicuius vel in stratis publicis seu viis consortalibus; De pena facientis fossatum seu scolantis aut cavantis ita quod aqua faciat dampnum in alienis terris* [Bianchi, Granuzzo, Mariani Canova and Varanini (eds) 1992 *Statuti di Verona*: t. II. b. V. rubr. 73. 74: 665].
[122] Orlando (ed.) 2010 *Statuto di Marano* 1429: rubr. 65: 116.
[123] Sacco 1932 *Statuti di Savigliano*: b. VI, rubr. 324: 139-140.
[124] Ronchini (ed.) 1857 *Statuta Communis Parmae*: b. IV: 367-368, 374-375, 383-384, 385. On the characteristics of this statutory drafting see Moglia 2022: 53-57.
[125] Fugazza (ed.) 2012 *Lo statuto di Piacenza*: b. V. rubr. 58. 60. 63-67: 120-122. See Galetti 2000: 40-42, 51.
[126] Mor (ed.) 1932 *Statuti di Quarona*: rubr. 43-45: 289-291.
[127] Nogara, Cessi and Bonelli (eds) 1927 *Statuti di Orzinuovi*: rubr. 127. 175. 177: 247, 262-263. See Toubert 1960: 466-468.

exploiting the resource;[128] and this reality continued, in many respects, into the modern age.[129] Also, water theft was mostly in the form of misappropriation of one private individual's property by another, rather than the violation of a common good.[130]

No article of law like those mentioned appears in statutes in central Italy. For example, the normative codes of Rome (1363) prohibited the drawing of water for private use from the public *Aqua Virgo* conduit using devices called *giottelli*.[131] The statutes of nearby Rieti banned the diversion of water from one public stream to another [*Dig.* 43.12.2; *Cod.* 11.43(42).4].[132] The same did the codes of the Pistoia territory (Uzzano, Monsummano, Buggiano).[133] The problem of illegal diversions from public pipelines seems to have caused much concern to the city authorities in central Italy.[134] Rome and the Lazio area seem to have held on to the provisions of Roman law whereby every citizen had the right to oppose any undue withdrawal from watercourses, and magistrates were empowered to remove any diversion made without their explicit consent.[135] The statute of Nocera (Central Umbria), printed in 1567, but derived from a 1371 draft, prohibited any modification of watercourses and any private derivation from them.[136] The statutes of the Marche city of Ascoli Piceno severely punished anyone who cut or drilled water pipes to activate diversions, and forbade the digging of private wells near pipes that collected water from public sources.[137] This code also encouraged private individuals to take responsibility for maintaining public sources at their own expense.[138] Conversely, despite including similar norms, the statute of Bergamo, in northern Italy, made provision for derogations to the withdrawal ban, if contractually agreed between the commune and private parties.[139] The community of Pons, in Canavese (Piedmont, 1344), prohibited the drawing of water from the community's canal (*rugia*), but only on days not agreed between each private individual and the local authorities.[140] On the other hand, it is surprising that, Bra, another important Piedmontese community and town in the historical Roero area on the left bank of the Tanaro River, barely mentioned water for public use in its vast, well-structured statute (1461) and did so only to prohibit the fouling of springs and wells with manure and other *vituperium*.[141] It would seem that the withdrawal and use of public water did not constitute an emergency worthy of regulatory attention.

Normative sources attest to undoubtedly greater freedom of action for private individuals in northern Italy than for their counterparts in central Italy and Sardinia. In my opinion, this was

[128] See, in this regard, Simonetti 2014.
[129] See Petracco 2010.
[130] Frola 1918 *Statuta Sancti Georgii*: rubr. 3: 266.
[131] Mendoza 2022 *Gli Statuti del Comune di Roma*: b. III. rubr. 131-133. 137: 596. See also Annoscia 2007: 164.
[132] *Si quis extraxerit aquam de aliquo rivo et miserit eam alio, ipsam remittere teneatur per cursum unde extraxit* [Caprioli 2008 *Lo statuto della città di Rieti*: b. IV. rubr. 7: 291-292].
[133] Vannucchi 2009: 17.
[134] Maire Vigueur 2023: 239-240.
[135] Costa 1919: 14; Fiorentini 2003: 67-68.
[136] *De aqua non derivanda extra cursum proprium* (*Statuta et iura municipalia Civitatis Nucerii*: b. V. cap. 11: 85).
[137] Zdekauer and Sella (eds) 1910 *Statuti di Ascoli Piceno*: b. III. rubr. 72. 74: 405-406.
[138] *Che se alcuno volesse governare ad soi spese la fonte de ponte Majore* (*ivi*: b. III. rubr. 77: 406-407). See in this regard Cherubini 1988.
[139] *Salvo quod predicta ... non derogent in aliquo aliquibus statutis comunis Pergami nec aliquibus contractibus factis per comune Pergami occasione aque ipsius seriole* [Forgiarini (ed.) 1996 *Lo statuto di Bergamo*: b. XV. rubr. 6: 303; *seriola* = a canal derived from the Serio River].
[140] Frola 1918 *Statuta Ponti et Vallium*: rubr. 3: 84.
[141] Mosca (ed.) 1958 *Gli statuti di Bra*: rubr. 241: 141.

due to the greater availability of water in the northern regions and the different significance attributed there to fountains, wells and other supply structures. From this point of view, Italy reflects the whole of medieval Europe, where, for example, miniatures in the thirteenth to fifteenth centuries depicted fountains in northern countries as large ornamental structures located in the centre of gardens and castle courtyards, whereas in the south they stood out in the heart of towns, where they acted as wells, that is as functional facilities.[142] And let us not forget that canals also ended up fulfilling different functions in the north and centre-south of the Italian peninsula, since, in the Po valley area, these structures were relatively large and served for both irrigation and navigation, while in many regions of central and southern Italy they were mere conduits built to regulate the distribution of autumn rains. South of the northern Apennines the traditional Roman model remained prominent and Cato's advice to dig ditches when it rained still held, so that the land would not dry out and also to prevent water stagnating.[143]

Squatriti points out that large hydraulic works had an enormous ideological impact on the exercise of power.[144] Moving to the issue of the relationship between water management legislation and self-representation by the ruling classes, the most representative and emblematic constructions of the Po region of Italy, hence the most widely monumentalised, were not so much the aqueducts or the fountains, but rather the bridges built over the territory's numerous rivers and canals.[145] The regions of northern Italy are home to numerous fortified bridges, designed as castles and used both for defence purposes and as toll collection points.[146] Most of the structures were originally built in wood. Some of them also served as drawbridges.[147] However, at least from the mid-fourteenth century, many of these wooden constructions, often destroyed by rivers or war events, were replaced by stone and brick bridges. Evidence of this is seen in the large late-medieval structures of Verona (Scaligero/ Castelvecchio bridge over the Adige River, second half of the fourteenth c., **Fig. 30**; *Ponte delle Navi*, fourteenth century, destroyed in the nineteenth, **Fig. 31**); the covered bridge of Bassano del Grappa (*Ponte Vecchio*, thirteenth c., **Fig. 32**), equipped since 1315 with two defensive towers; *Ponte di Rialto* (thirteenth to sixteenth c.) and the profusion of bridges in Venice (**Fig. 33**); the large structure in Pavia (1354, covered 200 years later; **Fig. 34 and 35**, before and after the contemporary post-World War II reconstruction); the analogous bridge of Alessandria (Piedmont, **Fig. 36**); and the artefact in Fermignano (Pesaro, fourteenth c., **Fig. 37**). It is seen in the statutes of these cities, which provided for their construction and maintenance.[148] In this respect, the only important exceptions in central Italy were Florence (Ponte Vecchio, rebuilt in the fourteenth c., **Fig. 38**, and Ponte Santa Trinita, thirteenth–sixteenth c., **Fig. 39**, although these constructions only acquired a monumental dimension in the early Renaissance), and Pisa

[142] See Alexandre-Bidon 1994; Verdon 2002: 28-30. On the fountains as public places in the Mediterranean region see Klapisch-Zuber 1987: 344.

[143] *Per hiemen aquam de agro depelli oportet. In monte fossas inciles [pellere] puras habere oportet. Prima autumnitate, cum pulvis est, tum maxime ab aqua periculum est. Cum pluere incipiet, familiam cum ferreis sarculisque exire oportet, incilia aperire, aquam diducere in vias et <extra> segetem curare oportet uti fluat* (Catonis 1982[2] *De agri cultura*: 155. 1).

[144] Squatriti 1998: 17-18. See also Maneglier 1991: 117-130.

[145] Bernardi, Fox and Adamoli 1988: 11-13.

[146] Coppola 1998: 3-10, 53-54. *Quod anciani populi Verone debeant habere singulam clavem cuiuslibet porte et pontis* [Bianchi, Granuzzo, Mariani Canova and Varanini (eds) 1992 *Statuti di Verona*: t. I. b. I. rubr. 68: 165-166].

[147] Fantoni 1990: 89.

[148] See, for exemple, Bianchi, Granuzzo, Mariani Canova and Varanini (eds) 1992 *Statuti di Verona*: t. I. b. I. rubr. 228-230: 241-242; t. II. b. V. rubr. 5: 629; Gloria 1873 *Gli statuti del comune di Padova*: b. IV. rubr. 1: 297-299.

(Ponte di Mezzo, eleventh-fourteenth c.).[149] Still on the subject of exceptions, but regarding fountains as visual manifestations of constituted power and its action for the common good, the famous monumental structure of *Madonna Verona* located in the centre of *Piazza delle Erbe* is the symbolic personification of this northern city (**Fig. 40**). The artefact was built in 1368 at the behest of Cansignorio della Scala, lord of the city, using reclaimed Roman materials. On the stem supporting the pedestal of the allegorical statue are carved the faces of the four rulers of the city: the legendary Vero, Alboin the king of the Lombards, Berengar and *Verona regina*. The monument had more of a symbolic and political function than a practical one, and despite the later civic tradition, was made primarily to celebrate the ruling dynasty, which needed a clear reference to classicism, and thus to an object that evoked the artistic heritage of the ancients and their morals, as the inscription on the cartouche shows: *est iusti latrix urbs hec et laudis amatrix* (this city is the bearer of justice and the lover of prise). In any case, this fountain is an important artefact perhaps built in conjunction with the restoration of the Roman aqueduct.[150]

Regardless of the differences we have highlighted, the actions of city authorities, aimed at ensuring a sufficient supply of water for all, emerge from statutes throughout the different areas of Italy we have examined. Indeed, it is significant that many normative texts in both northern and central Italy more or less explicitly imposed easements for the public good, referred to in legal historiography as *servitù di acquedotto* (servitude of aqueduct) or *acquedotto coattivo* (enforceable aqueduct), related to the more general right of passage through neighbours' land to reach one's own (*ius itineris*).[151] This meant that anyone who owned land that was not naturally irrigated, or an inadequately supplied lodge, could ask for or buy water from a neighbour, and then convey it across other people's land, provided that they caused the least amount of damage possible and provided that the owner of the land on which the diversion channel was built was adequately compensated.[152] All this revealed a need for water that was not always met by available natural sources and the will of the public authorities to act as guarantors of the fair distribution of both public and private water.

[149] Baldaccini 1947: 9-12; Salvestrini 2005: 21-25; Paolini *et al.* 2016. Even the first monumental fountain in Florence is not earlier than the sixteenth century (Cresti 1982: 9; Butters 2010; Ferretti 2016).

[150] Ambrogi 2005: 190-191, 286-288; Napione 2009: 533; Visentin 2016: 353-361.

[151] Bianchi, Granuzzo, Mariani Canova and Varanini (eds) 1992 *Statuti di Verona*: t. I. b. II. rubr. 101: 358; Leicht 1966: 92-94; Dani 2003: 288, note 92; Chiodi 2008: 562-567; Cavallar 2010: 118. See Caggese (ed.) 1921. Pinto, Salvestrini and Zorzi (eds) 1999 *Statuti della Repubblica Fiorentina*: t. II: *Statuto del Podestà*: b. II. rubr. 33: 102: *Quod liceat alicui ire per terras vicinorum ad terras suas*.

[152] See Ciampi 1872 *Statuto di Viterbo del 1251*: b. I. rubr. 65: 117; b. III. rubr. 152: 191. Frola 1918: *Statuta Clauisii* (Chivasso): rubr. 2: 189; *Statuta Sancti Georgii*: rubr. 3: 266; statuto di Balangero 1391: rubr. 1: 299; statuto di Barbania (fifteenth c.): rubr. 1: 322.

IV

Legal Norms for Water Management: Rural Areas

1. From countryside to city and back

As specified earlier, municipal statutes of communal Italy cover water management in both the urban context and rural areas, often within similar regulations. In town and country alike, landowners along rivers were naturally *rivales* and faced the common issue of the right to draw water.[1] This pattern can be seen in the normative legislation of several centres in the Veneto region. For instance, the statutes of Treviso (twelfth and thirteenth centuries) approved the reclamation of the swamp areas around the city,[2] perhaps inspired by what had already been accomplished for the marshland in the Verona suburbs during the last decades of the twelfth century.[3] In the municipal statutes of the areas surrounding the Po valley, where the agrarian economy relied on permanently irrigated meadows named *marcite* (a dominant feature of the landscape in this region, related to the extensive presence of rivers and canals), water resource regulations were mostly concerned with irrigation practices.[4] An analysis of the norms from Milan dating back to 1216, for example, demonstrates that two statute chapters (*titoli*), namely *De aqua* and *De iure molandinorum*, and each section therein, attempt to regulate the transmission and distribution of river water for public and private use and provide adequate supplies of the resource at a usable quality for irrigation in the surrounding area (*ex flumine publico vel privato ad irriganda sua prata vetera vel nova*). It also mentions that this practice should be carried out with consideration for the watermills located alongside the natural water sources of the region. Watermills were to be protected from any potential damage and supplied with a sufficient quantity of water.[5]

In the *Breve del Comune e del Popolo di Pisa* (1287), in the statutes of Arezzo of 1327 and in the later statutes of Massa in Lunigiana (Tuscan coast, 1591, but with prior legal material incorporated and declared in force), municipal governments authorised the annual election of an official to oversee natural and artificial waterways, aqueducts, wells, fountains, reservoirs and mains (note that Massa elected an official for each district or local community or *vicinia*). It was their duty to ensure that all locations were constantly supplied with clean water (*aqua munda*) and to manage irrigation water coming through the local springs.[6] We find a similar rule in the statutes of Ascoli Piceno, which entrusted the maintenance of the fountains to the *villae* and castles of the suburban territory (*districto*), and in the Latium code of Castel Fiorentino (1298), which required the inhabitants of the countryside to clean the community's major

---

[1] On the etymology of the term and its meaning in the *Digest* (fragment of Ulpianus), see Schiavon 2011: 117-119. See also Cavallar 2010: 103-106.

[2] *De paludibus extirpandis* [Betto (ed.) 1984 *Gli Statuti del comune di Treviso*: b. I. rubr. 158: 133-134].

[3] Castagnetti 1974; Varanini 1988: 339-341.

[4] Campopiano and Menant 2015; Campopiano 2018: 29-30.

[5] Besta and Barni (eds) 1949 *Liber consuetudinum Mediolani*: b. XIX. rubr. 20: 107-108.

[6] Ghignoli (ed.) 1998 *I brevi del Comune e del Popolo di Pisa*: b. IV. rubr. 4: 418; Camerani Marri (ed.) 1946 *Statuto di Arezzo*: b. I. rubr. 58: 39-41; *Statuta Massae* 1591/1991: b. IV. rubr. 1-3: 187-189.

fountain (*Fons maior*) twice a year, indicating exactly which families would have to pay for this work.[7] The statute for the *viarii* of the Republic of Siena dated 1290 devoted 19 sections (*rubriche*) to the management of the trenches and natural and artificial waterways in the nearby countryside.[8] The 1253 statute of Bologna mentions officials called *notarii aquarum et yscariorum* who were in charge of water management in the suburban area.[9] Elsewhere, taxation from local communities assisted by public services would pay for the compensation of magistrates like these.[10] The mid-thirteenth-century and the 1335 statutes of Bologna cover water transmission and distribution schemes from the various local torrents in great detail.[11] It was common for the city's judicial institutions to initiate canal-building works for conveying water to the countryside, even though it was the inhabitants of those areas who had to pay for it and provided the labour.[12] Under the 1265 statute of Reggio Emilia, the small waterways called *rioli* were to benefit the whole community, not only the landowners and private citizens who could pay for the service. This fact illustrates that, as they benefitted from the greater autonomy granted to private parties,[13] landowners in this northern Italian commune perhaps had the upper hand when it came to exploiting the resource.[14] It is worth noting that, while granting non-exclusive permission to irrigate agricultural areas by bringing in water from the city's pipes, canals and rivers, the 1255 statute of Parma also urged everybody to respect the rights of landowners (most of whom were town dwellers).

2. Countryside water in service to the city

We have already remarked that the populations of the Po valley area had greater freedom of access to water resources than those of central Italy. However, this freedom was not uniformly possessed by town dwellers and inhabitants of the countryside. Privileged water rights were legitimate for urban-based individuals and institutions. For instance, the fourteenth-century statutes of Forlì established a city water basin (*bignale*) from which Augustinian and Dominican friars could draw larger quantities of water than other subjects so they could water their vegetable gardens.[15] The statute legislation of Parma granted the Friars Minor and an unspecified abbot (*dominus abbas*) exclusive ownership and control of two tributaries of the large Parma stream.[16] Similarly, a law code of Bologna (1250) granted the Franciscans exclusive and continued access to the sources of running water from a torrent.[17] The statutes of the Tuscan municipality of Colle Val d'Elsa imposed higher penalties on anyone occupying or

[7] Tomassetti, Federici and Egidi (eds 1910): *Statuti di Castel Fiorentino*: rubr. 32: 342.

[8] Ciampoli and Szabó (eds) 1992 *Lo Statuto dei Viarî di Siena*.

[9] Frati (ed.) 1869 *Gli statuti di Bologna*: t. 1. b. I: 208. See Rinaldi 2000: 147-148; Cazzola 2021: 90. On the term *yscarii* or *scarii* (special officials), see Fasoli 1972; Geltner 2019: 87-88.

[10] *Statuta civitatis Cremonae* 1485: c. 133v; Bizzarri (ed.) 1933 *Gli Statuti del Comune di Torino*: rubr. 172-176: 83-85; Mordini (ed.) 2019 *Statuta civitatis Grosseti*: b. I. rubr. 23: 24-27. See Galetti 2000: 48-50; Foschi 2013; Geltner 2019: 51-65, 113-116.

[11] Frati (ed.) 1869 *Gli statuti di Bologna*: t. 2. b. IX: 374-388, 404-408; Trombetti Budriesi and Braidi (eds) 1995 *Per l'edizione degli statuti del Comune di Bologna. I rubricari*: 44-45. See also Pittarello (ed.) 2017. *Statuti di Padova*: b. IV. rubr. 13: 546-554; Rinaldi 2000: 151-153; Foschi 2000: 175-180.

[12] *Con ciò sia cosa che il fiume d'Arno, vagando e distrugendo, guasti et renda disutili del terreno ... del comune di Fighino ... li signori Priori del'arti ... possano ... elegere et diputare ... oficiali ... che possano diliberare et provedere ... et ... fare parate et opere ... alle spese degl'uomini del detto comune di Fighine et delli huomini che ànno terre in quella ysola* [Bambi, Salvestrini and Tanzini (eds) 2023 *Gli Statuti della Repubblica fiorentina del 1355 in volgare*: t. II: *Statuto del Podestà*: b. IV. 122: 601-602].

[13] Gamberini 2003.

[14] Campanini and Vasina (eds) 1997 *I rubricari degli statuti comunali di Reggio Emilia*: 45-46, 54. On the Reggio regulations governing water, see Fabbrici 2000; Campopiano 2018: 35-38; Cazzola 2020: 83-85; Campopiano 2023: 32-34.

[15] Rinaldi (ed.) 1913 *Statuto di Forlì*: b. V. rubr. 9: 316-317.

[16] *Statuta Communis Parmae* 1856: rubr. IV: 379-381.

[17] Frati (ed.) 1869 *Gli statuti di Bologna*: t. 2. b. VII: 147.

damaging the abbot's castle aqueduct, the conduit that brought water from the countryside to the residence of the abbot of Spugna Monastery, the first lord of the town.[18] The Parma statute gave greater tax freedoms to town-dwelling landowners, often at the expense of the freedom enjoyed by inhabitants of the countryside. This was especially the case if the latter took canal water away from the properties of the former. In fact, one section of the statute specified that, in cases of disagreement, and as a matter of course, one was to believe whoever accused the other person of having illegally taken the water away. Less credence was given to the oath of innocence sworn by the accused. However, this order only applied to town dwellers (*in civibus tantum*). If the disagreement involved a town dweller against a *rusticus*, the judge was to give more weight to the statements made by the *civis* in the first instance, even in cases where the latter was the accused. Further, if the town dweller was the complainant, his hearing would take place without delay. This only occurred provided that he was supported by the testimony of the local magistrate of the canals, who had to declare that he had seen the farmer take water from the town dweller's reservoirs without permission.[19]

The law favoured inhabitants of cities in various ways. Almost all construction and maintenance works carried out in the territory were planned within the urban walls and undertaken in the countryside at the expense of rural communities, although they were contributed to in part by town-dwelling landowners. These actions were designed for the protection of fields and urban settlements, but the planning decisions favoured the interests of urban society.[20] For example, the 1306-07 statutes of Modena, a lowland city located between the Secchia and Panaro tributaries of the Po, often subject to flooding,[21] entrusted the maintenance of river embankments to the rural community of Sorbara and others nearby, on the basis of actions decided by the civic authorities.[22] A similar provision can be found in the statute of Mantua of 1303, which tasked two officials (*ducalieri*), one from the city and one from the countryside (*rusticus*), with ordering the works in each rural community (*villa*) to be carried out at the expense of the peasants.[23] The 1266 and 1304 statutes of Parma required the inhabitants of the countryside to work on the maintenance of the *dugarie* (canals), which irrigated the land and provided access to the capital city.[24] The 1265 Reggio statutes did the same, stipulating that the city magistrates were to involve the rural community of Campagnola in the excavation and maintenance of the canals necessary for access to the city.[25] The 1287 statutes of Ferrara and those of Mantua (1311), Cremona (1339) and the Tuscan town of San Miniato al Tedesco of 1337, to name just a few, levied the cost of maintaining embankments (monitoring plant growth and goat grazing) on the localities under their political control, despite charging some of the work to the town-dwelling landowners who had interests in those areas.[26] A strict division of competencies between city and countryside is set out in the Ferrara statutes of 1287 and, above all, in the specific *Statuta ad Offitium Argerum* drawn up and reformed several

---

[18] Ninci (ed.) 1999 *Statuta antiqua Communis Collis Vallis Else*. 1407: b. VIII. 85: 386.

[19] *Statuta Communis Parmae* 1856: rubr. IV: 386.

[20] See Betto (ed.) 1984 *Gli Statuti del comune di Treviso*: b. I. rubr. 242: 194-195.

[21] Fumagalli 2007^2: 60.

[22] Vicini (ed.) 1929-32 *Respublica Mutinensis*: I: 181-82. See Dotti Messori 2000.

[23] D'Arco 1872: b. VIII. rubr. 5: 220-221.

[24] *Statuta Communis Parmae* 1856: 146-149; b. IV: 300, 382. See Parente 2000: 58-60.

[25] Campanini and Vasina (eds) 1997 *I rubricari degli statuti comunali di Reggio Emilia*: 191.

[26] Montorsi (ed.) 1955 *Statuta Ferrariae*: V: i-xi; Gualazzini (ed.) 1952 *Statuta et ordinamenta comunis Cremonae*: 267; Salvestrini (ed.) 1994 *Statuti del Comune di San Miniato al Tedesco*: b. IV. rubr. 82. 112: 374-375, 403-405; b. V. rubr. 56: 458-460. See Zupko and Laures 1996: 69; Roversi Monaco 2000: 98; Bacchi 2000: 111-116; Vaini 2000: 73-75. See also Bianchi, Granuzzo, Mariani Canova and Varanini (eds) 1992 *Statuti di Verona*: t. II. b. V. rubr. 6: 630; Cazzola 2021: 79.

times between 1320 and 1394.[27] The first of these texts, in fact, dedicates a specific section (rubrics 12–48) to the regulation of public works (therefore also hydraulic works) in urban and rural spaces. The second is a collection of rules specifically dedicated to the care of canals and ditches. The vast district of Ferrara was transected by various branches of the Po and was therefore subject to frequent flooding, also on account of its very low gradient. Space management involved defining individual hydraulic units (*pollicine*), whose surface area was determined by the hydrographic configuration of the river delta. Watercourse embankment works were divided between large public works pertaining to the magistracies in charge of the entire city domain (*laboreria que pertinent generaliter ad comitatum et districtum Ferrarie*), and local works (*laboreria specialia*) pertaining to each *pollicina*.[28] The system of interventions, especially the digging and cleaning of public canals, carried out from the end section of each ditch, came under the political responsibility of one *iudex* and 18 ditch bank guards (*superstites aggerum*). At the operational and administrative level, in addition to the notaries of the *iudex*, a number of operators (*cavarzellani*) acted as representatives of the individual territorial units. In time, it was ordered that the surveys the officers conducted on the state of ditches and embankments were to be recorded in special registers, one for each *villa*. This documentation was kept with the Friars Minor, the Friars Preachers and the Augustinians and, to all effects, became a registry of owners for the purpose of sharing out the burden of maintaining waterways. Generally speaking, although the system provided for the active participation of rural folk at the administrative level, the influence imposed by the city remained strong. Urban magistracies retained for themselves the planning phase and assigned the execution of works to the rural populations.[29]

Only the statutes of Treviso and Perugia of 1279 show that the cost of building some of the rural infrastructures, such as bridges, was met solely by the urban city-state.[30] The Treviso statutes also specified that maintaining an efficient road network should allow the normal flow of water (*consuetus cursus aquarum*). In a previous reform of this code, water was identified as being public (*aque que publice sint*), suggesting that only the commune was responsible for its management; whereas, in line with the legislation typically found in other towns in northern Italy, everything else was mostly left to private parties.[31] The city authorities' allocation of the burden usually followed the general principle whereby contributions were proportionate to the estimated direct benefit that individuals and communities derived from construction and maintenance work. Thus, contributions for embankments and drainage ditches were primarily made by frontier farmers and individual rural communities for the stretches of rivers and canals that belonged to them.[32] In some cases, as the Modenese code of 1327 shows, requirements were different for the excavation of drainage ditches next to roads. In the case of ditches next to public roads, the burden was to be shared per head (*per testata*), that is, by requiring rural dwellers to excavate and resurface the section of ditch facing the land they cultivated. When it came to collector ditches, on the other hand, the principle applied was

[27] Zucchini 1962.

[28] See Cazzola 2021: 93-97.

[29] See Zucchini 1965: 263-266.

[30] *Cum minori incomoditate et minoribus expensis poterunt* [Betto (ed.) 1984 *Gli Statuti del comune di Treviso*: b. I. rubr. 272: 217]. *Ut inde possint bene homines, equites et pedites pertransire* [Caprioli (ed.) 1996 *Statuto del Comune di Perugia*: b. I. rubr. 193: 200-201]. See Nico Ottaviani 2008: 74-76.

[31] Liberali 1951 *Gli statuti del Comune di Treviso*: rubr. 358: 133. See Geltner 2019: 53-54.

[32] Cazzola 2021: 88.

that of sharing the burden among the owners concerned.[33] There was, however, no strict division by degree of use, firstly because city owners were favoured over rural ones; and secondly, because city authorities could, for political reasons, grant exemptions and privileges to individual communities and landowners.

Generally speaking, what distinguished the duties of one rural population from another was the extent to which they depended on urban law. In fact, there were rural centres whose administration was directly mentioned in urban legislation, including as regards water management, as well as centres that had obtained the right to draft their own rules, as was often the case in the Bolognese and Florentine territories. Although each text depended on the legislation passed by the ruling towns and cities, the level of autonomy of those communities that were politically subordinate to it but had their own statutes, according to an albeit limited principle of subsidiarity, was obviously greater.[34]

It is important to highlight (as Campopiano has done) that civic governments often made full use of the skills of inhabitants of the countryside, by incorporating their legislation (legislation often of monastic origins)[35] into water-related matters. A clear example can be seen in the statute of the Lombard community of Nirone, near Parma (1260). This code has come down to us almost entirely in the regulations on public water of the territory of Milan (1346).[36] Another interesting case is that of Pernumia, south of Padua, whose statute, which was partly absorbed into the city's regulations,[37] provides important insight into the settlement and production dynamics related to marshland reclamation along the Bacchiglione River.[38] Nevertheless, it was clear that the integration that had taken place was urban-centric and that the provisions that had been selected were in the interests of the cities. As a result, urban governments exploited the water management experience that rural populations had acquired over time.[39]

Furthermore, urban public magistracies attempted to reconcile the varied interests of the entire population, as testified in the frescoes by Ambrogio Lorenzetti in his *Effects of Good Government in the city and the countryside* in the *sala consiliare* of Palazzo Pubblico in Siena (1338-39).[40] Under the 1342 statute of Perugia, any decision concerning contributions from rural communities for the construction and maintenance of bridges were to be taken by a Franciscan Brother of Penance appointed by the urban authorities. As a member of the clergy, the friar might have seemed a useful intermediary between the city government and the rural population.[41]

---

[33] Campori 1864 *Statuta civitatis Mutine*: b. V. rubr. 414.
[34] See Dondarini (ed.) 1995.
[35] See Canzian and Valenzano (eds) 2022; Destefanis and Garanzini (eds) forthcoming.
[36] Fantoni 1990: 120; Campopiano 2018: 30-32; Campopiano 2013: 378-380. See also Boucheron 1994: 123-138; Ostrom 2002.
[37] Gloria 1873 *Gli statuti del comune di Padova*. b. IV. rubr. 2: 300-303.
[38] Bortolami 1978 *Pernumia e i suoi statuti*; Bortolami 2008; Orlando (ed.) 2010: 127-128.
[39] See Cerlini 1933 *Consuetudini e statuti reggiani*: 136; Pistoia and Fusaro (eds) 2006 *Statuti di Feltre*: b. III. rubr. 81: 169 (Veneto region).
[40] See Frugoni 2019; Piccinni 2022.
[41] Salem Elsheikh 2000 *Statuto del Comune e del Popolo di Perugia*: t. II. b. IV. rubr. 20 and 69: 362-363, 423.

3. Wetland management

Worthy of close examination are the statutes produced by or for rural communities and consortia of landowners located in marshlands. In fact, wetlands had a considerable economic impact on the resources they provided for populations: fishing and fish breeding, the harvesting of aquatic plants, wild bird hunting, and so on. These were no less significant in symbolic terms, given that the communities living closing to them had often inherited ancient rights of collective use, which were then enshrined in local statute law. On the other hand, urban authorities claimed public prerogatives over these regions as heirs to imperial authority.[42] The special features and the productivity of these territories, considered to be completely unhealthy during the nineteenth and twentieth centuries, are revealed in important scientific literature, especially from the sixteenth to the eighteenth centuries.[43]

Significant examples of regulatory interventions dating back to the communal era emerge from the laws of the Mantuan *Oltrepò* and several statutes from central Italy. With regard to the first territorial area, that is, the lower plain surrounding Mantua, the 1303 statutes mention the existence of the *digagne*, which were consortium institutions for the self-government of water drainage works.[44] These collective organisations gradually defined their tasks and, in the fifteenth century, adopted their own statutes similar to those that had produced some comparable associations in central Italy.[45] In the Po delta area, a vast landed property had been created over the centuries, belonging to the ancient monastery of Santa Maria di Pomposa, located on a river island in the Ferrara area.[46] This vast, largely amphibious space was home to a population of monastery settlers for whom the abbots of Pomposa drew up a statute as early as 1295. This code was reformed several times during the fourteenth century and contained numerous provisions concerning the collective governance of water. Banks and ditches were monitored, following the model of Ferrara's municipal code (though undoubtedly in a one-to-one relationship between urban and rural-monastic legislation), by the *cavarzellano*. In this region, the task of planning interventions did not emanate from a town or a village, but from monks primarily interested in defending the abbey from flooding. In this sense, the statutes of Pomposa incorporated laws dating back to at least the twelfth century.[47]

In central Italy, Perugia's code (1389) gave prominence to the *Comunanze del Chiugi*, administrative and tax institutions covering an area of about 120 square kilometres largely occupied by farmland, which included both the coastal strip of lake Trasimeno and a section of the Val di Chiana marshes. This particular administration was established by the municipality of Perugia for the economic development of farmers and fishermen. This shows that, even when it came to managing these kinds of territories, the urban authorities' control was very tight.[48]

---

42 See Prosperi (ed.) 1995. For a 'positive' view of the marsh habitat between antiquity and the Middle Ages, see Cracco Ruggini 2008: 100-102. On wetlands in northern Italy, see Raviola 2011.

43 See Arquer 2007: 22; Malvolti, Micheli, Prosperi, La Tosa and Zagli (eds) 1990. For the contemporary age, see D'Amato and Nannucci (eds) 2004.

44 D'Arco 1872: lib. 8. rubr. 5: 177.

45 Masé Dari 1960 *Lo statuto gonzaghesco*.

46 See Mezzetti (ed.) 2016.

47 Samaritani (ed.) 1958. See also Cazzola 2021: 97-98.

48 Vallerani 1987: 663-698; Vallerani 1992; Francesconi and Salvestrini 2006: 208-211.

The actions of communal magistracies also emerge from the statute of neighbouring Foiano della Chiana, in south-east Tuscany (1387). This community was located in an area dominated by stagnant waters. The statute was drafted a few years after the locality was brought under Florentine control.[49] This code contains a rubric explicitly protecting fish ponds created for fish farming, which highlights the importance of the marsh economy for the local community.[50]

Undoubtedly noteworthy is the situation reflected in the statute of the Consortium of *Piano del Padule d'Orgia* to the south-west of Siena.[51] This authority was established around 1250 by the municipality of Siena in partnership with a large local landowner, the Abbey of Santissima Trinità e Santa Mustiola in Torri. The purpose of the agreement was to promote exploitation of water and reclamation of a vast marshy area located near the *Via Francigena*, between Siena and Valdelsa.[52] The consortium was a private entity made up of all the large and small landowners in this wetland area. It was structured so that it could essentially operate autonomously from the public authorities. However, in line with the more 'interventionist' choices of the municipalities of central Italy, its statute, largely composed between 1350 and 1392 from norms drawn up from 1303 onwards, was drafted following the model of urban regulations, and compliance was guaranteed by the city magistrates.[53] Unlike the Foiano code, this statute was less concerned with water management than it was with the reclamation of marshy areas for agricultural purposes. Nevertheless, it emphasises the careful maintenance of a complex system of drainage canals aimed at preventing water stagnation and obtaining fertile plots of land to be allocated and farmed. From this point of view, the law appears to be the result of a long experience of management gained mainly in the monastic circles involved in the consortium itself. The statute stresses that the members of this association were required to finance and promote regular maintenance work on roads, bridges and, above all, ditches and drainage canals. The latter were cleared of the debris obstructing the passage of water by means of a complex barrage system configured during the year to prevent the autumn and winter overflow.[54]

The statute of the Sienese consortium shows the heavy involvement of land owners in the management of the ecosystem of the marshland. From this point of view, the organisation it describes was similar to that of the consortium created in the mid-thirteenth century by the river users of the Lombard Nirone stream, described in the *Statuta Nironis* of 1260.[55] That said, even in this case, the city authorities' protection of the regulatory system governing water management in rural areas remains starkly evident.

One special territorial context was the Fucecchio Marshes, in central-northern Tuscany, a lake district located roughly in the centre of the Arno River basin.[56] The situation in the communal period emerges to a certain extent from the 1337 statute of the municipality of Fucecchio. Not many of its rubrics were devoted to the large marshy area bordering the community,

---

[49] Marrocchi 2003; Barbagli 2017: 14-15, 23; Buonora 2019: 99; D'Angelis 2021: 178-179.
[50] *De pena rumpentis pescheriam vel mittentis aliquid in ea* [Allegria (ed.) 2017 *Statuto del comune di Foiano*: b. 3. rubr. 75: 183-184].
[51] Banchi 1871 Statuto della Società del Piano del Padule d'Orgia. 1303-1375.
[52] Cortese 1997: 127.
[53] Gelli 2014: 40-42, 47, 50-53.
[54] Banchi 1871 Statuto della Società del Piano del Padule d'Orgia. 1303-1375: caput 5, 6, 26, 63, 64, 67. See Gelli 2014: 44-46.
[55] Fantoni 1990: 120.
[56] See Zagli (ed.) 2003; Corsi, Prosperi and Ceseri Frullani 2022.

nevertheless the code forbade fishing and the trade of fish to outsiders; it prohibited the construction of barrages along the Usciana Stream; it imposed the cutting of reed beds; and laid down rules for the proper maintenance of numerous ditches.[57]

Most of the statutes of communities located in wetland areas appear to have granted inhabitants broad freedoms to fish, and only punished excesses, destructive techniques and damage to property. However, in derogation of Roman law, the texts considered fishing almost everywhere to be for civic use reserved for local residents.[58]

[57] Carmignani (ed.) 1989 *Statuti del Comune di Fucecchio*: b. II. rubr. 48: 83-84; rubr. 63: 90; b. III. rubr. 38: 113; rubr. 51: 119; rubr. 58: 121-122.
[58] See Balestracci and Pasini (eds) 2001; Dani 2020: 34.

V

Conflicts and Regulatory 'Solutions'

1. Distribution disputes

In respect to the availability and distribution of water resources, as was also the case for other collective assets for public use, such as roads, pastureland and forests, there was a clear effort to reach a careful equilibrium between private interests and collective needs. This was because, following on from Roman law, water whose source was on public land not subject to *divisio* or *adsignatio* to private parties was in the public domain; however, this mostly benefited major centres.[1]

Starting from the assumption that is confirmed by legal doctrine that, owing to a perception of its infinity, the value of water was as a collective resource and not as an asset to be protected in its own right,[2] one of the chief objectives of statutes was to mediate the frequent disputes caused by unequal access to it, often granted officially on the basis of social and professional status. In doing so, *statuta* played a central role in trying to safeguard collective stability and enabling the urban burgher elite to exercise control over large territories.[3]

One interesting hypothesis proposed in anthropology highlights that, in pre-industrial societies (and, in various ways, in contemporary ones, too), there is no absolute shortage of water per se, but rather conflicts of interest and power plays that determine or prevent its scarcity locally.[4] Indeed, conflicts resulting from access to water were not just a part of the relationship between town dwellers and inhabitants of the countryside, but they characterised a large part of the social relations established around water, both inside and outside cities, and often resulted in irregular access to the resource, which municipal legislation sought to curb.[5] Differences arose especially among those who used river and canal water for irrigation purposes, those who used it as a waterway and those who employed it to power hydraulic machinery. Diversion of the resource during the summer period, particularly when there was greater need of it to irrigate the crops, risked compromising the functionality of watermills and fulling mills, as well as restricting navigation. Moreover, water infrastructures were often damaged by timber rafts and boat transit. At the same time, dykes, which were necessary for watermills or for creating fishing reserves – because the *ius commune* gave everyone the right to fish in perennial rivers, as they were by definition public (*Dig.* 43.12.2)[6] – hindered the free movement of navigators. Conflict prevention was therefore of prime importance to legislators. This is demonstrated, for example, in the small but ancient statute of the municipality of Claverano in the Canavese region of Piedmont (1251), which contained two regulations for

[1] See Costa 1919: 1-6, 38-41; Fusco 2011-13: 89-90; Dani 2015: 309-323. For a Europe-wide comparison, see Fournier and Lavaud (eds) 2012.
[2] See Caracciolo 1988: 45-47; Fiorentini 2003: 55.
[3] See Mocarelli 2011: 85; Barbot 2013a: 40-41; Di Tullio and Lorenzini 2019: 75-83.
[4] See Breda 2005: 9.
[5] See, e.g., Chiodi 2008: 513-414.
[6] Costa 1919: 31-32; Schiavon 2011: 155-176.

protecting the activities of fishermen on Lake Sirio and along the streams in the area and preventing damage to their boats and the infrastructure necessary for their work (*ingenia*).[7]

I have shown that the most pressing concern in northern Italy seems to have been water transfer and canalisation; whereas the most frequent conflict seems to have involved private parties (especially regarding use of the artificial canals known as *rogge*).[8] In the statutes of these regions, water saving was required by law, especially in the dry summer period. It can be deduced from the sources that many conflicts over the distribution of water arose during the warmer season. The statutes of Parma and Reggio stipulated that, from 29 June each year, watering was not allowed before Nones on Saturday and after the end of Sunday.[9] The 1360 Turin statute given by the prince Amadeus I of Savoy talks generally about hours and days on which every person can draw water for irrigation, but does not specify which.[10] The Bologna statutory code of 1250 established that, from mid-May to mid-September, water from the river Savena was not to be dispersed along roads, except – *quod deus avertat* – in case of fire. Water could only be taken from the torrent between September and May and only on one day and night a week.[11] The Veronese statutes of 1327 limited the drawing of water from the Riso Torrent to certain days of the week, but allowed millers to divert the water.[12]

Nevertheless, strict regulation of irrigation and a willingness to mediate between farmers and millers also features, and a fortiori, in many legislative texts of central Italy; here, often regardless of the season. For example, in Orvieto, the irrigation of vegetable plots was only allowed, at any time in the year, when mills were not in operation.[13] According to the Viterbo statutes of 1251-52, the four *boni homines* who rigorously oversaw the distribution of water to horticulturists let it flow from the ninth hour on Friday to the third hour on Monday, leaving it to power the mills during the rest of the week.[14] The fifteenth-century rural statutes of Rincine and Fornace (Casentino valley, north-east Tuscany) banned the drawing of water from public rivers and private canals.[15] According to the statutes of Sassari, in northern Sardinia, millers had the right to use running water throughout the week, except in the period between dawn on Saturday and dawn on Monday, when gardeners were allowed to divert channels and pipelines to irrigate the soil. The different shifts were overseen by *partidores de abba* (water dispensers). These were three officials chosen to represent the gardeners of each of the three sections (*De Levante*, *De Mesu*, *De Ponente*) into which the fertile irrigation valley of the Gurusele Stream, near the city, was divided. They used bulkheads to regulate the flow of water from canals and sources and directed it towards users, mediating the frequent disputes between garden owners and mill owners. The provisions suggest that the distribution system was operated via lifting systems and canals and locks; water flowed into them which ensured that, especially in summer, the areas exposed longest to heat during the day (in the eastern sector) were the last to be watered and therefore held on to moisture longer.[16]

---

[7] Frola 1918 *Statuta Clauerani*: rubr. 2: 289.

[8] Galetti 2000: 47-48; Chiodi 2008: 571-575; Barbot 2013a: 48; Barbot 2013b.

[9] Ronchini (ed.) 1857 *Statuta Communis Parmae*: IV: 370-374; Cerlini (ed.) 1933 *Consuetudini e statuti reggiani*: xxxv.

[10] Bizzarri (ed.) 1933 *Gli Statuti del Comune di Torino*: rubr. 154: 75-76. On the statute see Campopiano 2023: 36.

[11] Frati (ed.) 1869 *Gli statuti di Bologna*: t. 1. b. I: 114. See also Sabbionesi 2019: 113.

[12] Bianchi, Granuzzo, Mariani Canova and Varanini (eds) 1992 *Statuti di Verona*: t. II. b. V. rubr. 16: 635.

[13] Riccetti 1992: 145-146.

[14] Egidi (ed.) 1930 n.p. 2005 *Gli statuti viterbesi*: I: 98-99; Lanconelli and De Palma 1992: 44-48. See also Magnusson and Squatriti 2000: 235-236.

[15] Santarelli 1969 *Statuto dei comuni di Rincine e Fornace*: rubr. 48: 77.

[16] *Et fina a tantu qui aen aver abbatu tottu sos ortos de ponente, non pothat torrare ad abbare sos ortos de levante* [Finzi (ed.)

The norms aiming to regulate access by season, calendar and time of day had their roots in Roman law, which had provisions for a timetabled usage of the resource that clearly depended on the agricultural practices of ancient Italy.[17] Similar forms of organisation are found in various areas of the Mediterranean, from the Catalan-Aragonese and Andalusian contexts to the Maghreb regions.[18] In Italy, institutional figures similar to the aforementioned *partidores*, called *acquaroli*, are mentioned both in the statutes of Sulmona dating back to the first half of the sixteenth century, and in the code of Brescia printed in 1557.[19] The commune of Sulmona contracted out to these operators water distribution services for field irrigation. They were also tasked with the management and operation of a large, publicly owned bulkhead (*scerto grande*) which controlled the inflow of water from the river Gizio towards the city, where the water came through the monumental aqueduct referred to above. The *acquaroli* paid a charge to the commune in return for the fees paid by users based on rates set by the authorities and laid out in the statute itself.[20] It is worth recalling that, in the fourteenth-century statutes of Ravenna, the term *aquaroli* referred not so much to the men in charge of water distribution, as to the 'officers' who oversaw the banks and rivers, more often called *cavarzellani* in northern Italy.[21]

2. Drainage and ducting problems

Statutes regulated the collection of rainwater and placed great importance on the sewer system. The 1216 law code of Milan makes reference to the *stillicidium*, a Latin term denoting drops of moisture or rain falling from the eaves of a house. A concept mentioned in the Justinian code,[22] rainwater dripping into a neighbour's lodge or land was therefore subject to sanctions.[23] The fourteenth-century legislative framework of Genoa established more vaguely that rainwater should flow as usual (*aque pluviales decurrant ut consueverint*).[24] The fourteenth-century statutes of the Valsolda, a subalpine territory overlooking Lake Lugano, prohibited private individuals from allowing water to fall from the roofs of their loggias or from balconies onto the public street; this problem must have been especially prominent in these communities during the spring thaw.[25] The statute of San Marino (1352–53) prohibited the draining of water from privately owned fields to public roads or the fields of other owners.[26] Disputes over rainwater running off onto neighbouring property were so common that the 1252 statute of Bologna imposed restrictions on allegations or accusations for this type of offence.[27]

In an attempt to mitigate the consequences of water transfer in the Po valley area, the statute of Castel San Giovanni (in the Piacenza region, from the second half of the fourteenth century)

1911 *Gli Statuti della Repubblica di Sassari*: 89]. See also Borghero and Salvestrini 2023.

[17] Costa 1919: 45-48; Fiorentini 2003: 131, 136-145.

[18] Bazzana and Guichard 1981: 120; Milskaïa 1984: 23-28; Lauretano 2001: 144; Trillo San José 2002: 117; El Faïz 2005: 273-274; Chiodi 2008: 521-529; Campopiano and Menant 2015: 301-307; Furió 2015; Cadinu 2019: 794-796.

[19] *Statuta civitatis Brixiae* 1557: 16.

[20] Mattiocco (ed.) 2001 *Capitula civitatis Sulmonis*: 15, 76-80.

[21] See, in this regard, Lerner 1972: 160-161.

[22] Fiorentini 2003: 149-150; Spanò 2014: 12-13.

[23] Besta and Barni (eds) 1949 *Liber consuetudinum Mediolani*: b. XVIII. rubr. 7. 15: 105-107.

[24] Piergiovanni 1980: 407.

[25] *Quod nullus debeat projcere aquam a lobijs* (*Statuta totius comunitatis Vallisoldi*, in Barrera 1864: rubr. 62: 381).

[26] *Quod nemo mictat aquam de campo suo in viam aliquam vel campum alterius* [Balsimelli (ed.) *Gli Statuti di San Marino*: b. 1. rubr. 32: 28-29].

[27] Frati (ed.) 1869 *Gli statuti di Bologna*: t. 1. b. II: 275.

distinguished between canals used for irrigation (*rivos adaquatorios*) and those used to power mills (*rivos macinatorios*).[28] The strong demand for water from artisanal activities also led the Veronese authorities to distribute hydraulic machines more evenly along the three urban rivers (Adigetto, Fiumicello, Lori).[29] However, this distribution shows the relatively abundant availability of water. In this regard, we can add that, in the Milan area, conflicts over water distribution often arose, not because of water scarcity, but as a consequence of the division of land resulting from emancipation, inheritance or sale.[30] In cases where reserves of clean flowing water were less plentiful, areas of disagreement – as recorded by legal codes – mainly involved landowners and field workers versus public authorities. These magistrates did not appear in the statutes as mediators of conflicts, but rather as one of the main parties. This was the case in many hill towns in central Italy, but also in Piedmont and in several cities of the Veneto plain.

We have already mentioned the prohibitions on the drawing of water from public pipelines by private individuals in the statutes of Rome and Rieti. The codes of Deruta in Umbria punished anyone who removed water from public rivers and torrents without the explicit authorisation of government magistrates.[31] Legislators in L'Aquila stipulated the same provision.[32] In north-west Italy, the statute of Novara (1338–39) devoted a good portion of the fifth book to the question of excavation and maintenance of trenches, canals and sluices. It banned any form of unauthorised extraction, but particularly provided for penalties for the sale of water to landowners who were not under the authority of the city government (*Ne aqua rugie que vadit Casalinum vendatur vel alienetur*).[33] The desire of the urban magistrates to appoint themselves as the principal authorities for water management (regardless of the quantitative availability of the resource) emerges clearly from the Florentine statute of 1355. This code established that floodplains included the area within 20 arm's lengths of every running river and were to be considered state-owned property.[34] In the previous century, one of the oldest statutes of the Republic of Siena, dating to between 1226 and 1242, prohibited the construction of buildings along the Arbia Torrent, which flowed to the south of the city. The statute considered its banks to be public property.[35]

[28] Fumagalli 1985; Galetti 2000: 46.
[29] Varanini 1988; Cazzola 2021: 81-82.
[30] Chiodi 2008: 529-530, 538-543.
[31] Nico Ottaviani (ed.) 1991 *Statuto di Deruta in volgare*: b. III. rubr. 54: 228.
[32] Clementi (ed.) 1977 *Statuta Civitatis Aquile*: rubr. 286-290: 190-192.
[33] Cossandi (ed.) 2004/05: *Gli statuti di Novara*: b. V. rubr. 1-42: 467-482. One finds, however, similar rules in Montorsi (ed.) 1955 *Statuta Ferrariae*: b. V. rubr. 10. 74. 75: 286, 304.
[34] *Della pena di chi venderà del terreno o greto allato ad Arno* [Bambi, Salvestrini and Tanzini (eds) 2023 *Gli Statuti della Repubblica fiorentina del 1355 in volgare*: t. II: *Statuto del Podestà*: b. III. rubr. 171: 450].
[35] Mecacci 1993: 104.

VI

Water Quality

1. Water purity

One of the aspects regulated in the legal corpus examined here is water quality. Water purity was a common recommendation in much of the legislation of the time.[1] This stemmed from the awareness that, contrary to the widespread belief rooted in classical concepts summarised by Pliny the Elder, a good, uncontaminated, flavourless, odourless drink of water was a rare thing. This was especially the case in urban contexts, where close living conditions led to the dangerous proximity of supply wells and waste systems.[2] The oft-referenced professional activity of water carriers (*acquaioli*), quite widespread in the medieval Mediterranean area and regulated by numerous statutes, originated from the difficulty of finding clean water, which these carriers often drew from upland springs located in forests or pastures far away from human settlements.[3]

It should also be said that the ideas about water purity and cleanliness that emerge from regulatory contexts were not short on references to biblical images. Indeed, unblessed water was invoked to solemnise judicial procedures that, to one degree or another, were legitimised by symbolic and sacred elements.[4]

2. 'Ordinary' water

Norms specifically devised to protect water purity are commonly found in the legislative frameworks of communes to the south and to the north of the Apennines. For instance, a monetary fine (20 *soldi*) was levied under the 1309 *Costituto* of Siena against those who washed and watered livestock in the basins assigned for the collection of water for human use.[5] The Verona statutes of 1327 required tavern owners to keep containers of clean water (*aquam mundam*) to wash the dishes used in their establishments.[6] The communal statutes of San Gimignano (in central Tuscany) issued a decree for the construction and preservation of an aqueduct (*doccia sive aqueductus*) to supply the community with fresh water and specified that the cistern intended for use by residents should not be contaminated by rainwater.[7] The 1337 communal statute of Arezzo banned the watering or washing of visibly sick cattle (*bestiam morbosam*) in any of the town's water collection tanks.[8] Similarly, the vernacular statutes of the *podestà* of Florence (1355) condemned anyone who watered horses that were in poor health

1 See, for a comparative perspective, Leguay 2007.

2 Sorcinelli 1999: 127-131; Verdon 2002: 11-21; Montanari 2012: 136-137, 143, 148.

3 See Salem Elsheikh (ed.) 2002 *Il Costituto del Comune di Siena*: t. 1. b. I. rubr. 235: 202.

4 See Hidiroglou 2007: 16-19.

5 *De la pena di chi facesse soçura ne le fonti* (*ivi*: t. 2. b. III. rubr. 127: 57).

6 Bianchi, Granuzzo, Mariani Canova and Varanini (eds) 1992 *Statuti di Verona*: t. II. b. IV. rubr. 44: 569.

7 *Ita quod aqua pluvia non ingrediatur dictam docciam* [Brogi (ed.) 1995 *Gli albori del Comune di San Gimignano e lo statuto del 1314*: b. V. rubr. 16: 275]. See also Diacciati and Tanzini (eds.) 2016 *Lo statuto di San Gimignano del 1255*: b. III. rubr. 36: 99.

8 Capelli (ed.) 2009 *Statuto del Comune di Arezzo*: b. IV. rubr. 98: 339. See also Allegria and Capelli (eds) 2014 *Statuto del Comune di Cortona*: b. IV. rubr. 1. 3. 17: 353, 356-358, 373-374.

at the city's sources specifically designated for human consumption.[9] Under the fifteenth-century communal statutes of Grosseto, large monetary penalties for breaches of water policy regulations were imposed on whoever polluted the town's trenches with animal waste, olive pomace or human faeces.[10] The statutory code of the *podestà* of Pistoia dated 1296 was firmly determined to fight the detrimental habit of disposing of slaughterhouse waste (*intestina bestiarum*).[11] We find similar bans in the unpublished 1321 statutes of Lucca.[12] The Fonte del Poggiolo in Montefalco (PG) preserves on its back wall the writing of a passage from the municipal statute that forbade washing in the drinking water basin (*pena uno scudo chi lava qui*).[13] In this sense, statutory legislation framed and accompanied current legislation, often called upon to deliberate on the construction and maintenance of pipelines to supply cities with *aqua clara*, as was the case in Orvieto during the first half of the fourteenth century.[14]

Moving from the centre to the north of the Italian Peninsula, a typical distinction in Roman law was made in Bergamo ordinances for use of fountains to avoid cross-contamination, thereby keeping water for domestic purposes separate from water needed for watering or washing livestock (*lavellis et guazatoribus et vasis custodiendis*).[15] The law code of Ravenna articulated a series of regulations to prevent urban water resource pollution due to animal waste or other types of waste disposal. In order to discourage such practices, it banned barrel filling around wells, except at a distance of one *pertica*.[16] We can safely assume that this procedure was most likely conceived to avoid infrastructure damage and water contamination, at the same time as monitoring equal access to the resource.[17] A penalty was provided for in the statutes of Verona for anyone who threw animal waste into the Adige River.[18] The 1245 statute of Bologna focused particularly on both the drainage and sewage systems (*clavige*) and their complex network of pipes and conduits to free public water facilities from polluted water and deposits of dirt and refuse matter.[19] In order to avoid affecting water quality in the community's two streams, Flumisella and Clerinzone, the fourteenth-century statute of Lecco, in the Po valley, issued a ban on garbage (*glaream, turpitudinem*) removal.[20] Similarly, a rubric from the 1287 statutory code of Ferrara prohibited animal slaughter and the cleaning of salty fish in the city ditch,[21] whereas the statute of Cittadella forbade the disposal of crabs, shrimps or dead

---

[9] *Neuno cavallo o altra bestia ch'abia il male del vermine o capomorbo o altra infirmitade di male apiccaticcio sia menata o si debba menare a bere o a lavare alla fonte overo al'abbeveratoio fatto alla fonte di Santo Ylario o alla fonte al Porto* [Bambi, Salvestrini and Tanzini (eds) 2023 *Gli Statuti della Repubblica fiorentina del 1355 in volgare*: t. II: *Statuto del Podestà*: b. IV. rubr. 76: 566-567].

[10] Mordini (ed.) 2019 *Statuta civitatis Grosseti*: b. IV. rubr. 31: 271-272.

[11] Zdekauer (ed.) 1888 *Statutum Potestatis Comunis Pistorii*. b. III. rubr. 162: 150. See also *ivi*, *Tractatus offitii judicis deputati super dannis datis*: rubr. 110: 189; *De actandis necessariis ad cloachis* [Diacciati and Tanzini (eds) 2016 *Lo statuto di San Gimignano del 1255*: b. IV. rubr. 23: 118].

[12] Lucca, Archivio di Stato, Statuti 3. V. LI. LXII: cc. 245-246, 255-256; examined in Geltner 2019: 70-71.

[13] Merli 2000: 48; Visentin 2016: 133.

[14] Riccetti 1994: 255-258.

[15] Forgiarini (ed.) 1996. *Lo statuto di Bergamo*: b. XV. rubr. 20: 309.

[16] A unit of length = approx. m. 3, 270.

[17] Pasolini (ed.) 1868, repr. 1985 *Gli Statuti di Ravenna*: b. V. rubr. 74. 78: 119.

[18] Bianchi, Granuzzo, Mariani Canova and Varanini (eds) 1992 *Statuti di Verona*: t. II. b. IV. rubr. 103: 588-589.

[19] Frati (ed.) 1869 *Gli statuti di Bologna*: t. 2. b. IX: 517. See also Greci 1988; Geltner 2014; Geltner 2019: 85-112.

[20] Anderloni and Lazzati (eds) 1915 *Statuti dei laghi di Como e di Lugano*: Statuto di Lecco del secolo XIV: 3-11.

[21] Montorsi (ed.) 1955 *Statuta Ferrariae*: b. IV. rubr. 76. 77: 277; b. V. rubr. 7. 27. 33. 63: 285, 291, 295, 300. Similar rules in Rinaldi (ed.) 1913. *Statuto di Forlì*: b. III. rubr. 49: 242-243; Bizzarri (ed.) 1933 *Gli Statuti del Comune di Torino*: rubr. 156. 292: 76, 121-122; Betto (ed.) 1984. *Gli Statuti del comune di Treviso*: b. I. rubr. 244: 195; Gaddoni (ed.) 1932 *Statuti di Imola*: b. III. rubr. 53: 205-206.

fish in streets and public squares.[22] At the beginning of the fourteenth century, the Venetian authorities tried unsuccessfully to force boatmen selling water in the city to draw relatively clean water from a canal branching off the river Brenta.[23]

Various norms laid down similar rules in the statutes examined governing the treatment of sewage. It was generally forbidden to throw dirty water out of windows before the night curfew (after the third toll of the vespers bell), that is, before road sweepers had started cleaning the streets at night. It was particularly important not to do so without first warning any passers-by with exclamations such as 'watch out, watch out!'[24] According to the *Ordinazioni* of the councillors of Cagliari Castle in Sardinia, it was forbidden to pour waste water from windows and along canals.[25] It was not permitted to build latrines between houses and public walls or even in squares. Only those who had already had them for no less than 20 years were allowed to replace them, at their own expense, with channels and wells.[26] It is interesting to compare the thirteenth-century statutes of Spoleto, which required residents to cover the sewage drains from their homes to the public street, so that neighbours and passers-by would not have to endure the bad smell.[27] It is also interesting that the codes refer almost exclusively to buried sewers running alongside or across public streets, whereas no such obligation emerges for private spaces.[28] These are norms that we find, with few differences, in very different geographical contexts. For example, in Padua a 1236 statute article required those with toilets and latrines (*cloaclam vel sedile*) near the street to conceal them with a wall; and another forbade the depositing of manure and dirty water on church parvises.[29] In the roughly contemporary statutes of Vicenza, similar provisions appeared to prevent *fetor et immundiciia*.[30] We can also liken them to the statutes of Ravenna, which formally disallowed the discharge of waste into public spaces to prevent potential harm to passers-by (*transeuntes possint offendi*).[31] The 1352 statute of San Marino associated, by prohibiting it, the discharge of dirty water ('corrupted' water) with the discharge of any other 'ugly thing' (*bructura*).[32] The 1377 statute of Ascoli Piceno forbade the opening of ditches and drainage canals from which bad smells emanated, justifying the dictate with a requirement not to annoy neighbours and not to offend the decorum of certain religious buildings and other buildings of public use.[33] Let us not forget the 1355 codes of the Republic of Florence written in the vernacular, which

[22] Ortalli, Parolin and Pozza (eds.) 1984 *Statuti di Cittadella*: b. II. rubr. 38: 125.

[23] Maire Vigueur 2023: 231-232.

[24] Examples can be numerous. See Bellandi, Berti and Mantovani (eds) 1984 *Statuti della lega del Borgo a San Lorenzo*: b. II. rubr. 2: 98 (North Tuscany); Camerani Marri (ed.) 1963 *Statuti dei comuni di Castelfranco di Sopra (1394) e Castiglione degli Ubertini (1397)*: b. II. rubr. 43-46: 95-96 (Arezzo and Valdarno); Morandi (ed.) 1966 *Statuto del Comune di Montepulciano*: b. IV. rubr. 120: 367; Marrocchi (ed.) 2019 *Lo statuto duecentesco del Comune di Radicofani*: rubr. 23: 60-61 (South Tuscany). See also Bocchi 1995: 104.

[25] Pinna (ed.) 1929 Le Ordinazioni dei Consiglieri del Castello di Cagliari: b. II. rubr. 62: 124-125.

[26] *Fossa cuberta en la qual caygua la sutzura*: *ivi*: b. II. rubr. 63. 64. 65: 126-127. See also Artizzu 1992: 74; Bocchi 1995: 77-88, 91, 94-95, 103-105.

[27] Antonelli (ed.) 1962 *Statuti di Spoleto. Breve populi*: rubr. xxv. lxi: 40, 55; see Geltner 2019: 42.

[28] See Bizzarri (ed.) 1933 *Gli Statuti del Comune di Torino*: rubr. 283: 120 (*De non tenendis cloacis in viis publicis*).

[29] Gloria 1873 *Gli statuti del comune di Padova*: b. 3. rubr. 8. c. 790. 791: 263-264.

[30] Lampertico (ed.) 1886 *Statuti del comune di Vicenza*: IV: 149.

[31] Zaccarini (ed.) 1998 *Statuto ravennate di Ostasio da Polenta*. 1327: b. III. rubr. 25: 235-236.

[32] *Quod nullus prohitiat ... aliquam bructuram in plateas dicti castri sive aquam putridam vel coructam* [Balsimelli (ed.) *Gli Statuti di San Marino*: b. 3. rubr. 115: 85-86]; *De pena mictentis vel prohitientis bructuram in citernam de fossis* (b. 3. rubr. 121: 88); *Quod terrena existentes circa fontes terminentur* (b. 3. rubr. 127: 90-91).

[33] *Onde possa sequire fetore overo suççura overo prejuditio overo tedio de li vicini overo de lu comune usu de li homini* [Zdekauer and Sella (eds) 1910 *Statuti di Ascoli Piceno*: b. III. rubr. 68: 402].

prescribed that those who dwell near the Arno bring forth from their houses the filth and cover up the stench (*Che coloro che abitano presso ad Arno facciano uscire delle loro case il fracidume et puzura sotterra*);[34] or the statute of the Mugello community of Scarperia (between Tuscany and Romagna), which speaks of inappropriate discharges that can offend or cause injury to neighbours' (*offendere o a' vicini fare ingiuria*).[35] In the same vein, the statutes of the vicariate of Podere Fiorentino (Palazzuolo sul Senio, Tuscany-Romagna Apennines) and those of Bassano in Veneto forbade the discharge of sewage water into the streets, to the detriment of public spaces and those of neighbours, for the purpose of clearing the private spaces of individuals.[36]

Often bans were placed on discharging polluted waste water from craft production, especially textiles and tanning. In addition to the already mentioned 1313 statutes of L'Aquila, which prohibited spillage into canals and roads of *molza* (tannery water) that *civitatem deturpat*, we also mention the royal rules imposed on Palermo by King Frederick III in 1330 to prevent those who treated leathers from *gitare mortilla in lo fiumi de la conciria*; and lastly the statute of the Tuscan commune of San Miniato al Tedesco (1337), which heavily punished anyone who poured *multiccium, pelles seu choria bestiarum* into the road (note the similarity in the terms used in the statutes of places very distant from one another).[37] The statute of San Marino provided for a fine for anyone who washed leather in running water.[38] The statute of the manufacturing city of Chieri in Piedmont (1313) forbade the washing (*deayquare*) of linen, hemp and leather in the stream running through the community.[39] The statute of San Marino also prohibited washing clothes in the public cistern.[40]

Only rarely do codes include an explanation for the bans. The most frequent definition encountered is that of water polluted by *turpia*, or malodorous sewage (*fetor*), which certainly appeared unhealthy,[41] but whose removal was affixed to general requests for a polysemic *munditia*, or propriety, in significant areas of the urban context, and safeguard of public or private goods, not always (or at least not only and, above all, not explicitly) attributable to disease prevention.[42] A clear example of this are the norms of the fourteenth-century statute of San Gimignano that forbade the taking of animals to the municipality's cemetery, as well as urination or defecation (*De turpitudinibus non faciendis*) at certain symbolic places, such as the *Romite* or *domine Nobilis* hospital. Such actions were considered a physical and moral offence against the dead or suffering and were unrelated to hygienic and sanitary considerations.[43]

---

[34] Bambi, Salvestrini and Tanzini (eds) 2023 *Gli Statuti della Repubblica fiorentina del 1355 in volgare*: t. II: *Statuto del Podestà*. b. IV. rubr. 64: 559.

[35] Arrighi (ed.) 2004 *Gli statuti di Scarperia*: rubr. 38: 90. On the town, see Brunori Cianti and Lazzi (eds) 2005.

[36] Vignoli 2001 *Statuti del Vicariato del Podere Fiorentino*: b. IV. rubr. 5: 210-211; Orlando (ed.) 2010 Statuto di Bassano 1259, b. II. rubr. 71: 80.

[37] Clementi (ed.) 1977 *Statuta Civitatis Aquile*: rubr. 269: 182; De Vio 1706 *Felicis et fidelissimae urbis panormitanae privilegia*: 101; Salvestrini (ed.) 1994 *Statuti del Comune di San Miniato al Tedesco*: b. II. rubr. 35<36>: 159. See Nada Patrone 1989: 185-186, 189-190; Magnusson and Squatriti 2000: 254-258; Tosi Brandi 2007: 13-14.

[38] *De pena lavantis coria prope aquam vivam* [Balsimelli (ed.) *Gli Statuti di San Marino*: b. 3. rubr. 128: 91].

[39] Cognasso 1913 *Statuti civili del Comune di Chieri*: rubr. 120: 71.

[40] *De pena lavantis pannos vel quid turpe prope citernam de fossis* [Balsimelli (ed.) *Gli Statuti di San Marino*: b. 3. rubr. 122: 88].

[41] See Geltner 2019: 195, note 129.

[42] Geltner writes in this regard that "health-related prescriptions in the sources usually assume that rather than explain why fecal matter, grease, and industrial waste are dangerous (*periculosum*)" (*ivi*: 96). Tosi Brandi 2007: 7; and Albertani 2007: 19-21, mention the close connection existing between hygiene and decorum, in relation to the statutory regulations of Emilia-Romagna. For a comparison with the similar situation in fifteenth-century Castilian cities, see del Val Valdivieso 2007: 175-176.

[43] Brogi (ed.) 1995 *Gli albori del Comune di San Gimignano e lo statuto del 1314*: b. IV. rubr. 183: 241-242; b. IV. rubr. 184: 242. See also Canzian 2022a: 109-110.

It should also be remembered that the 1287 statutes of Ferrara regulated waste disposal *pro decore civitatis* (for the decorum of the city).[44]

As we have already said, Galenic principles undoubtedly viewed the channelling of waste water as a way to avoid infections. However, we cannot be sure that they were behind the regulatory choices of municipal governments. The rules in the Florentine statutes, for example, required sewers to be sealed off and discharged into urban canals and the river Arno;[45] in other words, where, in the famous View of the Chain (*Veduta della catena*) – the first realistic representation of the city dating back to the late fifteenth century – we see people fishing, swimming, drawing water and sailing (**Fig. 41**).[46] Another *rubrica* of the same code allowed for textile processing residues to be thrown from one of the city's bridges.[47] A provision in the same statutes required that fresh produce sold at the market should first be washed in the Arno or another river.[48] Similar rules with similar outcomes are found in relation to the Adige River in the 1327 statutes of Verona, which specify that drainage channels (*scancie* or *aquaroli*) for sewage and other *turpitudo* could flow freely alongside roads as long as they were not higher than one foot.[49] Again in relation to the first half of the fourteenth century, the Milanese friar and chronicler Galvano Fiamma recalls that Azzone Visconti, lord of the city, had several underground *cloacae* built for the specific purpose of preventing the formation of slush that hindered the flow of street traffic.[50] After all, at the time it was normal in Milan for much of the sewage to flow into the gardens adjacent to houses.[51] The Milanese statutes of 1396 refer to the aforementioned *cloacae*, and thus to the existence of a city sewer system. However, the texts suggest that these structures consisted mainly of modest drainage canals, often open (*magolzia*), which carried sewage to private land or directly into the Seveso and Nirone Rivers.[52]

We could make comparable observations about the channelling of waste at Cagliari Castle, since the local statute only required waste water to be removed from squares and areas in front of the defensive wall, but allowed it to be discharged in nearby areas of no particular symbolic significance or strategic and military value. The 1295 statutes of Bassano (Veneto region) forbade the use of the castle porticos as latrines.[53] Similar considerations are suggested by the *androne* (covered sewers) mentioned in the 1255 statutes of Parma, and by the code of San Gimignano of 1314, which required covered sewers to be dug in secluded places in the

[44] Greci 1990: 439-441.
[45] Bambi, Salvestrini and Tanzini (eds) 2023 *Gli Statuti della Repubblica fiorentina del 1355 in volgare*: t. II: *Statuto del Podestà*. b. IV. rubr. 64: 559. See also Salvestrini 2005: 109-111, 116.
[46] Berlin, Kupferstichkabinett, Ludovico degli Uberti, from (attr.) Francesco di Lorenzo Rosselli, View of Florence known as *della Catena*, early sixteenthth-century xylographic copy of a c. 1472 painting, 6 sheets. Regulate fishing and navigation in the Arno Bambi, Salvestrini and Tanzini (eds) 2023 *Gli Statuti della Repubblica fiorentina del 1355 in volgare*: t. I: *Statuto del Capitano del Popolo*: b. III. rubr. 19: 473; t. II: *Statuto del Podestà*: b. III. rubr. 176: 452; b. III. rubr. 202: 484-486. On Florence as the epitome of medieval Europe's economic expansion and social organisation beyond ecological limits, see Hughes 1996.
[47] *Sia licito a ciascuno di gittare il pastaccio in Arno di sopra dal ponte Rubaconte* [Bambi, Salvestrini and Tanzini (eds) 2023 *Gli Statuti della Repubblica fiorentina del 1355 in volgare*: t. II: *Statuto del Podestà*: b. III. 119: 410].
[48] Ivi: t. I: *Statuto del Capitano del Popolo*: b. I. rubr. 120: 194.
[49] *Scancia Domus Nove per quam descendit aqua coquine taliter ordinetur quod aqua vadat subtus terram* [Bianchi, Granuzzo, Mariani Canova and Varanini (eds) 1992 *Statuti di Verona*: t. II. b. IV. rubr. 109: 591. See also rubr. 110. 116: 591, 593].
[50] Ceruti (ed.) Fiamma 1869: 469; Castiglioni (ed.) Fiamma 1938: 1018.
[51] Fantoni 1990: 109-111; Canzian 2022a: 114, 116.
[52] Milano, Biblioteca Ambrosiana, ms. B.19: *Statuta Civitatis Mediolanensis de anno MCCCXCVI*, c. 191v. See Bocchi 2009.
[53] Greci 1990: 444.

districts of the community (with the exception of the *Contrada di Piazza*), but permitted the use of these deposits, even if located within the walls and therefore close to homes, as latrines.[54] Along the same lines is the regulatory code of Uzzano (1389, Pistoia countryside) which prohibited the conversion of natural depressions in roadways into pockets for collecting sewage and other waste, so as not to obstruct transit and disturb passers-by, although these substances were allowed to accumulate elsewhere.[55] Finally, the most illuminating example is perhaps the thirteenth-century *Fontana dei Leoni*, originally built in front of the upper church of the Basilica of Saint Francis in Assisi. The city's 1319 statute forbade the washing of people, animals or things in this monumental structure and in the city's other major fountains. This was out of respect for the sacredness of the entire town and for the decorum of the basilica, which drew large numbers of pilgrims, rather than consideration for the cleanliness of the flowing water.[56]

It is useful to remember that it was customary at the time to wash clothes in urine, which has bleaching properties. Also, while there was widespread protection of rivers from various forms of pollution, especially as a way of safeguarding private and municipal property,[57] there were generally no rules for preserving the cleanliness of the sea, which was considered *res communis omnium* (that is susceptible to anyone's use and appropriation). For example, the statutes of the Sardinian coastal town of Castelgenovese (now Castelsardo) stipulated that washerwomen, flax workers and tanners should get their water from the mouth of the river Frigianu. This way they would avoid other carefully identified points further upstream, so that the section assigned for the irrigation of vineyards and other crops would stay clean. Meanwhile, dirty water could be discharged freely at the point of outlet of the stream into the sea.[58] The statutes of the communal era expressed a strong ambiguity regarding the legal status of the sea and the shores (*litora*), which, ultimately, for some Roman jurists like Neratius and Pomponius were to be considered *res nullius* (*Dig.* 41.1.14 pr.; 41.130.4). Therefore, regardless of the legal status of maritime areas, their waters were not the direct concern of either the public administration or private owners and, for this very reason, they were not subject to any form of environmental protection.[59] The major communal cities with important maritime statutes understood this type of legislation, mostly divorced from the Romanesque tradition,[60] as the law of navigation relating to commercial or military matters, not as legislation protecting a public good.[61]

Use of certain terminology is never unintentional, in my opinion. In the statute of the Piedmontese community of Masio, in the territory of Alessandria (1372), sewage was referred

[54] Greci 1990: 447-448; Brogi (ed.) 1995 *Gli albori del Comune di San Gimignano e lo statuto del 1314*: b. IV. rubr. 208: 247 (*De cloachis fiendis*); Sabbionesi 2019: 28-33; Canzian 2022a: 117-118.
[55] Vannucchi 2009: 16.
[56] Cenci 1974-76: 16.
[57] See, for example, the regulations prohibiting the poisoning of running waters with lime or the use of poisonous plants as a fishing technique found in Tuscan, Sardinian and Castilian legislative texts [Finzi (ed.) 1911 *Gli Statuti della Repubblica di Sassari*: 72; Caggese (ed.) 1921, and Pinto, Salvestrini and Zorzi (eds) 1999 *Statuti della Repubblica Fiorentina*: t. II: *Statuto del Podestà*: b. III. rubr. 82: 217 (*De piscibus non tossicandis*); Murgia (ed.) 2016 Carta de Logu: rubr. 85: 326; del Val Valdivieso 2007: 176-177; Sznura 2010: 270-271, 277-278; Borghero and Salvestrini 2023]. *Nemo audeat piscari, cum maza vel quaraguasco, calcina vel simili artificio [...] in fluminibus vel aliquis aquis, per quod pisces moriantur vel infirmentur* [Gualtieri (ed.) *Gli Statuti di Vernio*: rubr. 29: 47, Tuscan Apennine mountains, fourteenth c.].
[58] Besta 1899: 216, 218, 219; See also Bocchi 1995: 106-107.
[59] See Vallocchia 2011-12 (access October 2023).
[60] Tangheroni 2001, p. 165.
[61] See Musarra 2021.

to as *bruterium* (with an obvious concern for the protection of decorum), and it was established that these substances should be kept, just as in the Tuscan town of San Gimignano, within walled spaces between individual properties, and between houses and the public street.[62] The *putredo, soczura, bruttura* often mentioned in the legislative texts[63] referred to contaminated substances that undoubtedly equated physical dirtiness with immorality.[64] In the statutes of another Tuscan town, Colle Val d'Elsa, *aliquid turpe* is used to refer to sewage; while the code of the Veneto municipality of Portogruaro (1434) speaks of *aliquam aquam immondam* and *putrida substantia seu turpia*.[65]

Ultimately, regulatory sources mention the cleanliness or, in a broader sense, the purity of water. In my opinion, however, this is not only in relation to its physical qualities. Water could be beneficial or harmful. It could be characterised in terms of 'goodness' or 'malice', as Pier de' Crescenzi wrote in the first decade of the fourteenth century. According to the famous agronomist, the difference between the various waters present in the soils undoubtedly depended on the physical structure of the terrains through which they flowed (stony or non-stony soils), the direction in which the streams flowed (the waters of streams sloping towards the east were preferable for drinking), or its weight.[66] It is more than likely that experience led to a preference for better, more pleasant drinking water, perhaps flavoured and mixed with wine.[67] However, the 'moral' nature of this element also played a role in the choice of what water was to be used or protected. It was purity in terms of simplicity, 'neutrality' and tasteless humility that gave value to water. Moral purity recalled the dignity of the element at the expense of its consubstantial 'banality'. The *munditia* of water redeemed its 'inferiority', which made it, for example, less valuable than wine and unsuitable for the privileged classes to drink.[68] Water could assume a sacramental value or be an expression of the most fetid bodily ejections. It could be a symbol of life and regeneration or a cause of corruption,[69] but it was above all man's actions and the rules imposed by social contexts that determined these alterations in status, rather than its intrinsic physical quality.

As Douglas argued from an anthropological perspective, law and institutions helped to define the quality of food and drink and whether or not it was permissible to consume them, on the basis of moral dictates or, more generally, collective ethical and religious consensus. The rejection of 'dirty' water was not necessarily due to a need to protect people's physical health, but was often meant to uphold the symbolic categorisations that enabled the application of social rules and order.[70] Moreover it was better not to abuse even good water: the well-being conferred by ablutions and baths or even the simple ingestion of fresh, good water could

62 Guasco 1975 *Statuti di Masio*: rubr. 272: 132.

63 *Niuna persona ... ardisca ... fare alcuna socçura né bruttura a neuna fonte de la corte di Trequanda* (in Sienese area). See Ciampoli and Turrini (eds) 2002 *Statuti Medievali e Moderni del Comune di Trequanda*. 1369: b. III. rubr. 29: 66.

64 Duranti 2023: 21-22.

65 See Ninci (ed.) 1999 *Statuta antiqua Communis Collis Vallis Else*: t. I. 1341. b. III. rubr. 26, 27: 361; Orlando (ed.) 2010: 128. See Morrison 2008: 7-8; Bocchi 2009: 334-338, 342-347; Bayless 2012; Geltner 2019: 43-44.

66 De' Crescenzi 1995. I: 31-36. See, in this regard, Montanari 2012: 146.

67 Montanari 2012: 143-145, 149-150.

68 Comparing the perceptions of people in the Middle Ages with those of contemporary societies, Squatriti writes of "asimmetrie fra purezza microbiologica e tolleranza culturale dell'acqua" (see Squatriti 2008: 584-600). See also Pibiri (ed.) 2018: 31-32.

69 Piscitelli forthcoming.

70 Douglas 1966: 7-29.

lead to sin, lasciviousness, moral corruption and, thus, also to physical disease.[71] Meanwhile, in papal Rome, the use of *balnea* of classical origin long endured through the Middle Ages, despite the condemnation of bodily pleasures. This was the result of continuous use and shared social practices that were justified by both the desire for cleanliness and the need for ritual purification.[72]

Water participated in the polysemy that characterised the quest for well-being in the centuries of the Middle Ages; a quest that could not separate the satisfaction of material needs from the aspiration for eternal salvation.[73] For lawmakers, water could of course be dirty or clean. However, the dirtiness and purity of water had a significance that went beyond its organoleptic properties, its composition, its condition and its odour – in short, its merely physical status.

3. Thermal waters

To demonstrate the social, rather than the strictly healing value of the 'beneficial' liquid element, the subject of thermal waters deserves separate discussion. In some cases, the properties of these springs had been known to the surrounding populations since ancient times, and the beliefs of philosophers and doctors about them were relatively widespread.[74] Although they may not have been entirely aware of the springs' real therapeutic properties,[75] urban and rural dwellers, particularly the wealthier among them, would frequent the sites that gave forth relatively famous waters, to drink there and mainly to bathe. Considering the fact that drinking water generally tasted bad and was often replaced by fermented drinks, thermal water was one of the few liquids that could also be ingested or, rather, could be bathed in, for curative reasons.[76] Places like the Bormio and Masino baths in Lombardy, those of Bagnolo and Vinadio (Piedmont), *Aquae Patavinae* (Terme Euganee, in Veneto), Acqui on the Ligurian Apennines, the sources of Salso (Salsomaggiore, in Emilia, known from at least the eighth century); Bagno di Romagna; Montecatini, Monsummano, and the other spa towns in the Lucca–Pistoia area; Bagno a Corsena, Monte Pisano, Bagno a Morbo (Volterra) in the Tyrrhenian region; Petriolo, Bagno Vignoni, Bagni di San Filippo and San Casciano dei Bagni south of Siena; Bagni di Roselle, Gavorrano and Saturnia in the Maremma district; the *Balnea* of Fontecchio in Umbria; the sulphurous springs of Bullicame near Viterbo, and the Roman and medieval baths of Fordongianus in Sardinia were mentioned and described by epistolographists and treatise writers of the time; and we know that they were frequented intensively in the late thirteenth and early fourteenth centuries.[77] As early as the end of the twelfth century, the chronicler Pietro da Eboli (or, according to other attributions, Alcadino of Syracuse) wrote the treatise *De balneis puteolanis* dedicated to the thermal waters of the Campi Flegrei near Naples.[78]

[71] Vigarello 1987: 20-22, 39-42; Montanari 2012: 140-142.
[72] Annoscia 2007: 114-115; De Francesco 2017: 85, 88-91.
[73] See *La ricerca del benessere individuale e sociale* 2011.
[74] Bacci 1571; Sorcinelli 1998: 113-128; Nicoud 2022.
[75] On this topic see Guérin-Beauvois and Martin 2007; Chandelier 2010.
[76] See, on the topic, the missive of the Pratese merchant Francesco di Marco Datini on the water of Montecatini and Porretta in Tuscany (Nigro 1994: 132).
[77] Barbini 1975; Cherubini 1986; Graziani 1986; Premuda 1988-90; Melis 1989; Chambers 1992; di Lollo 1996: 5; Boisseuil 2002: 2-3, 253-319, 393; Boisseuil 2010: 492-495.
[78] Clark 1989-90; Maddalo 2000.

It is the legislative records that reveal that the fame of these baths spread even further after the 1348 plague, when interest in places of healing undoubtedly grew;[79] although for some locations the effect of the epidemics seems to have been the opposite, namely to induce fear of promiscuous places where infections were thought to be easier to contract.[80]

Since, from a legal point of view, thermal springs were not different from other perennial sources, they were linked to the land on which they were located, and it was possible to take possession of them by channelling water and building basins. These unusual circumstances outside of the ordinary management of public and private waters were especially recorded in central Italy and along major international routes, such as the *Via Francigena*. Here spa sites arose which, as Boisseuil suggests, were locations identified by place names with one or more baths fed by springs, and larger spa areas, in which waters rose from various springs and flowed into distinct baths surrounded by infrastructure designed to welcome bathers.[81] Some important cities especially located south of the Apennines, such as Siena, Lucca, Pisa, Viterbo and Volterra, but also Padua, expressed a clear desire to have control over these places, both by purchasing them and, above all, by formulating statutory articles dedicated to the *publica utilitas* of their waters.[82] The local political authorities had attained an awareness of the, if nothing else, economic importance of the hot and/or mineral springs situated in their territories (*balnea*). For this reason, they devoted a great deal of normative measures to these resources. As the statute of Viterbo sums up effectively, local sulphurous pools had to be maintained in good condition to facilitate access for bathers, whose presence benefited the community (*taliter quod ex ipsis Comunitas possit habere utilitatem*).[83]

The communal legislation on spa waters in places in *Tuscia* has been published and analysed in an important work by Didier Boisseuil.[84] From the collections of statutes that he has examined and recorded we can draw interesting insight into the way communes designed legislation on this subject. First, it emerges that legislators never presented the potential therapeutic virtues of the waters within their jurisdiction. The studies conducted, at least since the twelfth century, by physicians such as Pietro da Eboli (ca. 1150–1220), Pietro d'Abano († 1316) and Michele Savonarola (1385–1468) on the health-giving properties of certain waters are not mentioned and appear not to be reflected in the statutory texts.[85] As we have said, the authorities were, however, aware of their economic and social importance and mandated that special care be taken of the sources, and that new veins be found, in addition to the construction and maintenance of conduits, proper management of drainage ditches and other infrastructure needed for transporting the water. At the same time, they prohibited or limited the creation of branches and obstacles (like mills) that would weaken the flow of water;[86] and it was of course forbidden to throw rubbish into springs and pools or make improper use of

[79] Boisseuil 2002: 129-238.
[80] Guarducci 2021: 26.
[81] Guarducci 2021: 27, 34-36; Boisseuil 2018.
[82] Boisseuil 2002: 70, 274-276; Esposito 2012; Gloria 1873 *Gli statuti del comune di Padova*: b. 4. rubr. 2: 300-303; b. 4. rubr. 4: 308-312.
[83] *De ducenda aqua ad piscinas ionketi* (Ciampi 1872 *Statuto di Viterbo del 1251*: b. I. rubr. 34: 462).
[84] Boisseuil 2002; see also Boisseuil 2009.
[85] Mantelli and Temporelli 2007: 114; Simonetti 2012b.
[86] Fumi (ed.) 1874 *Gli statuti di Chianciano*: rubr. 146, 203, 337: 76, 84, 161; Boisseuil 2002: 346-348 (Siena 1293); rubr. 22, 24: 354 (Siena 1293); *ivi*: t. III, rubr. 121, 123, 125, 265, 268, 271, 277: 341, 343-346 (Siena 1262); *ivi*: 376-377 (Siena 1337-39); Lucca 1454: Giambastiani (ed.) 1996: 493-499 (Lucca 1454). See also Boisseuil 2002: 329-332; Boisseuil 2003: 351-352.

thermal water for, say, macerating flax or softening leather.[87] Some communes managed these sources themselves, forbade their privatisation, either entirely or in part, and levied duties on them.[88] In the mid-thirteenth century, the municipality of Siena sent a member of the *podestà*'s family to several spa locations (Bagni di Petriolo and Macereto) as rector of the baths, whose activity was regulated from 1293 by specific *ordinamenta balneorum*. During the fourteenth century his area of competence was expanded and transformed into an administrative district called the *Podesteria dei bagni*.[89] The thirteenth-century statute of Acqui, a town located between Liguria and Piedmont, established the public nature of the space surrounding the thermal pool located in the cathedral square.[90] Smaller localities, like Gavorrano in the Siena area, preferred to tender out the management of spas and the collection of the resulting proceeds to the highest bidder every year.[91] Statute makers also made provisions for hospices and other accommodation facilities for bathers, which were required to be orderly at all times and suitable for ensuring the physical and moral safety of visitors to the spas.[92] There was never any distinction between the importance of keeping facilities efficient and running smoothly and that of separating the sexes and monitoring conduct in places where men and women bathed naked, once again showing that safeguarding the health of the body and the soul always went hand in hand.[93]

We know that different kinds of people with many different types of diseases, especially of the skin, went to spas. However, legislation only made explicit reference to certain individuals, such as lepers. The statutes of the spa resort of Chianciano in the Siena area, for example, prohibited them from washing their clothes in the waters where members of the community came to wash theirs. The tone of the measure was certainly in defence of public health (although this is not made explicit in the text), but it is interesting that it only concerned the skin disease with widely known religious connotations and subject to moral stigmatisation originating from the Bible.[94]

Aside from these, other statute rules were geared to ensuring other forms of safety for bathers, such as the ban on carrying weapons to places where naked, and therefore defenceless, people gathered; or the prohibition of gambling; and the injunction on fighting and disorderly conduct, most likely because of the large numbers of visitors.[95] The statutes also laid down rules on the markets that formed more or less spontaneously in these locations.[96]

---

[87] Soffici and Savino (eds) 2003 *Statuto di Monsummano*: rub. xlvii: 53-54; Fornarese (ed.) 1971 (1st ed. 1905) *Statuta Vetera Civitatis Aqui*: p. 35. See also Vannucchi 2009: 18-20.

[88] *Quod inveniatur unus operarius ad actandam aquam calidam* [Soffici and Savino (eds) 2003 *Statuto di Monsummano*: rub. xlvi: 53]; Giambastiani (ed.) 1996: b. V, rubr. 38. 39. 113. 114: 443-449 (Lucca 1331); *ivi*: 464-467 (Lucca 1372); Boisseuil 2002: 359-360 (Siena 1305-25); *ivi*: b. III. 66: 362 (Siena 1309).

[89] Boisseuil 2002: 31.

[90] Fornarese (ed.) 1971 (1st ed. 1905) *Statuta vetera civitatis Aqui*: pp. 25, 81.

[91] Boisseuil 2002: 323-324 (Gavorrano 1465).

[92] Boisseuil 2002: 331, 333, 336-337 (Lucca, 1454, 1469, 1485).

[93] Ciampi 1872 *Statuto di Viterbo del 1251*: b. IV. rubr. 93: 592; Boisseuil 2002: 386; Guarducci 2021: 29-32.

[94] Fumi (ed.) 1874 *Gli statuti di Chianciano*: rubr. 262: 137-138; Ascheri (ed.) 1987 *Chianciano 1287*: rubr. 158-162: 153-154; Boisseuil 2002: b. IV. rubr. 94: 388 (Viterbo 1469). On the image of lepers in medieval culture, see Bériac-Lainé 1998.

[95] Boisseuil 2002: rubr. 16, 18, 19: 352-353 (Siena 1293); *ivi*: b. III. rubr. 159: 363 (Siena 1309); *ivi*: 387-388 (Viterbo 1469).

[96] Boisseuil 2002: rubr. 23, 28, 29: 354-356 (Siena 1293); *ivi*: b. III. rubr. 165-167: 365-366 (Siena 1309).

VII

Water-driven Machinery

1. Grain mills and fulling mills: the economy and the law

Watermills and fulling machines (*gualchiere*) appeared along the banks of rivers and torrents. Among these were the water-driven machinery used for grinding or processing cloth, as well as hammers used to mint coins (and in Florence to stamp florins, the most prestigious currency in the Medieval Europe) which required running water.[1] During the fourteenth century, the silk mill technique was discovered and perfected in Bologna. Hydraulic machines were used to increase productivity and improve the quality of these processes.[2]

Until the thirteenth century, these factories were in major cities in communal Italy, such as Bologna, Reggio Emilia, Padua, Verona and Milan, especially on church-owned property.[3] Roughly speaking – although there is wide variation in the availability of documentary and regulatory sources on this subject for the various Italian regions –[4] from 1250, with the advent of the *Popolo* regimes came the communal authorities' growing interest in these workshops that were essential to the survival of the overall community. Communes not only took possession and direct management of numerous machines,[5] but also kept them efficient and sound, mostly by incorporating masonry constructions into wooden structures and by fortifying them against potential sieges or river floods.[6] This policy went hand in hand with control of the grain trade and taxes on milled products.

To regulate the use of these machines, the drafters of statutory texts had to resort to the experience of public administrators and economic operators, since technological developments had distanced jurists from the precedents of Roman law in this field. It was necessary, however, to rely on Romanistic tradition to assess, for example, whether the construction of a watermill altered the course of a river and whether the owners of land or buildings downstream of this hydraulic machine suffered harm from its construction or lost any advantage they previously enjoyed.[7] One of the most interesting products of this interaction is undoubtedly the statute of the consortium of mill owners located on the right bank of the Bisenzio River, in and around the Tuscan city of Prato (*Statuto dell'Arte dei padroni dei mulini sulla sponda destra del fiume Bisenzio*, 1296–1484). During the communal period, Prato had a strong craft and manufacturing base, which had long made industrial use of the nearby river.[8] Numerous grain mills and fulling

---

[1] Salvestrini 2005: 30; Arnoux 2008: 740; Coli and Pranzini 2023: 58.

[2] Guenzi and Grandi 2010: 474-475; Cazzola 2021: 89; Maire Vigueur 2023: 268-274.

[3] See Dussaix 1979: 115-119; Pini 1987: 16; Bortolami 1988: 289-291; Balestracci 1994: 115.

[4] Chiappa Mauri 2003a: 236-237.

[5] See Muendel 1991: 370, 372-374. The progressive acquisition of rights to water and hydraulic power facilities by the *Populus* communes was systematic and led to the expropriation of structures in centres such as Reggio Emilia and Bologna. It remained, however, limited to strict control of water and machines in Milan, Padua and Viterbo. On this topic, see Dussaix 1979: 127-139; Pini 1987: 15-19; Bortolami 1988: 299; Balestracci 1992: 447-450; Lanconelli and De Palma 1992: 46-47; Boucheron 1994: 126-127; Chiappa Mauri 1998[2]: 105-107.

[6] Papaccio 2008.

[7] See Cavallar 2008: 111-116; Cavallar 2010: 114-120. See also Arnoux 2008: 715-720.

[8] Braudel and Cherubini (eds) 1991.

mills for processing textiles lined the banks of the Bisenzio. Between 1293 and 1296, the lists of millers registered by the public authorities indicated as many as 67 mills; whereas in the early fourteenth century Florence only had 14 millers who were heads of families. To avoid conflicts and to exert a calming influence on the milling industry, the municipality of Prato acted as impresario and for a long time constructed hydraulic machines. However, private enterprise also grew during the late thirteenth and fourteenth centuries. In order to continue exercising a mediating role, the commune encouraged the emergence of an association of owners interested in this activity. This association soon became a guild, albeit without the political role held by other professional associations. The municipal authorities delegated to the association part of the management of the water intended for motive power.[9] As early as the thirteenth century, guilds of mill owners were required to draft a statute. This legal text represented the consortium of owners, that is, those who normally rented their machines to millers.[10] The primary purpose of the statute was to regulate the maintenance and cleaning of bulkheads and canals. This activity was financed by the owners in the consortium.[11] For the distribution of water, the code stipulated the election of two council members, whose task was to ensure that sufficient water reached all operators, especially during the summer season.[12] Just like the *partidores* in the Sassari statutes,[13] these appointees had the task of mediating between the needs of the millers and those of the farmers.[14]

If we disregard the interesting Prato *codex*, it is the regulations on milling machines that highlight the gap that sometimes existed between the economic importance of these structures, ascertained from various property and administrative records, and the relative scarcity of references in statutory texts. This is the case, for example, of the community of Montalcino in Val d'Orcia (south of Siena), whose fifteenth-century statute only mentions mills in a single rubric aimed at defending them from possible damage, in the context of a local economy heavily reliant on these hydraulic machines.[15]

2. Machine typologies

There were, in cities and countryside, many different types of machines.[16] For example, in thirteenth- and fourteenth-century Florence, wooden mills stood along the urban stretch of the Arno, either suspended over the river but built along the exposed gravel bed (*molendinum pendulum*), or floating anchored to the banks (*molendinum in navibus*); both types had vertical wheels. There were also *terranei* mills, which stood near the artificial canals (*rogge*). The floating mills had the advantage of being faster to build and movable to where the current was stronger to draw maximum benefit from the motive force provided by the water. Yet they were rather fragile structures, subject to being uprooted and overturned by the waves. One interesting record in the form of a protocol of the notary Biagio Boccadibue for 1306 details the sale made by Nera, daughter of the late Ranieri, from the people of San Niccolò, who, for four gold florins, sold to Tuccio, son of Feci, all her rights to a quarter share in two ships with

[9] Piattoli (ed.) 1936 *Lo Statuto dell'Arte dei padroni dei mulini*: 77-84, 87-88, 97-98.
[10] Ivi: 88-90.
[11] Ivi, rubr. 11, 12, 14, 36, 37: 119-120, 128.
[12] Ivi, rubr. 27: 124.
[13] See chapter 6.
[14] Piattoli (ed.) 1936 *Lo Statuto dell'Arte dei padroni dei mulini*: rubr. 30, 38: 126, 128-129.
[15] Viola 2018 *Montalcino. Lo statuto dei danni dati*: 75-77, 131-132.
[16] For an overview, see Cortese 1997: 47-58.

mill and tools in bad repair, that is, sunken and swept away by the waters of the Arno. It also gave permission for these items to be searched for in the river, so they could be recovered and restored to function.[17] Alongside these main types were the above-mentioned *terranei* or *terragni* mills, which had horizontal wheels and were also distributed along lesser streams.[18]

To give one more example, in Verona, many machines afloat on the waters of the Adige had similar structures to the Florence mills (**Fig. 42**). The *Chronicon veronense* by Paride da Cerea reports that a flood submerged more than 50 in 1239.[19] Even in Turin, a smaller town at the time, duties on milling facilities was a significant source of income for the public purse, and was therefore regulated by communal *ordinati* (statutes and deliberations). The 1360 code forbade the branching of new canals from the course of the river Dora and imposed a requirement to make use of existing canals.[20]

In almost all the normative texts analysed here, references are found to these types of infrastructure, especially watermills, since the presence of windmills was scarce in Italy for environmental reasons.[21] The government authorities of smaller communes intervened to encourage the installation of new wheels, particularly, as in the case of San Gimignano, during the thirteenth century, when the municipality allowed landowners wishing to build machinery to dig canals that cut through neighbouring property. The law code of this populous, 'minor' centre in Tuscany even required landowners to sell their plots of land to whoever intended to implement such infrastructure.[22]

The statutes of the most important cities that were already equipped with machinery regulated various activities and aimed to encourage and protect them.[23] For example, the early fourteenth-century codes of Ravenna protected canals with mills by prohibiting people from crossing over them with wagons and from watering animals there. This prevented them from getting damaged. It was also forbidden to dig further into any trench; only the owners of adjacent land had access to them.[24] A similar attitude can be seen in the statutes of Perugia from the thirteenth and fourteenth centuries, which focused on the disputes (*scandagle*) that often arose between landowners who wanted to extract water for irrigation and managers of mills who needed running water.[25] The statutory code from Poggibonsi in Valdelsa (central Tuscany, 1332), a community with an out-of-town monumental fountain (**Fig. 18**), stipulated the maintenance of the *fontes*, *puteos* and *aqueducti*. These supplied water by order of the commune leaders, although the maintenance costs were charged to landowners and mill owners.[26] On this point, many law codes seem to agree: mills and fulling machines were fundamental resources for the economies of some centres situated along rivers or torrents (as

[17] De Angelis, Gigli and Sznura (eds) 1984: 27-28.
[18] See Beggio 1977: 549-550, 557; Muendel 1984: 215-218, 222, 224-225; Dockès 1991: 120-123; Comba (ed.) 1993.
[19] Vaccari (ed.) 2014 *Il «Chronicon Veronense»*: I. 1.
[20] Bizzarri (ed.) 1933 *Gli Statuti del Comune di Torino*: rubr. 154: 75-76.
[21] See Basing 1990: 39-42.
[22] Diacciati and Tanzini (eds.) 2016 *Lo statuto di San Gimignano del 1255*: b. IV. rubr. 94: 139.
[23] Besta and Barni (eds) 1949 *Liber consuetudinum Mediolani*: b. XX. rubr. 1-3: 108; Bianchi, Granuzzo, Mariani Canova and Varanini (eds) 1992 *Statuti di Verona*: t. II. b. III. rubr. 132. 133: 508; Pesci, Ugolini and Venturi (eds) 1994.
[24] Pasolini (ed.) 1868, repr. 1985 *Gli Statuti di Ravenna*: b. V. rubr. 115: 112. See also Roversi Monaco 2000: 85-103; Pirani 2014: 191-192.
[25] Caprioli (ed.) 1996 *Statuto del Comune di Perugia*: rubr. 451: 404, 406; Salem Elsheikh (ed.) 2000 *Statuto del Comune e del Popolo di Perugia*: t. I. b II. rubr. 56: 436-443.
[26] Pucci and De la Roncière (eds) 1995 *Poggibonsi e il suo statuto*: b. I. rubr. 3; b. I. rubr. 39: 57, 83-84.

was the town of Colle di Valdelsa in Tuscany),[27] but such machinery was an important source of earnings for its owners and managers. For this reason, it was the latter's duty to bear the cost of the upkeep of mill runs, canals, dykes, splint walls and other necessary structures.[28] In northern Italy, the municipality of Treviso explicitly required mill owners to install access stairways and bridges.[29] The previously mentioned Milanese statutes on roads and water stated that, if disposing of water after use without discharging it into the same torrent, the owner was required to close mill races fed with water from the Olona River and used to rotate waterwheels.[30]

Despite the substantial repetition of norms relating to grinding machinery, they nevertheless highlight some details that are worthy of mention. For example, the 1325 statute of Cortona introduced a distinction between dry mills – powered by animals – and watermills. This differentiation allows us to deduce, from the maximum wages of operators, that the latter were on average more profitable than the former.[31]

[27] Salvestrini 2007.
[28] Ninci (ed.) 1999 *Statuta antiqua Communis Collis Vallis Else*: b. I. rubr. 29. 32. 34. 60: 136-139, 141-142, 162; Mendoza 2022 *Gli Statuti del Comune di Roma*: b. I. rubr. 131: 168.
[29] Betto (ed.) 1984 *Gli Statuti del comune di Treviso*: b. I. rubr. 287. 288: 224-225. On mills in the Veneto area, see Canzian 2014: 239-242.
[30] Stella, Farina and Balestreri (eds) 1992 *Gli statuti delle strade e delle acque del contado di Milano*: 67: 77-78.
[31] Allegria and Capelli (eds) 2014 *Statuto del Comune di Cortona*: b. I. rubr. 17: 138-140.

VIII

Transportation of Merchandise and People. Timber Rafting

1. Waterways

During the Middle Ages, interaction between land and water routes was very common. It was normal for a journey made by people or goods to begin, say, on a path and continue along a navigable river, across a lake or marshland, and perhaps proceed further by sea. In contrast to what seems to have happened in England from the thirteenth century onwards,[1] navigation continued to develop in communal Italy during this and the following periods, along with the transportation of goods by waterway.[2] According to a convincing hypothesis by Szabó, the reorganisation of the medieval road network from the thirteenth century onwards was in part due to the interaction between land and river routes.[3] In principle, navigable rivers served to speed up and ease travel. The large number of statutory regulations that we find in the codes of the Po Valley area, aimed at enforcing the cleaning of rivers and canals, was motivated more by the need to maintain waterways than by the fear of floods.[4] Major rivers like the Po, the Ticino, the Adige, the Piave, the Arno and the Tiber provided the quickest and safest routes of communication and goods transportation on the Italian Peninsula. For this reason, more or less large urban and rural settlements had sprung up mainly along their banks or close to them. We know that, until modern times, Venice was connected via various canals and rivers to Lake Maggiore. The development of communities in the lower Veneto plain was related to the excavation of canals at least as early as the twelfth century.[5] Particularly evident was the joining of land and water routes in the Friuli area, at the extreme north-eastern edge of Italy (*Caput Adriae*), where the Adriatic Sea penetrated deep into the European continent and a network of rivers, canals and paths linked the coasts to Alpine routes and passes.[6]

Between the eleventh and twelfth centuries, Donizone, the biographer of Matilda of Canossa (1046 – ca. 1115), called the Po a road and Matilda its mistress (*Ipsa Padi stratam tenet*).[7] Between the thirteenth and fourteenth centuries, the delta branch of the river which reached the Adriatic Sea between Ravenna and Comacchio became particularly important for the transportation of salt. The waterway was long the object of dispute between the local municipalities (Comacchio, Ravenna, Cervia) and the capitals of the largest territorial domains in the region (Venice and the Papacy).[8]

1 Blair (ed.) 2014.
2 Maire Vigueur 2023: 262-263.
3 Szabó 1986: 30.
4 See Fantoni 1990: 43-45; Maire Vigueur 2023: 254-255.
5 Simonetti 2019: 33-35.
6 Degrassi 2007: 162-165, 182.
7 Donizone 1984: 134, v. 335. See Andreolli 2008: 444-446.
8 Soranzo 1964; Cazzola 2021: 99-102.

Moving to central Italy, all cities in northern Tuscany (Florence, Prato, Pistoia, Lucca and Pisa) could be reached by waterways.[9] The intersection of water and land routes and the connection between river and sea transport constituted the backbone of the communication system both in the Po valley and in central Italy, albeit with marked regional differences.[10]

In 1183, the year of the Peace of Constance between the emperor and the communes, the Italian municipalities obtained from the sovereign the right to keep their *consuetudines in aquis*, to build and manage roads and to collect *ripaticus* (mooring fees).[11] These rights had been in the hands of local authorities since ancient times. For instance, in Porto, near Verona, there is evidence of them as far back as the tenth century.[12] The communes' victory over the imperial authority led to a decisive takeover of the territories bordering the cities, which, in the Po Valley area, also extended to control of communication routes. These included waterways. Therefore, from this period onwards, it was mainly the cities that promoted the excavation of new canals linking urban and minor centres.[13] Organising transport became an important aspect of municipal planning, which is why it inevitably made its way into statute law. Naturally, the statutes devoted more attention to the management of overland routes, which required intensive and complex maintenance. However, they also deal with waterways, which were the main routes for transporting large quantities of goods. One barge, in fact, could normally carry up to 300 times the weight that a mule could.[14] The strategic importance of the transportation of people and goods in lake regions is seen in the statute of Como, drafted immediately after the city came under Milanese rule (1335). In fact, several rubrics of the code mention the maintenance of the wharves and ports overlooking the eponymous lake.[15]

Of course, water transport had its costs. The duties levied at landfall points, updated forms of the ancient *telonaei*, mainly benefited the coastal municipalities, which, not surprisingly, drew up meticulous levy statutes. In communal period and, in some cases, up to the mid-modern age, some ancient tolls were still being levied by local, mostly ecclesiastical lords, who had long been in charge of this important source of income.[16] Moreover, the dynamics of the relationship between cities and subject towns also emerged in relation to water transportation and related charges. For example, the statute of the Tuscan municipality of Santa Maria a Monte charged different tolls on grain and salt transported along the road and the river in the Arno valley depending on the parties involved, favouring hauliers of the municipality of Florence, the dominant city public authority, and demanding more from individual merchants.[17] The community of Verona also imposed taxes and strict control over the transport of salt by river.[18] The statute of the commune of Modena (1327) devoted no fewer than 364 articles of its fifth book to the protection of waters and roads. In 1336, the municipality decided to further increase this legislation by isolating it from the rest of the law and creating a separate statute that would be periodically reformed until 1525. It was

[9] Raviola 2006; *Il Tevere* 2006; Salvestrini 2010b; Orlando 2011; Campopiano 2018: 34-35; Coli and Pranzini 2023: 53-55.
[10] Rossiaud 2005; Chiodi 2008; Greci 2010; and, for a comparison with the modern French context, Szulman 2014.
[11] Balestracci 1992: 438; Dani 2020: 40.
[12] Castagnetti 1976: 35; Stella 2022: 281.
[13] Rippe 2003: 519; Simonetti 2012a: 61-81.
[14] Fasoli 1978; Scavizzi 1991: 7; Foresti and Tozzi Fontana (eds) 1999; Sydow 2000; Salvestrini 2005: 30-34.
[15] Manganelli (ed.) 1936-57 *Statuti di Como del 1335*: I: 83, 87; II: 39, 243. See also Duvia 2007: 213-214.
[16] On rural river lords, with a focus on Piedmont, see Rao 2016: 14-17.
[17] Casini (ed.) 1963 *Statuto del Comune di Santa Maria a Monte*: rubr. 243: 245-246. On salt transportation during the period see Wyrozumsky 1986: 166-168.
[18] Bianchi, Granuzzo, Mariani Canova and Varanini (eds) 1992 *Statuti di Verona*: t. II. b. III. rubr. 156: 516.

published for the first time in 1545 as *Statuta civitatis Mutinae ad iudices aquarum pertinentia*, and reprinted thirty years later.[19] According to this complex, stratified legislative tradition, a judge was specially charged with ensuring that these infrastructures were not damaged by frequent flooding events (*aquarum superabundancia*), which could interrupt the supply of goods.[20] While it is true that most articles in all of Modena's statute drafts concerned the maintenance of the road network and, to a lesser extent, the waterways, it was maintenance of the former that required strict supervision of running water, particularly the nearby Secchia and Panaro Rivers.[21]

For the municipality of Asti, a city in Piedmont with a strong merchant tradition, strategically located in the Tanaro River valley, the *pedagium canalium* that it temporarily ceded to King Robert of Anjou in 1312 was an important source of income.[22] In any case, the duties levied on river traffic ('passages') were less frequent and lower than those on roads, fords and bridges.[23]

From the twelfth century onwards, the countryside around many major centres in the Po valley and northern Tuscany was torn up to create a growing number of artificial canals, defended by main and intermediate banks, which became the main access routes connecting cities. The river transport network in the Lombardy and Veneto areas is documented at least as far back as the eleventh century and was encouraged primarily by Venetian and Milanese merchants, who used both urban and suburban ports and moorings located along the principal river arteries, and managed primarily by the bishops and, later, the municipal authorities.[24] Even 'minor' cities like Padua, Bologna and Udine invested in digging canals: Padua in order to have a direct connection to the Venetian lagoon from the river Brenta; Bologna in order to intercept the waters of the Reno and Savena torrents and to build a canal for navigation (Navile, thirteenth century); and Udine to draw conduits (*rogge*) from the Friulian Torre creek.[25]

After the Peace of Constance, against a backdrop of difficult agreements between the victorious Lombard cities against Frederick I, Holy Roman Emperor, Milan claimed navigation rights on the river Lambro. Similarly, in 1198, after the wars fought alongside Piacenza and Brescia against Pavia, Cremona, Lodi, Como and Bergamo, Milan took direct possession of Lodi's river port on the Adda and reserved the right to transport and unload essential goods (grain, pulses and wine) anywhere within the territory of Lombardy.[26] Although nearby Bergamo had, since 1168, allowed the Milanese full access and complete exemption from tolls between the Adda and Oglio Rivers, the Lambro's draught was too shallow for boats in the summer, which persuaded the Milanese to turn to the far more important Ticino. This river offered the advantage of a direct, convenient link to the Po and therefore the possibility of extending trade towards Lake Maggiore and all the sub-alpine regions.[27] The excavation of the largest Milanese canal, initially called Ticinello and then Naviglio Grande, can be traced back

[19] *Statuta civitatis Mutine* 1575.
[20] Campori 1864 *Statuta civitatis Mutine*: b. I. rubr. 128 and 129.
[21] Ivi: b. IV. rubr. 188.
[22] Gabiani and Gabotto 1906: *Atti della Società del Popolo di Asti*: 434.
[23] Orlando (ed.) 2010 *Statuti di Belluno* 1392: b. IV. rubr. 134. 135. 172: 93, 97.
[24] Biscaro 1908: 285-286; Fantoni 1990: 23-25; Varanini 2009; Mussini 2010: 232-233; Canzian 2019: 25.
[25] Molà: 447; Guenzi and Grandi 2010: 476; Vergani 2010: 507-508; Simonetti 2012a: 62-65; Maire Vigueur 2023: 259-260.
[26] Fantoni 1990: 25.
[27] See Andenna 2002.

to 1177–79, although it was only enlarged and made suitable for navigation in 1269.[28] In 1220, the other Lombard city, Cremona took steps to avoid the duties levied by nearby Mantua, by joining forces with Reggio Emilia to construct a canal originating from the Po between Guastalla and Luzzara and entering the Secchia River at Reggiolo, to provide direct contact with the larger river.[29]

The magnificent system of canals in the Veneto region was begun roughly at the same time as the Milan network in order to regulate the waters of the numerous alpine rivers and streams, and provide convenient transport routes and energy for hydraulic machines.[30] One of the first canals to open seems to have been the Bisatto, which the Vicentines excavated in 1140–43 by diverting the Bacchiglione towards Este along the ancient Sirone canal. In 1314, in order to ensure the city was not left without water, the Paduans derived a new canal from the Brenta River, calling it the Brentella and joining it to the Bacchiglione.[31] Paduan municipal statutes of 1362 (written during the rule of the Carrara family) mention almost all the canals in the town and its territory, including the Piovego, completed in 1209 to reach the town at the Brenta; the Battaglia, excavated perhaps in 1189 along the Rovigo road; the Bovolenta canal and the Montagnana, built in 1338 by Umbertino da Carrara.[32] Padua was able to capitalise on the experience accumulated during the first half of the twelfth century, when an initial diversion of the Brenta carried out to favour navigation caused a disruption of the local ecosystem and major swamping phenomena.[33] The city took advantage of the waterways that linked it to Monselice.[34] Several regulations in its statutes were designed to ensure the efficiency of canals for the flow of merchandise within the urban walls.[35]

In Romagna, the 1287 law code of Ferrara regulated the transport of ships that carried salt to the communities of Adria and Arcoada.[36] The statute of the guild of river navigators in the Emilian city of Modena, going back to 1252, is a useful source for understanding the types of vessel (*navi, burchielli*) that travelled along rivers and canals and what they transported (wood, merchandise).[37] Longitudinal navigation down rivers and streams was mainly on lighter, narrower vessels (*sandali*), known in Tuscany as *navicelli*.[38] The Modena statutory code obliged owners of suspension and floating mills to raise this mobile machinery, as well as any part jutting out into the water streams, on Saturdays and Sundays, thereby allowing navigation on those two days. Still on the issue of facilitating transport, the statute prohibited the construction of splint walls (*steccaie*) and stakes in navigable river beds or in close proximity to their shores. This norm is also found in the 1327 Ravenna statute, which prohibited the placement of obstacles (*columpnam*) on the city's canals (*flumicellos*).[39] The code of Lendinara (Veneto region, 1321) forbade the construction of any structures on the Adige River that might

[28] Pecorella 1962; Di Gianfrancesco 1975: 203-206; Fantoni 1990: 27-31.
[29] Zimolo 1939: 243; Schiavini 1977: 201-208; Mancassola 2012: 122-125.
[30] Orlando 2011.
[31] Canzian 2019: 21.
[32] Di Gianfrancesco 1975: 207-208; Vallerani 1993: 12-14. See also Canzian 2003.
[33] Maire Vigueur 2023: 261-262.
[34] Simonetti 2009: 117, 119.
[35] Gloria 1873 *Gli statuti del comune di Padova* 1236: b. IV. 2. c. 892-894: 302-303; *ivi* 1265-67: b. IV. 2. c. 889-891: 300-302; Pittarello (ed.) 2017 *Statuti di Padova*: b. IV. rubr. 11: 533-538. See also Orlando (ed.) 2010.
[36] Montorsi (ed.) 1955 *Statuta Ferrariae*: b. II. rubr. 157: 104; b. V. rubr. 122. 123. 128-139, 213: 320-324, 344-345.
[37] Vicini (ed.) 1938 *Statuti dell'Arte dei navigatori di Modena*: 7-21.
[38] Orlando (ed.) 2010 *Statuti di Ariano* 1328: b. II. rubr. 115: 79.
[39] Zaccarini (ed.) 1998 *Statuto ravennate*: b. III. rubr. 31: 239-240.

obstruct its flow and use.[40] The Vicentine statutes of 1264 established that navigation along the Bacchiglione River was unrestricted in the entire area of the city, especially for transit to nearby Padua.[41] The statutes of Chivasso, near Turin, (1306) punished anyone attempting to change the course of the stream that ran through the community and to take water from the section within the castle, which was undoubtedly used for motive power and as a drainage channel.[42] These provisions were based on *ius commune*, which defended the navigability of perennial rivers by rigidly regulating the construction of infrastructure along waterways by waterside landowners.[43]

Having long acquired the right to collect *ripaticus*, as mentioned earlier, in the thirteenth and fourteenth centuries, communes were able to force the owners of land alongside waterways to allow mooring and the unloading of goods, as required, for example, by the statute of the Ligurian community of Rossiglione (second half of the fourteenth century).[44] Legislative codes of larger towns and smaller communities along the Arno (*Breve della Degazia del Mare* of Pisa, 1362; *Statuto della gabella* of the town of Fucecchio, 1352; *Statuto delle gabelle* of San Miniato al Tedesco, 1364, and the legislative code of Santa Maria a Monte, 1391) mention duties on road and river transportation between the port of Pisa and the city of Florence, revealing information about the types of goods that were transported to Tuscany's largest commune. Indeed, we discover that the main commodity transiting through these mooring places, where taxes were usually paid, was wheat, which Florence imported from southern Italy, Sicily and Provence, and, in smaller quantities, Tunisia, Catalonia and the Lazio coast. Also coming into the city, especially via the river, were salt, spices from the East, 'Greek' wine from southern Italy and Monemvasia from the Peloponnese peninsula, oil from Campania and Provence, Spanish, French and English wool, and construction materials from nearby Maremma. Semi-finished textiles produced in Florence were taken, again via the Arno, from urban workshops to fulling mills built on the outskirts of town, thereby contributing to boat traffic on the river.[45] A similar, though less varied assortment of produce (among which wheat and other cereals were prominent) emerges from the customs records from the harbour on the Tiber for goods entering Rome during the fourteenth century.[46]

Naturally, river navigation, especially upstream, was very slow.[47] Sail boats exploited the wind when travelling along the Po, the Arno and the Tiber, whereas smaller barges only used poles. *Navicelli*, especially those travelling upstream on the Tuscan river, often had to be towed from the riverbank by men and animals. A horse could tow up to 15 tonnes by rope. More often, however, cattle and donkeys were used and the intervention of men was necessary on the steepest banks. In the valleys of both the Po and the Arno, these workers were usually called

[40] Statute of Lendinara 1321: Orlando (ed.) 2010 *Statuto di Lendinara*: b. II. rubr. 7: 115.
[41] Lampertico (ed.) 1886 *Statuti del comune di Vicenza*: IV: 188.
[42] Frola 1918 *Statuta Caluaxii*: rubr. 2: 185.
[43] Indicative, in this respect, is an account by Cassiodorus (sixth century), according to whom Theoderic, king of the Ostrogoths in Italy, had issued an edict *ne quis in fluminibus nauigeris diuersis territoriis meantibus, id est in Mincio Ollio, Ausere, Arno, Tiberi, audeat fluminum alueos piscandi studio turpissima saepe concludere* [Fridh (ed.) 1973 Cassiodori *Variarum libri XII*: V. xvii: 197; V. xx: 199. See also Costa 1919: 17-21, 25-26].
[44] Pesce 1914 *Statuti di Rossiglione*: rubr. 62: 105.
[45] Casini 1979: 389-395, 397-420; Casini (ed.) 1963 *Statuto del Comune di Santa Maria a Monte*: rubr. 243: 245-252; Salvestrini 1992: 97-104; Valori 2006; Tognetti 2008: 129, 131-133; Maire Vigueur 2023: 265-266. On this type of texts see Castiglione 2004. On trade relations between Florence and Pisa, traditionally enemy cities, see now Quertier 2022.
[46] Palermo 1979: 142-143; Scavizzi 1991: 83-87; Fara 2023.
[47] Andreolli 2008: 456-458.

bardotti or *redaroli*. They were young men who wore a harness with ropes known as *alzaie* (from the Latin *helcium*, tow rope) or *restare*. They towed the large barges, while moving along small paths marked out on the riverbank. On average, it took at least seven men to do the work of one horse.[48] Towing required there to be stretches of riverbank clear of thick vegetation and constructions. Therefore, towpaths could not be created where there were large natural or artificial obstacles. It was not uncommon for the *bardotti* and the towing animals to have to cross several times from one bank to the other on wooden barges (*navi*), which therefore needed to be available at all times.[49] Under optimum conditions, the journey from Florence to Pisa took approximately two days and it took three days in the opposite direction, but only with the aid of sails and if cargos were not too heavy. Of course, navigation on the Arno and on the end sections of the Tiber was only relatively smooth in the winter and autumn months, when rains increased the water levels.[50] The situation was different in the Po, the only major river in Italy, whose flow rate allowed year-round traffic, bringing activity to a good number of port facilities;[51] however, the transport methods used were no different from those on rivers in central Italy, except numerically. Indeed, rafts were also towed upstream on the large river of the North along towpaths and using various types of boats (*burchiello*, *sandalo*, *barbotta*, *peota* and others).

In the fourteenth and fifteenth centuries, the 'lock' system (*conche di navigazione* or *chiuse*) was introduced on the Po, perfected by Leonardo da Vinci. It enabled navigation along the tributaries and to reach the main stream of the river, while gently overcoming the differences in level between the various waterways caused by the morphology of the land and, therefore, the river and canal beds. It was this system that facilitated the linkage of the major cities to the Po. Examples include the canals of Cremona (derived from the Oglio River), Sabbioneta, Ravenna, Rovigo on the left bank of the main stream, and those of Parma, Reggio Emilia, Correggio, Mirandola, Modena, Bologna and Imola on the right side.[52]

What counted on all navigable rivers in Italy was not so much the speed at which vessels travelled, but rather how punctual they were when delivering their cargos. It was essential for riverside communities, especially towns and cities, to have guaranteed supplies of produce every day, regardless of when these set out or how long each boat took to make the journey. For this reason, departures were frequent and the waterways must have seemed extremely crowded, especially at certain times of the year.[53]

The importance of navigation on inland waters for Italian trade at the time is demonstrated in some records from 1401, the year in which a convoy of Venetian boats coming from the North Sea found it convenient to unload at Pisa three-fifths of its cargo headed in part for Florence and in part for Venice. Thus, the portion that was directed to the lagoon city went via the Arno as far as Florence, then by land to Bologna and finally along the Po and its tributaries from Ferrara to Venice. This took no more than fifteen days, whereas the ships, which continued circumnavigating the peninsula by sea, took forty-five days to reach Venice.[54]

---

48 See Ohler 2000: 117; Patitucci Uggeri 2002: 14.
49 See *Difesa* 1826^4: 105.
50 Cherubini 2003: 39; Salvestrini 2005: 31.
51 See Covini 2010.
52 Calzolari 1990; Cazzola 2021: 85-86.
53 See Pierotti 2005: 35.
54 See Tangheroni 1996: 269. See also Figliuolo 2022.

In cities and in the countryside, there was also trajectory navigation, which allowed river crossings when no bridge was available (bridges were much fewer in number at the time, and were unable to withstand heavy loads).[55] Around the few fixed structures that were built outside the urban centres a number of 'bridge areas' were created, which usually provided, alongside the suspended passages, diagonal navigation, necessary for the transportation of the heaviest loads.[56] Nevertheless, statutes rarely dealt with the latter form of transport.[57] In Umbria, the codes of Todi (1275) and Deruta of 1465 mention the *navi* that were employed to this end.[58] *Nave* was, in fact, the term adopted for the large barges that were normally used to cross rivers and the larger canals in central Italy.[59] The Florentine statutes of 1355 mention two different types of navigation operators: the *barchaiuoli* and the *navalestri*. The former, also called *navicellai*, were the navigators who moved along the course of rivers to various locations. The latter were the operators of the *navi*, the aforementioned barges that allowed people to cross waterways from one bank to the other.[60]

2. Timber rafting

One particular type of water transport involved timber rafts brought down from mountains and hills to lowland centres. This method was deployed on the rivers of northern and central Italy from ancient times.[61] It primarily involved construction wood, which was particularly in demand in towns and cities, but also in many villages.[62] Control over the supply of tree trunks and beams defined the hegemony of the communal lay magistrates regarding, for example, the management of the construction site for Florence's cathedral,[63] or the transportation of wood from the forests of Cadore and Trentino to the Venetian Arsenal.[64]

There were not too many differences between timber rafting in Alpine and Apennine areas. The activity is well documented in the Alps from the early fourteenth century and highlights the way Venetian dominance over north-eastern Italy benefited from self-regulating forms of local wood exploitation and transportation to accommodate urban needs.[65] If we look closely at Cadore, one of the best-documented and well-studied alpine valleys, given that the Venetian Arsenal relied on supplies from this basin,[66] we see that the transportation of timber from the mountains to the city began in high-elevation woodland areas. Here, trunks were stacked on the edge of forested areas, where large locks were built for collecting the material (*rastere*). The owners of these enclosures were usually merchants and woodland concession holders, who were territorial lords in Tyrol, such as Welsperg, the archduke of Austria and

[55] Greci 2016.
[56] Frati 2017-18: 174-177. For a comparison see Balossino 2022.
[57] See Mugnaini 1999.
[58] Ceci and Pensi (eds) 1897 *Statuto di Todi*: rubr. 85: 58; Nico Ottaviani (ed.) 1991[2] *Statuto di Deruta*: 135.
[59] Nico Ottaviani 2008: 79-81; Salvestrini 2009a: 23-25.
[60] Bambi, Salvestrini and Tanzini (eds) 2023 *Gli Statuti della Repubblica fiorentina del 1355 in volgare*: t. I: *Statuto del Capitano del Popolo*: b. I. rubr. 41: 168-169.
[61] Lewin 1983; Molfetta 1998; Küster 2003: 160-170; Salvestrini 2005: 32-33; Diosono 2008; Salvestrini 2016; Faleschini 2018.
[62] Bechmann 1984.
[63] Salvestrini 2010b: 215-218; Becattini 2015.
[64] No mention of timber rafting is made in some of the recent works on the timber trade in Piedmont and the Pavia market (Bertoni 2022; Bufanio 2022b).
[65] Braunstein 1988; Caniato and Dal Borgo (eds) 1988; Perco (ed.) 1988; Agnoletti 1993: 76; Asche, Bettega and Pistoia 2010: 55-99; Canzian 2022b: 144-147.
[66] Fabbiani 1959.

the mountain communities. These structures were flooded with water and then broken when strategically placed wedges were lifted. This enabled the trunks to roll down the slopes along wooden channels called variously *ludali*, *borrali*, *giavate*, or *risine*, which were raceways and slides that converged all the wood at the bottom. Once the trunks had reached stacking points near small dams (*stue*), they were transported via the waterway (*menada*), mainly in springtime, when the thaw and the rains increased the water levels in the torrents. In this regard, a distinction was made between the *menada piccola*, which took place from February to March when snowmelt caused the Piave or Adige rivers to rise and timber was allowed to flow freely, and the *menada granda*, which involved the transportation of timber in all seasons from stacking points to the lagoon in the form of large rafts.[67] The workers in charge of transferring them were usually called *zattieri* or *menadàs* and they were documented from at least the late twelfth century. Information about them is provided in the statutes of the guilds and those of the communities involved in transportation, including Bassano (1259 and 1295) and Belluno (1392).[68]

In the steepest sections and at the start of their journey along the Cismon, Travignolo and Avisio torrents, or even the rivers of which these were tributaries, such as the Brenta and the Adige, the trunks could be left to float unrestrained as far as the main sluice gates (*cidoli*). Here, they were bound into large rafts onto which climbed the raftsmen whose job it was to deliver the material to the lowland towns and Venice. At the start, fir, larch and beech trunks were numbered and marked with the merchants' signs; they were counted frequently along their journey for the purpose of duty payments. In the Dorsoduro district of Venice, the *Fondamenta delle Zattere*, the canal-side area along the Giudecca Canal, was one of the main sorting areas for material arriving via the lagoon.[69] In Appuhn's opinion, timber rafting was most intense on the Piave and Livenza Rivers. This was because the Brenta and the Adige had already experienced massive exploitation of their riparian woodlands in ancient times.[70] However, the statutes of the centres along all the main rivers suggest that this activity persisted for a long time at significant levels. If anything, we can differentiate between the rafting of logs and beams from the mountains that was prevalent on the Piave and the Brenta, and the transportation of lowland timber along the Livenza, a relatively short backwater river (*fiume di risorgiva*), which could not intercept material cut at high altitudes.

Moving from the Alps to the Apennines, we know that, even before the thirteenth century, much of the fir needed to restore the great basilicas in Rome came down the Tiber from the woodlands of the Massa Trabaria region between modern Tuscany, Umbria and Marche.[71] In Tuscany, from around the late twelfth century, when the areas alongside the river Arno were undergoing economic and demographic development, raw materials for building infrastructure were transported along the main stream and its principal tributaries. Playing an especially important role in supplying cities were the great woodland assets of the Camaldoli hermitage, Vallombrosa abbey and Florence's Opera del Duomo. These institutions, which owned woodland around the Apennine peaks, produced large quantities of beech trees,

[67] Corrà 1993: 81-85.
[68] Orlando (ed.) 2010 *Statuto di Bassano* 1259: b. III. rubr. 29: 80; *ivi* 1295: b. IV. rubr. 16: 83; *ivi* Statuti di Belluno 1392: b. IV. rubr. 134: 93; b. IV. rubr. 172. 174: 97.
[69] See Agnoletti 1996; Agnoletti 1998; Zanoboni 2009.
[70] Appuhn 2009: 40-44. See also Canzian 2012: 17-29.
[71] Codignola 2005; Cortonesi 2022: 79-80.

chestnuts and Turkish oak, and, mainly from the fifteenth century, firs.[72] For the Florentine authorities, purchasing timber from these landowners was a chance to obtain large quantities of material at good prices and to deal with only a few, large suppliers, with the assurance that they would be reforesting frequently and extensively, thereby curbing excessive soil depletion.[73] Trunks and beams sold to city merchants were transported along the Arno, tied into rafts similar to those on the Veneto rivers – only here they were called *foderi* – and steered by *foderatori* using long poles (**Fig. 43 and 44**). In Florence, timber rafting was regulated in the statute of the Woodcutters Guild, preserved in an early draft from 1301. This text stipulated the election of two officials, whose task was to monitor the efficient utilisation of rivers used as waterways (*due sufficientes homines pro viis faciendis aperiri*).[74] For a long time the municipality of Florence tried to intercept most of the material that was driven from the upper Valdarno (*Valdarno Superiore*) to the city. The republic's statutes of 1322–25 and 1355 forbade trunks from Casentino and Valdarno from continuing along the river any further than the urban settlement, except for small, heavily taxed quantities.[75] This law ensured Florence's monopoly in the supply of wood from the Apennine mountains. Furthermore, the city authorities' interest in importing boards, trunks and planks is revealed in a *provvisione* (resolution of the communal council) from 1290, which introduced a tax on large-sized timber and on the *foderi* to be collected at Porta Ruggero da Cuona, open on the river at the port of San Francesco, in the centre of the city.[76] In 1452, materials arriving in Florence for use by the Opera del Duomo for the construction and maintenance of the cathedral were exempted from the duties levied on the transportation of timber. Before they were shipped, these pieces were branded with the UFO (*ad usum florentine Operis*) mark, which led to the expression, *viaggiare a ufo*, which in the Florentine vernacular meant to transport goods without paying unfair taxes and, more generally, to pass free of charge.[77] A similar mark, AUF (*ad usum fabricae*), was placed on timber, on Val d'Ossola marble and other materials transported along the Ticino and the Naviglio Grande for the construction sites of Milan cathedral.[78]

Timber floating could be hampered by shallows, rapids, bridges and rocks. In some cases the entire course of larger rivers could be disrupted by dams and locks that made navigation and the transit of timber difficult. Some such barriers were the large sluice gate installed in the Tiber at Umbertide in Umbria (Fratta dam) in perhaps the thirteenth century;[79] or the sluice in the Bruna in the Sienese Maremma, an interesting project for an artificial lake originally designed for a 'feudal' setting and later developed by the commune in the early 1400s.[80] However, the most obstructive encumbrances involving the entire Arno (although

[72] Vannini and Cosi 2004: 107-108; Salvestrini 2008: 129-148; Salvestrini 2009a: 33-39.

[73] Becattini 2015; Salvestrini 2015a.

[74] Morandini (ed.) 1958 *Statuti dell'arte dei legnaioli*: rubr. 73: 51.

[75] *Di coloro che rechano legna a Firençe, a la città di Firençe, per lo fiume d'Arno, e di coloro che pigliano essi legni e de la restitutione d'essi; Dela pena di chi tollesse alcuna gabella overo passaggio del legname el quale si conducesse per lo fiume d'Arno overo dela Sieve altrove che ale porte dela città di Firençe* [Bambi, Salvestrini and Tanzini (eds) 2023 *Gli Statuti della Repubblica fiorentina del 1355 in volgare*: t. I: *Statuto del Capitano del Popolo*: b. IV. rubr. 12. 13: 512-514]. See Salvestrini 2005: 112-113; Salvestrini 2009a: 36-39; Grifoni 2016: 71-73.

[76] Firenze. Archivio di Stato. *Provvisioni, Registri*. 2: c. 117r (1290, agosto 3; approvaz. c. 120r); Firenze. Archivio dell'Opera di Santa Maria del Fiore. II. 1. 79: c. 12r; *ivi*: 80: c. 57v; *ivi*: II. 4. 9: c. 29r; *ivi*: II. 4. 12: c. 2v; *Statuta Populi et Communis Florentiæ, anno salutis MCCCCXV* 1778: t. III. b. V. tract. III. rub. 60: 446-448.

[77] Salvestrini 2009: 34-35.

[78] See Fantoni 1990: 32-34, 41; Lapucci 1993: 316; Carlotti and Saltamacchia (eds) 2012; Grillo 2017: 41-47, 129-135.

[79] Tosti 2002.

[80] Francovich and Citter (eds) 2003.

there were similar structures on shorter waterways in Romagna)[81] were the so-called *pescaie* or weirs, built near mills and fulling machines in both the city and the countryside (**Fig. 45 and 46**).[82] These weirs were oblique structures (more elevated when closer to the riverbed and lower on the other side) which consisted of a frame and a series of vertical wooden poles alternating with shorter stakes, all embedded in the river basin. These in turn were connected to more beams laid horizontally to form a wall against the current. The dual purpose of these constructions was to prevent enemy boats gaining access to the city and to concentrate the river current near one of the two banks during periods of minimum flow. In fact, the canals leading off from these sluices, known as *gore*, accumulated and directed the water to power hydraulic machinery during the summer season.[83] To facilitate the movement of wood, through-ways called *foderaie* gates were constructed at the lowest part of the weir. These were narrow slipways open in the dykes and were regulated by vertically sliding bulkheads (**Fig. 41, 45 and 46**). This process allowed material to pass through (although not without some difficulty).[84] As for river logging, the statutes of the Florentine republic stipulated that any construction wood floating down to the city on the Arno and its tributaries had to be pulled out on arrival at the aforementioned *Piazza Ruggiero da Cuona*, also known as *Piazza delle Travi* (Beam Square), that is, the landing place situated near Rubaconte Bridge (**Fig. 47**).[85]

Timber floating was mainly practised near the major mountain ranges. However, it was so important for the building industry of the time that it was even undertaken on shorter, more-difficult-to-navigate rivers. For example, we know that local statutes regulated the transportation of small logs to be used in the construction of ships' oars. These materials were transported on smaller rivers, such as the Sieve, a tributary of the Arno upstream of Florence, the Ombrone Pistoiese, which flowed into the Arno downstream of this city, the Magra River in Lunigiana,[86] and the end sections of Liguria's short waterways.[87] We also know from a 1339 general inventory of the properties owned by the Opera della Cattedrale di Santa Maria in Pisa that timber floating was practised along the river Tirso in western Sardinia (*ad flumen magnum [...] et caput ad viam maiorem publicam ubi calantur lignamina ab aqua*).[88] However, no trace of these activities can be found in the island's surviving statutory documentation.[89]

As always, the main task of statutory regulations was to ensure the proper pursuit of activities and therefore, in these cases, to punish the frequent thefts of timber that occurred during transportation, as did, for example, the Bassano statutes of 1259 and 1295 for logs in transit on the Brenta.[90]

---

[81] Caruso 2004: 190-194.
[82] Firenze, Archivio di Stato. *Arte dei legnaioli*. 1: cc. 10v, 29r. See Bellinazzi 1993: 213.
[83] Falqui and Prati 1937: 618-619; Salvestrini 2005: 21-22.
[84] Bambi, Salvestrini and Tanzini (eds) 2023 *Gli Statuti della Repubblica fiorentina del 1355 in volgare*: t. II: *Statuto del Podestà*: b. III. rubr. 176: 452: *Della pena di chi farà callaia nelle pescaie de' mulini*.
[85] Morandini (ed.) 1958 *Statuti dell'arte dei legnaioli*: rubr. 73: 51; Bambi, Salvestrini and Tanzini (eds) 2023 *Gli Statuti della Repubblica fiorentina del 1355 in volgare*: t. I: *Statuto del Capitano del Popolo*: b. IV. 11. 12. 13: 511-514.
[86] Morandini (ed.) 1958 *Statuti dell'arte dei legnaioli*: rubr. 46: 96; Lazzerini 2001: 34.
[87] Balletto (ed.) 1971 *Statuta antiquissima Saone*: t. 2. b. I. rubr. 61-64: 82-85; Genova. Biblioteca Universitaria. *Manoscritti*. B.VI.27: *Statuta et Conventiones Albisolae* 1389: rubr. 64; Hayward 1981; Caniato (ed.) 2007; Ciciliot 2007.
[88] Pisa. Archivio di Stato. *Opera della Primaziale*. 16: c. 76v. See Artizzu 1961: 77; Artizzu 1974: 108.
[89] Borghero and Salvestrini 2023.
[90] Orlando (ed.) 2010 *Statuti di Bassano* 1259 and 1295: b. III. rubr. 29: 80; b. IV. rubr. 16: 83. See also, in this regard, Occhi 2021: 137.

IX

Protection from Flooding and the Religious Dimension

1. Prevention, perception, resilience

One of the main concerns for governments regarding running waters was how to protect cities and rural areas from flooding.[1] Justinian law gave political authorities the right-cum-duty to carry out works to preserve communities and also to ensure that infrastructure installed by private parties to defend their own properties did not conflict with the public interest.[2] There are many accounts regarding floods and attempts to reduce their impact, especially on centres located along the Po, the Adige, the Arno and the Tiber.[3] It should, however, be stated that, again, there were differences between northern and central Italy. In fact, although the Po is the longest and most important Italian river, the cities located along its course are few and mostly situated on one bank (e.g. Turin, Piacenza, Cremona). It was the road, however, especially the Via Emilia, built alongside the Apennines, that attracted most of the settlements from the Roman era onwards.[4] The reason for this is to be found in the fear prompted by the great river, along with the idea that the most populous settlements should be kept from its course. Over time, towns and cities were linked to the major waterway via the dense network of canals we mentioned earlier. That Polesine settlements resulted from structural choices determined by a long-standing familiarity with the river and its frequent threats is demonstrated by the fact that it was not so much flooding that determined the abandonment of certain localities on the irrigated plains during the fourteenth century, as it was the broader and more complex socio-economic crises that were only partly caused by the episodic instability of climatic adversity.[5] This can be observed in three particularly significant examples. The first is the great flood known as the *Rotta di Ficarolo*, which took place near Ferrara (1152) and was caused by both natural and human-made phenomena. This event affected almost the entire Veneto plain and altered the course of the Po, giving rise to its Venice branch (*Po di Maestra*), which flows into the Adriatic sea with no fewer than three outlets.[6] The second example is the great, albeit insufficiently documented, flood known as the *Rotta della Malopera*, which caused a change in the course of the Adige River in the autumn of 1438, perhaps as a consequence of certain military operations, but without profoundly affecting the resilience and settlement of the affected region.[7] The third took place at the start of the modern period. The *Rotta dell'Adda* of 1520 brought about a change in the course of this river and to some extent affected the distribution of the population in Valtellina.[8]

---

1 For a comparison with the emblematic Dutch context, see van Dam 2017.

2 Costa 1919: 21-23; Fiorentini 2003: 169-171.

3 Bianchi, Granuzzo, Mariani Canova and Varanini (eds) 1992 *Statuti di Verona*: t. II. b. IV. rubr. 145: 607-608; t. II. b. V. rubr. 4: 628-629; Schenk 2007; Cazzola 2010; Salvestrini 2010a; Esposito 2010: 257-275; Benucci 2015; Salvestrini 2017a; Tognana 2019: 42.

4 Sterpos 1961; Orsini 2006.

5 See Rao 2022.

6 Buonora 2019: 101; D'Angelis 2021: 114.

7 See Traniello (ed.) 1988; Luzzini 2016: 289-290; Tognana 2019: 43; Cazzola 2021: 42-43. On the frequency of floods in Friuli region, see Ciconi 1862^2: 27-28.

8 Scaramellini 2007: 23, 29, 36.

In this regard, however, it should be remembered that, despite the threat posed by the tributaries of the Po and the Adige (Italy's second longest river), there was no lack of important centres, like Verona and Mantua, located along their banks. Mantua was surrounded by large bodies of water created artificially during the twelfth century with dams across the river Mincio. These were long part of the city's defences against attacks and sieges, but the very abundance of water made it prone to recurring and sometimes disastrous flooding of the built-up area.[9] This is amply demonstrated by the detailed statutes of 1303, which provided for frequent raising of embankments and monthly inspections of them, and the organisation of periodic *corvées* with rural labourers working on retaining walls, culverts (*chiaviche*) and bridges.[10] Moreover, frequent floods in these regions were caused not only by large rivers, but also by torrents, even where their flow was relatively constant. This was the case, for example, for the Colmeda creek and its floods in the Veneto region of Feltre.[11]

The situation has always been a little different for the rivers of central Italy. These were less sizeable and seemingly familiar, such that many important cities, like Rome, Florence and Pisa, developed and grew astride watercourses (Arno, Tiber) and, consequently, endured their disastrous floods. Towns and cities in this part of the peninsula demonstrated a strong capacity to react to these events, although not as effectively as their counterparts in the Po valley area.[12]

The *statuta* analysed in this research govern the prevention of calamitous events and, to a lesser degree, the compensation due for damages caused by disasters. For example, the statutes of Parma of 1255 and, especially, 1266 address the issue of 'bad weather' and imply that the Emilian countryside had undergone frequent flooding in the years leading up to the eruption of the Samalas volcano. From literary sources (Salimbene de Adam, *Chronicon Parmense*) we learn of floods in the area from at least 1276 to 1331.[13] The 1266 statutes hint at this situation and many of the regulations concerning the maintenance of canals must be seen in the context of a long period of bad weather.[14] We know that during those years (1316), the neighbouring municipality of Novellara, near Reggio, passed a regulatory resolution to divide the Crostolo della Modolena stream into two sections, in order to limit its flow and facilitate the control of its waters.[15]

Padua's statutes contain a series of meticulous provisions mandating the construction and maintenance of embankments along its rivers and canals from at least 1236, although the height of the period of legislation on this subject was in 1267 (*podestà* Giacomino Rosso).[16]

[9] Settia 2008: 372-373.
[10] D'Arco 1872: b. VIII. rubr. 5: 220-221.
[11] Melchiorre 2023: 87-89.
[12] See Salvestrini 2005: 73-86; Aldrete 2007; Esposito 2017.
[13] "E l'anno stesso [1276], un martedì, sul finir di Giugno, vigilia di S. Giovanni Battista, si rovesciò un diluvio strabocchevole d'acque; tantochè il Crostolo gonfiò in modo che, da Rivalta sino a Bagnolo, tutto il territorio era allagato, e molte persone perirono annegate; e le biade furono travolte da luogo a luogo, e ruinarono i ponti dei torrenti, le case furono rese crollanti, o atterrate dall'inondazione, le biade sommerse, le ghiaie che erano sulle strade trasportate su' campi o ne' fossati, sicchè diluvio tale non fu mai più veduto, nè i vecchi ricordavano che mai l'eguale in antico fosse avvenuto" (Salimbene de Adam 1882: II: 37, a. 1276); "De mense octobris [1331] maior plena aquarum et fluminum fuit in districtu Parme [...] tam per Parmensem quam per Cremonensem, omnes terre, domus, ecclesie et habitationes fuerunt submerse et suposite aquis et plene" (Bonazzi *Chronicon Parmense* 1902: a. 1331. c. 30-44: 217).
[14] See Fumagalli 1985.
[15] Mancassola 2012: 125; Cazzola 2021: 34-35.
[16] Gloria 1873 *Gli statuti del comune di Padova*: b. IV. rubr. 3. 4: 304-312.

Florentine chroniclers report disastrous overflow of the Arno in the city in 1269.[17] The loss of all the Tuscan republic's statutes from before 1322 prevents us from knowing the event's impact on local regulations. We do, however, find similar measures in north-west Italy relating to other periods. We might mention, for example, the statute of Chivasso, a community along the Po north-east of Turin (1306),[18] prohibiting the construction of obstructions and dams on rivers; or the text of the nearby community of Chiaverano (1251), which banned alterations to waterways.[19] In central Italy, the 1327 statute of Arezzo stipulated that tenants of land transferred by emphyteusis were not contractually liable to the landlord for repairs and improvements, if damage was caused by natural events.[20]

Regarding other forms of prevention, the thirteenth-century statute from Parma stipulated that it was the responsibility of rural communities to clear away plant material from embankments and riverbanks. Rivers and canals were to be periodically dredged to remove sand islands.[21] The statutory code, furthermore, prohibited any construction along embankments, both within the city and on suburban land.[22] In the Veneto region, the statutes of Cittadella (second half of the fourteenth c.), a newly founded town planned in 1220 by the municipality of Padua, bestowed powers on the *podestà* to require the periodic and extraordinary maintenance of bridges, embankments, canals and public ditches.[23] The 1264 statutes of Vicenza mandated the frequent cutting of plants along riverbanks *ut cursus fluminum non impediatur* (so that the flow of water would not be impeded).[24] In Tuscany, the Florentine statutes of 1355 encouraged boatmen to dredge the course of the Arno and other rivers in order to clear their beds and also as a way of obtaining building materials (sand and gravel).[25] Another chapter of this statute prohibited throwing stones and loam into streams, canals and ditches.[26] According to the fourteenth-century statute of Ravenna, within the first month of taking office the *podestà* was required to appoint engineering experts (*unum ingignerium vel plures bonos et expertos*) to monitor rivers and canals.[27] We should also mention the statutes of the Tuscan communes of Santa Croce sull'Arno, San Miniato al Tedesco and Fucecchio, located along the Arno where the river crossed the plain in the middle of its basin, dividing into many branches and occupying a riverbed of almost five kilometres. The texts contain articles devoted to banks and ditches, as well as bans on the building of dams and embankments. Finally, the statutes of the *Magistri viarum* of Rome (1452) mandated that the riverbed of the Tiber should be cleared of rubble and large items of refuse, and introduced penalties for dumping in the river and certain areas.[28]

---

17 Salvestrini 2017a: 39.
18 Frola 1918: *Statuta Clauisii* (Chivasso): rubr. 2: 170-171.
19 Frola 1918: *Statuta Clauerani*: rubr. 2: 291.
20 Camerani Marri (ed.) 1946 *Statuto di Arezzo*: b. III. rubr. 27: 139-140.
21 On seasonal river islands in the Roman law, see Costa 1919: 25.
22 *Statuta Communis Parmae*: IV: 368-380.
23 Ortalli, Parolin and Pozza (eds) 1984 *Statuti di Cittadella*: b. II. rubr. 38: 125.
24 Lampertico (ed.) 1886 *Statuti del comune di Vicenza*: b. IV: 161.
25 Bambi, Salvestrini and Tanzini (eds) 2023 *Gli Statuti della Repubblica fiorentina del 1355 in volgare*: t. I: *Statuto del Capitano del Popolo*: b. IV. rubr. 23: 518-519.
26 Bambi, Salvestrini and Tanzini (eds) 2023 *Gli Statuti della Repubblica fiorentina del 1355 in volgare*: t. II: *Statuto del Podestà*: b. III. 177: 452.
27 Pasolini (ed.) 1868, repr. 1985 *Gli Statuti di Ravenna*: b. IV. rubr. 347: 123. See Roversi Monaco 2000: 92-94.
28 Re 1920: 100; Carmignani (ed.) 1989 *Statuti del Comune di Fucecchio*: b. III. rubr. 71: 126; Salvestrini (ed.) 1994 *Statuti del Comune di San Miniato al Tedesco*: b. IV. rub. 82. 112: 374-375, 403-405; b. V. rubr. 56: 458-460; Salvestrini (ed.) 1998 *Statuti del comune di Santa Croce* 1409: rubr. 8: 63.

These were fairly standard norms mainly addressing the proper management of embankments, the prohibition of grazing on them and the maintenance tasks required in rural communities.[29] Nevertheless, despite these provisions, what was lacking in most of the local legislation was a comprehensive or coherent design for environmental planning. In fact, communal authorities could rarely exercise political control over short sections of larger rivers and even some minor ones. Nor did governments have full control over hydrographic basins. Thus, statutory norms solved some problems, but inevitably created others. For example, the raising of embankments in the countryside caused an influx of water and flooding in the city on some occasions. On the other hand, hydrographic areas were sometimes managed with the risk of compromising the security of border lands under a different territorial power. A clear example on a micro-territorial level is Pistoia and its territory, which were affected by several embankment works on streams and short rivers between the twelfth and thirteenth centuries. However, the demographic increase and the urbanisation of the plain on which the city stood at the foot of the Apennines rendered the river works implemented by the municipality ineffective.[30]

2. The case of Florence

The Florentine statutes of 1355 provide particularly interesting insight into flooding, since they contain an example of the contemporary norms that were enacted following a serious event, namely the great flood of 1333.[31] Florence is a city whose relationship with its river has been the subject of numerous studies. The same cannot be said, for example, of Rome: a recent important exhibition on the theme of the city in the Middle Ages completely ignored the relationship between its inhabitants and the Tiber.[32] In a comparison of the regulatory codes of 1322-25 and 1355, the older Florentine statutes mention few restrictions on the construction of worksites and weirs along the Arno. Such construction was forbidden for 300 Florentine *braccia* (about 700 m) upstream of Ponte Rubaconte in the centre of the city. In November 1333, the municipality took just seven days to enact more severe measures following the tragic event of the flood, which caused some 300 deaths. A *provvisione* (deliberation) dated the 12th of the month banned the construction of mills and other types of machinery along any stretch of the river that extended 2,000 *braccia* from Ponte Rubaconte, and 4,000 downstream from Ponte alla Carraia (the last bridge in the urban area). The penalty for transgressors ordering any new construction was up to 2,000 lire. Non-payers could find themselves in jail or facing capital punishment.[33] Such deliberations were made an integral part of the new edition of the statute of 1355.[34] They can be seen as political decisions taken as an emotional response to such a serious event. In this sense, we do not know the extent to which Florentines and other people living along the banks of the Arno (and other Italian rivers) were aware of the deleterious effects of dam construction and deforestation, mainly in mountain areas, and the

[29] See Carusi and Sella (eds) 1930 *Statuti di Udine*: b. IV. rubr. 4: 67 (North-East of the peninsula); Brogi (ed.) 1995 *Gli albori del Comune di San Gimignano e lo statuto del 1314*: b. I. rubr. 37: 115-116; b. V. rubr. 19. 33-35: 275-276, 279-280; Allegria and Capelli (eds) 2014 *Statuto del Comune di Cortona*: b. IV. rubr. 10: 367-368.
[30] Berti and Landi (eds) 2019: 59-67.
[31] On Which, Salvestrini 2005: 114-116; Frati 2017; Salvestrini 2017a: 49-50.
[32] Righetti and D'Achille 2022.
[33] Firenze. Archivio di Stato. *Provvisioni, registri*. 26: cc. 66v-67v. See Salvestrini 2005: 74-75, 98-100.
[34] Bambi, Salvestrini and Tanzini (eds) 2023 *Gli Statuti della Repubblica fiorentina del 1355 in volgare*: t. II: *Statuto del Podestà*: b. III. 202: 484-486.

consequences of the wash-out produced by meteoric waters.[35] Deforestation, therefore, also produced consequences for the seasonal swelling of rivers on the valley floor.[36] It seems clear from contemporary chronicles and records, as well as from studies carried out by some modern historians, that there was a widespread perception of there being a correlation between the different elements.[37] The larger landholders of the properties where woods and forests grew, such as the Camaldolese and Vallumbrosan monks, had drawn up strict regulations on the cutting of wood.[38] Furthermore, statutes from other places allow us to see the importance of mountain stream management for proper governance of wood or grazing areas situated further down the valley.[39] Nevertheless, in fourteenth-century Florence the situation was destined to change quickly. Measures that limited plant cutting were sorely lacking at the end of the fourteenth century because of the need for timber, as was the previously mentioned moratorium on construction sites along the urban section of the Arno between the *quartiere* of San Frediano and Ponte alla Carraia. This is the same section where, 30 years prior, building was subject to capital punishment.[40] Nevertheless, the government abandoned its rigour prompted by the need to allow for new mills within the city walls to deal with the threat of famine in case of military siege. The strict regulations designed to prevent such acts, therefore, had a sense of emergency about them. Since their coercive intent could not be enforced in all areas subject to flooding, and since there was a need to deal with more urgent economic circumstances, these regulations were slowly but surely flouted (**Fig. 48 and 49**).[41]

The only effective protection from floods that the Florentines of the fourteenth century sought was that offered by prayers to the Madonna of Impruneta (a sanctuary located on the hills closest to the city), by devotion to St John the Baptist, the city's patron saint,[42] and by those of the penitent women voluntarily confined in the cells of Ponte Rubaconte and Ponte Santa Trinita.[43] This was an otherworldly safeguard analogous to that 'guaranteed' by the hermitage of the Holy Cross which, again under the aegis of the municipal institutions and the protection of their laws, had risen near the springs of the Perugia aqueduct to guarantee a constant flow of water to the city.[44]

3. 'Ordeal' and legislative metaphors of baptism

In this regard, other aspects are worthy of note. The concern about floods necessarily evoked the fear of divine intervention in the close relationship between humans and their use of one of nature's most sacred elements.[45] In fact, floods were a tragedy insofar as they involved human settlements and, by God's will, transformed a natural element created to be dominated by man into a nemesis totally beyond his control.[46] The dichotomy between life and death and

[35] See in this regard Williams 2006.
[36] Schenk 2012; Salvestrini 2017b.
[37] Villani 1990: t. 3. XII. 1: 5, 8-9, 12; Salvestrini 2010a: 240-252.
[38] Salvestrini 2008: 129-148; Salvestrini 2014: 84-87.
[39] For example, the statute of Ragusa-Dubrovnik of 1272, speaking of land or vineyard, states: *que recipit aquam ex alto* [Šoljić, Šundrica and Veselić (eds) 2002 *Liber statutorum civitatis Ragusii*: b. V. rubr. 33: 312].
[40] Salvestrini 2005: 80.
[41] Salvestrini 2013b; Salvestrini 2015a.
[42] Salvestrini 2023b.
[43] Salvestrini 2005: 54-55; Pucci 2017: 47-51, 77-85, 111-119.
[44] Silvestrelli 1996: 90.
[45] See Salvestrini 2005: 35-36; Arnold 2017.
[46] See Squatriti 2008: 583-584, 611-612.

between salvation and punishment that water offers was always a double-edged sword for medieval society. Indeed, water symbolised spiritual rebirth through the Christian ritual of baptism, but was also the cause of death and an instrument of divine punishment in cases of flood.[47] In a broader sense, the sacredness of water stemmed not so much from the exaltation of its albeit undeniable spiritual dimension, but from the particular functional dignity that men recognised in it. Since objects and actions only become symbols if they are perceived as such by dint of the meaning assigned to them within a communicative union,[48] water, like fire, was viewed as a source of purification, precisely because of its ambivalent nature.[49]

Although the statutes were rooted in civil law, their pages were not short of references to the relations between political power and ecclesiastical institutions, and the religious life of the people. All the codes open with invocations to the deity and patron saints,[50] meanwhile religious festivities and the protection of churches and other places of worship occupy large sections of the provisions. However, there are only marginal references to the use of water as a sacralised element and an instrument of sacramental rituality for inflicting punishment through the medium of the forces of nature. The image of lustral ceremonies inspired by baptism or the vision of water as a tool of purification rarely emerge from the pages of these codices. Statutes show the symbolic value of water as a religious element, but they do it only in reference to its use in judicial practices.[51] For example, the *Liber consuetudinum Mediolani* of 1216 mentions trial by ordeal, whereby a final judgement of guilt in civil and criminal cases was determined via the medium of freezing water (*iudicium aquae frigidae*).[52] This involved submerging a child into a river. If he survived, it implicitly invalidated the accused's defence.[53] Legislators maintained that they had to justify such a cruel practice by having direct recourse to divine will. While these tests appear harsh, it is precisely for this reason that they were also considered efficient.[54]

The power to purify justified the use of water as an instrument of punishment, although we do not find drowning as a penalty in Italian statutes. The *Breve Pisani Communis* of 1286 provided for ritual bathing in the Arno for those who organised gambling and were unable to pay the prescribed fine. In the Florentine statutes of 1415, this punishment was metaphorically referred to as baptism, as this renewed 'sacrament' gave deliverance to the guilty, who were thereby reborn into legality by means of a civil and religious pact (*debeat cum aqua baptizari*).[55] This type of derisory punishment was often referred to as *corbellatio* and was almost always administered in flowing waters, similarly to the initiation ritual precepts set out in the ancient *Didaché*, the oldest 'manual' of catechesis (*Doctrine of the Twelve Apostles to the Gentiles*), compiled between the years 80 and 120 (βαπτίσατε ... εν ύδατι ζωντι, *baptizate ... in aqua viva.*

[47] See Bärsch 2017.
[48] Melville 2009: 57-58.
[49] Van Dülmen 1990: 6, 88; Tonutti 2007; Siniscalco 2009; Neuheuser 2017.
[50] See Bartoli Langeli 1987.
[51] Zorzi 2010a: 124-125, 129-131.
[52] Besta and Barni (eds) 1949 *Liber consuetudinum Mediolani*: b. XVI. rubr. 31. 32: 101.
[53] *Fit autem iudicium aquae frigidae per puerum virginem ligatum et in aquam per cordam dimissum. Et si illum aqua non receperit, nec submersus fuerit, qui fuerat accusatus subcumbat* (*ivi*: b. XVI. rubr. 32: 101).
[54] *Iudicium autem calentis ferri seu aquae frigidae non proprie pugna dicitur quia non ex viribus corporis certatur, sed potius divino alias iudicio relinquitur* (*ivi*: b. XVI. rubr. 2: 95).
[55] Bonaini (ed.) 1870 *Breve Pisani Communis*: b. III. rubr. 35: 398-399; *Statuta Populi et Communis Florentiæ*: t. IV. 28. b. 2: 406. See Taddei 1996: 339, 341.

7. 1).[56] Reference to this custom recurs in many statutes in northern Italy: Verona (1228 and 1327), Vicenza (1264), Como (1281), Mantua (1303), Adria (1442).[57] The Veronese code specifies that the punishment was to be inflicted in winter (*suppozetur ter in aqua de yeme*).[58] In this kind of contexts, baptism recovered its cathartic, not only initiatory and purifying, dimension. Baptism was an image of the impending passion, of the rebirth after a metaphorical death induced by suffering;[59] which, however, in the courtroom and before the lay magistrate, took the form of humiliation. In these Christian legislative contexts we can make out the distant echo of the caricatures of Islamic ablutions that were spread by missionaries and travellers in the thirteenth and fourteenth centuries, including the Florentine Riccoldo da Montecroce (1242-1320), and derided as a ridiculous image of baptism.[60]

In any case, where the punishment of 'propaggination', that is the capital execution of a condemned person who was suffocated upside down in a pit filled with water, slime or dung,[61] *corbellatio* was a milder punishment that emphasised the desire to cleanse and purify the offender. Many statutes reserved this type of punishment for blasphemers, whose vile sin had to be 'washed' away by cathartic ablution. For instance, a pole was permanently erected on the Pavia bridge from which insolvent swearers were plunged into the Ticino River.[62] Some Piedmontese statutes, such as those of Cuneo (1380), ordered the condemned party to be exhibited in the town square and 'washed' with four large buckets of water. The code of nearby Savigliano established that the blasphemer was to be pilloried or forced to jump into the waters of the Maira Torrent. In Garessio (Cuneo, 1278), offenders were to be flogged and watered three times; in Genola (Cuneo, 1449), they were to be thrown into the castle moat; in Ormea (Cuneo, thirteenth/fourteenth c.), a bucket of water was to be emptied over their heads; in Ivrea (Torino, 1329), they were to be publicly flogged all over town, or plunged three times into the Dora Baltea River.[63] These rules were perfectly mirrored in the statute of Piacenza (1264) and in the seigneurial laws of Spilimbergo (Pordenone, 1326), in other words, in the codes of two communities located respectively at the heart and at the opposite end of northern Italy.[64]

The religious and magical significance of sources emerges, however, from some statutes, such as that of Deruta (1465), which included a prohibition on performing magic rites (*alcuna malia fare*) near local fountains.[65]

---

[56] See Righetti 1959². IV: 32-33, 97, 525; Baroffio and Magrassi 1977: 474-475; Goppelt 1984: 69-73, 78-91, 101. On the purifying power of running waters see Ström 1942: 173.

[57] Zorzi 1994: 406; Zorzi 2010a: 125-126, 129-131.

[58] Bianchi, Granuzzo, Mariani Canova and Varanini (eds) 1992 *Statuti di Verona*: t. II. b. III. rubr. 106: 495.

[59] Quasten 1980. I: 42-43, 88-89, 99-100, 150, 495-501.

[60] Biosca i Bas 2013: 38-41.

[61] In fact, the term is said to derive from the name of the technique used mainly in viticulture, whereby plants were propagated by folding and then burying a branch (the offshoot, or propagation). See Dante Alighieri, *Inferno*, 19, 49-50.

[62] Pertile 1892: 346.

[63] Sacco (ed.) 1932 *Statuti di Savigliano*: rubr. 189: 82; Barelli, Durando and Gabotto (eds) 1907 *Statuti di Garessio*: Il Libro della Catena del comune di Garessio: 20; *ivi*: *Il libro degli statuti di Ormea*: rubr. 111: 168-169; Pene Vidari (ed.) 1968 *Gli statuti del comune di Ivrea*: b. 2. rubr. 13: 165-166; Camilla (ed.) 1970 *Corpus Statutorum Comunis Cunei*: rubr. 243: 131; Comba (ed.) 1970 *Gli statuti di Genola*: rubr. 38: 45. See Artifoni 1985: 237-238.

[64] Begotti 2001 *Gli Statuti di Spilimbergo*; Zorzi 2010a: 130. See also Fugazza 2009: 164-166.

[65] Nico Ottaviani (ed.) 1991 *Statuto di Deruta in volgare*: b. I. rubr. 64: 116.

X

Concluding Remarks

Various conclusions on several levels can be drawn from the analysis made in this book. Water is life, yet its use is inherently linked to political decision-making. It is no surprise that this unique, essential resource has always been a key focus of normative and regulative forces. The statutory legislation of communal Italy shows that water was a fundamental and strategic natural resource for economies, mainly for cities in flat areas with access to streams and intersected by rivers, especially if located in the north of the peninsula. However, in this context, it is only freshwater that is the object of legislators' interest. When it came to the sea, the regulatory focus was almost entirely on navigation, rather than the protection of certain types of water, in this case saltwater, whose availability at the time appeared to be infinite.[1] Closely related to this is the fact that the regulatory sources were mainly concerned with two of the many features of water, which is quintessentially polymorphous: namely its geographical dimension (particularly rivers, lakes and wetlands) and the ergological aspects of it, involving human intervention (canals, wells, dams and so on). Little emerges of what we might call the meteoric side of water (rain, snow, hail, the relationship between water and air, apart from the effects of floods), which remained largely confined to theoretical reflection, only minimally known to the drafters of the statutes.[2] Finally, human action was of interest to legislators mainly in terms of the greater or lesser availability of the resource, which had to be guaranteed or, in other cases, limited.

It is difficult to say how effective the policies adopted by individual municipalities were at securing this supply through legislative programmes. It is nevertheless clear that in no case was the availability of water ever linked to property regimes. To take up the famous thesis of the 'Tragedy of the Commons' formulated by Hardin in the 1960s,[3] the traditional existence of collective rights of access to water was never perceived by legislators as a form of overexploitation of the resource. On the contrary, it was regarded as municipal authorities intervening to defend a commodity needed by the community and to protect the common right to use it, with the aim of ensuring a fair and constant supply for all.

A sufficient supply of good quality water seems to have been the main objective of all the regulatory sources examined. However, the legislative interventions for important new, expensive and monumental infrastructures needed to transport and distribute this fundamental element, including large aqueducts, sources and pipelines, appear to have been more of a concern for the hilly communities of central Italy and Sardinia, which, in the thirteenth and fourteenth centuries, had limited access to water. Meanwhile, the communes of the Po area, home to the country's main rivers, were able to give freer rein to the initiatives of private parties when it came to diverting waters from canals and streams flowing on private land, and even from publicly owned perennial rivers. This was because, during the early centuries of the Middle Ages, the north of the Italian peninsula boasted a dense network of artificial canals that

[1] See Pradi 2011: 27.
[2] Lago 1983: 117-153.
[3] Hardin 1968.

had been excavated by rural populations on the initiative of large ecclesiastical owners and peasant communities. Thus, urban municipal authorities did nothing more than continue the intervention that had been started before they themselves had even come into being, and plan new works with the certainty that access to water resources would always be available.

Therefore, the Tuscan-Emilian and Tuscany-Romagna Apennines, separating the Po Valley from central Italy seem to have acted as a frontier between differing attitudes to the relationship between local laws and water usage. An area that could be defined as a buffer zone was northern Tuscany (Arno valley), with hybrid characteristics common to the north and centre of the peninsula.

Although water was crucial for town dwellers and farmers alike, and while the urban ruling classes acknowledged the right of individuals to have access to this natural resource, government elites nevertheless exerted power over the governance of water, in favour, initially, of their own needs. Also, this research has shown that the economic and strategic interests of the main urban classes had higher and stronger priorities than environmental concerns, such as the protection of public health–which does not emerge clearly from the examined texts–and hydrogeological equilibrium, especially with regard to flood risk management.[4] For this reason, written rules encouraged forms of exploitation of the available resources that the legislators themselves knew were not always desirable from a strictly environmental perspective. To this end, more stringent norms were enacted only after particularly serious events had occurred, showing that government magistrates preferred, especially when it came to flood defence, repairing damage that had already occurred (intervening after the fact) rather than preventing it.[5] Prevention would have required lengthy negotiation and mediation processes between the defence of public assets and the legal proceedings brought by landowners, businessmen or owners of hydraulic devices (including many religious institutions). These were tactical political manoeuvres designed to help people affected by flooding events, rather than oppose the social groups capitalising on the use and misappropriation of local water resources.[6]

Adopting terminology that has recently come into use in the exact sciences and which distinguishes resilience – that is, the ability to maintain, or, when challenged, quickly restore conditions considered highly desirable – from antifragility – the capacity of individuals and people to learn from adversity and emerge improved from it[7] – we could say that the Italic populations of the communal era and their laws reveal a general resilience but little antifragility in the face of environmental calamities caused by water.

In any case, the emphasis that all communities with a constitution placed on developing good water resource management programmes, albeit to differing degrees of intensity and with results not always equal to expectations, highlights that communal Italy was able to devise suitable responses to the requirements of complex social contexts, at least in terms of legislative planning, and did so by combining the tradition of Roman law with the normative experimentation, the institutional dynamism, and the political culture of the later Middle Ages.

[4] For an analysis of social behaviour in the face of natural disasters see Campbell 2016; van Bavel, Curtis, Dijkman, Hannaford, de Keyzer, van Onacker and Soens 2020; Soens 2020.

[5] Fiorentini 2003: 65-66; Buonora 2019: 98.

[6] See, in this regard, Squatriti 2008: 612-614; Rohr 2021.

[7] See McAnany and Yoffee (eds) 2009; Taleb 2012.

List of statutes examined

Northern Italy (north of the Tuscan-Emilian and Tuscany-Romagna Apennines)

Acqui (AL) 1276 ca.	Adria (RO)	Albisola (SV) 1389
Ariano (RO) 1328	Asti 1312	Balangero (TO) 1391
Barbania (TO) 15th c.	Bassano (VI) 1259	Bassano (VI) 1295
Belluno 1392	Bergamo 1353	Bologna 1245
Bologna 1250	Bologna 1252	Bologna 1253
Bologna 1267	Bologna 1335	Bra (CN) 1461
Brescia 13th c.	Brescia 1557	Castel San Giovanni (PC) 14th c.
Chiaverano (TO) 1251	Chieri (TO) 1313	Chivasso (TO) 1306
Cittadella (PD) 14th c.	Como 1281	Como 1335
Cremona 1339	Cremona 1485	Cuneo 1380
Feltre (BL) 1388–90	Ferrara 1287–88	Ferrara (*Statuta Communis Ferrariae ad Offitium Argerum*) 1320–94
Forlì 1359	Forlì 1373	Garessio (CN) 1278
Genola (CN) 1449	Genova 1375–82	Imola (BO) 1334
Ivrea (TO) 1329	Lecco 14th c.	Lendinara (RO) 1321
Lodi 1390	Mantova 1303	Mantova 1311
Marano Vicentino (VI) 1429	Masio (AL) 1372	Milano 1216
Milano 1256	Milano 1346	Milano 1396
Modena 1252	Modena 1306–07	Modena 1327
Modena (*Statuta civitatis Mutinae ad iudicem aquarum pertinentia*) 1336-1575	Nirone (PR) 1260	Novara 1338–39
Oltrepò mantovano (*Statuto gonzaghesco delle «Digagne»*) 15th c.	Omegna (NO) late 14th c.	Ormea (CN) 13th–14th c.
Orzinuovi (BS) 1341-87	Padova 1236	Padova 1265–67
Padova 1362	Parma 1255	Parma 1266
Parma 1304	Pavia 1393	Pernumia (PD) 13th–14th c.
Piacenza 1264	Piacenza 1323	Polesine di Rovigo (*Statuta totius Policinij*) 1440–49

Pomposa (FE) 1295	Pons (TO) 1344	Portogruaro (VE) 1434
Quarona (VC) 1384	Ravenna 1327–46	Reggio 1265
Rossiglione (GE) 14th c.	San Giorgio (TO) 1343	San Marino 1352–53
Savigliano (CN) 1305	Savona 1345	Spilimbergo (PN) 1326
Torino 1360	Treviso 12th–13th c.	Treviso 1231–33
Treviso 1260–63	Udine 14th c.	Valsolda (CO) 1373
Venezia 1242	Verona 1228	Verona 1276
Verona 1327	Vicenza 1264	

Central Italy (south of the Tuscan-Emilian and Tuscany-Romagna Apennines)

Arezzo 1327	Arezzo 1337	Ascoli Piceno 1377
Assisi (PG) 1319	Borgo San Lorenzo di Mugello (FI) 1374	Buggiano (PT) 1378
Castel Fiorentino della Provincia Romana (RM) 1298	Castelfranco di Sopra (AR) 1394	Castiglione degli Ubertini (AR) 1397
Chianciano (SI) 1287	Colle di Val d'Elsa (SI) 1307–1407	Cortona (AR) 1325
Deruta (PG) 1465	Firenze 1301	Firenze 1322–25
Firenze 1355	Firenze 1415	Foiano (AR) 1387
Fucecchio (FI) 1307–08	Fucecchio (FI) 1352	Gavorrano (GR) 1465
Grosseto 1421–22	L'Aquila 1313	Lucca 1321
Lucca 1331	Lucca 1372	Lucca 1454
Lucca 1469	Lucca 1485	Massa in Lunigiana 1591
Monsummano (PT) 1331	Montalcino (SI) 1452	Montepulciano (SI) 1337
Montisi (SI) 1494	Nocera Umbra (PG) 1371/1567	Orvieto (TR) 1313–15
Perugia 1262	Perugia 1279	Perugia 1342
Perugia 1389	Pescia (PT) 1339	Piano del Padule d'Orgia (SI), Consorzio 1303-1375
Pisa 1287	Pisa 1313	Pisa 1362
Pistoia 1284	Pistoia 1296	Poggibonsi (SI) 1332
Prato, *Statuto dell'Arte dei padroni dei mulini sulla destra del fiume Bisenzio 1296*	Radicofani (SI) 1255	Rieti 1350
Rincine e Fornace (FI) 1446	Roma 1363	Roma 1452

San Gimignano (SI) 1255	San Gimignano (SI) 1314	San Miniato al Tedesco (PI) 1337
San Miniato al Tedesco (PI) 1364	Santa Croce sull'Arno (PI) 14th c.–1422	Santa Maria a Monte (PI) 1391
Scarperia (FI) 15th c.	Siena 1226–42	Siena 1262
Siena 1290	Siena 1293	Siena 1298
Siena 1305–25	Siena 1309–10	Siena 1337–39
Spoleto (PG) 1296	Stroncone (TR) 1707	Sulmona (AQ) 16th c.
Todi (PG) 1275	Trequanda (SI) 14th c.	Uzzano (PT) 1339
Uzzano (PT) 1389	Vicariato del Podere Fiorentino (Palazzuolo – FI) 1406	Viterbo 1251–52
Viterbo 1469	Volterra (PI) 1210–24	

Sardinia

Arborea (kingdom, *Carta de Logu*) 1389–92	Cagliari (*Casteddu*) 14th c.	Castel Genovese (Castelsardo – SS) 14th c.
Sassari 1294 – 14th c.	Villa di Chiesa (Iglesias – CI) 1303–04	Villa di Chiesa (Iglesias – CI) 1338

Sicily

Palermo 1330		

Dalmatian Coast

Ragusa (Dubrovnik) 1272		

Bibliography

Primary sources

Alberti, Leon Battista 1988. *On the Art of Building in Ten Books*. transl. by J. Rykwert with N. Leach and R. Tavernor. Cambridge Mass: The MIT Press.

Allegria, S. (ed.) 2017. *Statuto del Comune di Foiano del 1387*. Firenze: Associazione di studi storici Elio Conti.

Allegria, S. and V. Capelli (eds) 2014. *Statuto del Comune di Cortona (1325-1380)*. Firenze: Olschki.

Anderloni, E. and A. Lazzati (eds) 1915. *Statuti dei laghi di Como e di Lugano dei secoli XIII e XIV*. II. Roma: Loescher.

Andreani, L. 1986-87. Un frammento di statuto del comune di Orvieto (1313-1315). Note a margine. *Bollettino dell'Istituto storico-artistico orvietano* 42-43: 124-172.

Antonelli, G. (ed.) 1962. *Statuti di Spoleto del 1296*. Firenze: Olschki.

Arquer, S. 2007. *Sardiniae brevis historia et descriptio*. Laneri, M. T. and R. Turtas (eds). Cagliari: CUEC.

Arrighi, V. (ed.) 2004. *Gli statuti di Scarperia del XV secolo*. Firenze: Edifir.

Ascheri, M. (ed.) 1987. *Chianciano 1287. Uno Statuto per la storia della comunità e del suo territorio*. Chianciano-Roma: Viella.

Baldo degli Ubaldi 1616. *In primam Digesti veteris partem commentaria*. Venetiis: Giunta.

Balletto, L. (ed.) 1971. *Statuta antiquissima Saone (1345)*. Genova: Istituto Internazionale di Studi Liguri.

Balsimelli, F. (ed.) 1943. *Gli Statuti di San Marino del 1352-1353, con aggiunte le riforme dal 1356 al 1488*. San Marino: Arti grafiche sammarinesi.

Bambi, F., F. Salvestrini and L. Tanzini (eds) 2023. *Gli Statuti della Repubblica fiorentina del 1355 in volgare*. I: *Statuto del Capitano del Popolo*; II: *Statuto del Podestà*. Firenze: Olschki.

Banchi, L. 1871 (ed.) Statuto della Società del Piano del Padule d'Orgia. 1303-1375, in *Statuti senesi scritti in volgare ne' secoli XIII e XIV*. II. Bologna: G. Romagnoli: 73-153.

Barelli G., E. Durando and E. Gabotto (eds) 1907. *Statuti di Garessio, Ormea, Montiglio e Camino*. Pinerolo: Chiantore-Mascarelli.

Barrera, C. 1864. *Storia della Valsolda con documenti e statuti*. Pinerolo: Chiantore.

Begotti P. C. (ed.) 2001. *Gli Statuti di Spilimbergo del 1326, con le aggiunte fino al 1421*. Spilimbergo: Pro Spilimbergo.

Bellandi, F., F. Berti and M. Mantovani (eds) 1984. *Statuti della lega del Borgo a San Lorenzo di Mugello (1374)*. Firenze: Olschki.

Besta, E. and G. L. Barni (eds) 1949. *Liber consuetudinum Mediolani anni MCCXVI*. Milano: Giuffrè.

Betto, B. (ed.) 1984. *Gli Statuti del comune di Treviso (sec. XIII-XIV)*. Roma: ISIME.

Bianchi, S. A., R. Granuzzo, G. Mariani Canova and G.M. Varanini (eds) 1992. *Statuti di Verona del 1327*. Roma: Jouvence.

Bizzarri, D. (ed.) 1933. *Gli Statuti del Comune di Torino del 1360*. Torino: Società Storica Subalpina.

Bonaini, F. (ed.) 1870. *Breve Pisani Communis, an. MCCCXIII*, in *Statuti inediti della città di Pisa dal XII al XIV secolo*. II. Firenze: Vieusseux.

Bonazzi, G. (ed.) 1902. *Chronicon Parmense ab anno MXXXVIII usque ad annum MCCCXXXVIII*. RIS: Città di Castello: Lapi.

Bortolami, S. 1978. *Territorio e società in un comune rurale veneto (sec. XI-XIII). Pernumia e i suoi statuti*. Padova: Deputazione di Storia per le Venezie.

Brogi, M. (ed.) 1995. *Gli albori del Comune di San Gimignano e lo statuto del 1314*. Siena: Cantagalli.

Caggese, R. (ed.) 1910/1921, and G. Pinto, F. Salvestrini and A. Zorzi (eds) 1999. *Statuti della Repubblica Fiorentina*. I: *Statuto del Capitano del Popolo degli anni 1322-25*; II: *Statuto del Podestà dell'anno 1325*. Firenze: Olschki.

Camerani Marri, G. (ed.) 1946. *Statuto di Arezzo (1327)*. Firenze: Olschki.

Camerani Marri, G. (ed.) 1963. *Statuti dei comuni di Castelfranco di Sopra (1394) e Castiglione degli Ubertini (1397)*. Firenze: Olschki.

Camilla, P. (ed.) 1970. *Corpus Statutorum Comunis Cunei 1380*. Cuneo: Società per gli Studi Storici della Provincia di Cuneo.

Campanini, A. and A. Vasina (eds) 1997. *I rubricari degli statuti comunali di Reggio Emilia (secoli XIII-XVI)*. Bologna: La Fotocromo Emiliana.

Campori, C. (ed.) 1864. *Statuta civitatis Mutine anno 1327 reformata. Monumenti di Storia Patria delle Provincie Modenesi. Serie degli statuti*. I. Parmae: Fiaccadori.

Capelli, V. (ed.) 2009. *Statuto del Comune di Arezzo (1337)*. Arezzo: Società Storica Aretina.

Caprioli, M. (ed.) 2008. *Lo statuto della città di Rieti dal secolo XIV al secolo XVI*. Roma: ISIME.

Caprioli, S. (ed.) 1996. *Statuto del Comune di Perugia del 1279*. Perugia: Deputazione di Storia Patria per l'Umbria.

Carmignani, G. (ed.) 1989. *Statuti del Comune di Fucecchio (1307-1308)*. Fucecchio: Comune di Fucecchio.

Carusi, E. and P. Sella (eds) 1930. *Statuti di Udine, sec. XIV*. Udine: Deputazione Friulana di Storia Patria.

Casini, B. (ed.) 1963. *Statuto del Comune di Santa Maria a Monte, 1391*. Firenze: Olschki.

Casini, B. 1979. Il "Breve" delle gabelle della Porta della Degazia del Mare di Pisa del 1362, in *Studi per Enrico Fiumi*. Pisa: Pacini: 373-429.

Castiglioni, C. (ed.) 1938. Galvano Fiamma. Opusculum de rebus gestis ab Azone, Luchino et Johanne Vicecomitibus ab anno MCCCXXVIII usque ad annum MCCCXLII, in G. Carducci, V. Fiorini and P. Fedele (eds) *Rerum Italicarum Scriptores*. 12. Bologna: Zanichelli.

Catonis, M. Porcii 1982. *De agri cultura ad fidem Florentini codicis deperditi iteratis curis*, ed. by A. Mazzarino. Leipzig: B.G. Teubner (2nd ed.).

Ceci, G. and G. Pensi (eds) 1897. *Statuto di Todi del 1275*. Todi: Trombetti.

Cenci, C. 1974-76. *Documentazione di vita assisiana 1300-1530*. Grottaferrata: Ed. Collegii S. Bonaventurae.

Cerlini, A. (ed.) 1933. *Consuetudini e statuti reggiani del secolo XIII*. Milano: Hoepli.

Ceruti, A. (ed.) 1869. Galvano Fiamma. Chronicon extravagans et chronicon maius, in *Miscellanea di Storia Italiana*. 7. Torino: Regia Deputazione di Storia Patria: 439-785.

Cessi, R. (ed.) 1938. Gli statuti veneziani di Jacopo Tiepolo del 1242 e le loro glosse. *Memorie del reale Istituto veneto di Scienze, lettere ed Arti* 30/2: IV-XV, 3-231.

Ciampi, I. 1872. *Cronache e statuti della città di Viterbo*. Firenze: Cellini. *Statuto di Viterbo del 1251.*

Ciampoli, D. (ed.) 1984. *Il Capitano del Popolo a Siena nel primo Trecento*. Siena: Consorzio Universitario della Toscana Meridionale.

Ciampoli, D. and D. Gatti (eds) 1994. *Lo Statuto di Montisi del 1494*. Siena: Cantagalli.

Ciampoli, D. and Th. Szabó (eds) 1992. *Viabilità e legislazione di uno stato cittadino del Duecento. Lo Statuto dei Viarî di Siena*. Siena: Accademia Senese degli Intronati.

Ciampoli, D. and P. Turrini (eds) 2002. *Statuti Medievali e Moderni del Comune di Trequanda (secoli XIV-XVIII)*. Siena: Cantagalli.

Clementi, A. (ed.) 1977. *Statuta Civitatis Aquile*. Roma: ISIME.
Cognasso, F. 1913. *Statuti civili del Comune di Chieri (1313)*. Pinerolo: Società Storica Subalpina.
Comba, R. (ed.) 1970. *Gli statuti di Genola*. Torino: Deputazione Subalpina di Storia Patria.
Corsi, A. and A. Prosperi (eds) 2022. Ceseri Frullani da Cerreto Guidi. *Gl'avvenimenti del lago di Fucecchio e modo del suo governo* [1599]. Fucecchio: Edizioni dell'Erba.
Cossandi, G. (ed.) 2004/05. *Gli statuti di Novara nel XIV secolo. Studio ed edizione della legislazione di Giovanni e di Galeazzo II Visconti*. Phd. Thes. Milano: Università Cattolica del Sacro Cuore.
D'Amato, M. and S. Nannucci (eds) 2004. *Fra la terra, l'aria e l'acqua. Memorie, volti e luoghi del Padule di Fucecchio*. Firenze: Polistampa.
D'Arco, C. 1872. *Studi intorno al Municipio di Mantova dall'origine di questa fino all'anno 1863, ai quali fanno seguito documenti inediti o rari*. III. Mantova: Viviano Guastalla.
De Angelis, L., E. Gigli and F. Sznura (eds) 1984. *I notai fiorentini dell'età di Dante, Biagio Boccadibue (1298-1314)*, I: *Fascicolo III (novembre 1305 - maggio 1309)*. Pisa: Giardini.
De Regibus, A. (ed.) 1946. *Statuti del Lago d'Orta del secolo XIV: Riviera ed Isola, Omegna, Gozzano*. Milano: Giuffrè.
De Vio, M. 1706. *Felicis et fidelissimae urbis panormitanae privilegia*. Panormi: Cortese.
De' Crescenzi, Pietro 1995. Ruralia Commoda. *Das Wissen des vollkommenen Landwirts um 1300*. I. Einleitung mit Buch I-III. W. Richter (ed). Heidelberg: Editiones Heidelbergenses.
Diacciati, S. and L. Tanzini (eds) 2016. *Lo statuto di San Gimignano del 1255*. Firenze: Olschki.
Donizone. 1984. *Vita di Matilde di Canossa*, ed. by V. Fumagalli and P. Golinelli. Milano: Jaca Book.
Egidi, P. (ed.) 1930, n.p. 2005. *Gli statuti viterbesi del MCCXXXVII-VIII, MCCLI-II e MCCCLVI*, in V. Federici (ed.) *Statuti della Provincia Romana. S. Andrea in Selci, Subiaco, Viterbo, Roviano, Anagni, Saccomuro, Aspra Sabina*. I-II. Roma: ISIME: 27-282.
Finzi, V. (ed.) 1911. *Gli Statuti della Repubblica di Sassari*. Cagliari: Dessì.
Firenze. Archivio dell'Opera di Santa Maria del Fiore. II. 1. 79; II. 1. 80; II. 4. 9; II. 4. 12.
Firenze. Archivio di Stato. *Arte dei legnaioli*. 1.
Firenze. Archivio di Stato. *Provvisioni, Registri*. 2. 26.
Fiumi, E. (ed.) 1951. *Statuti di Volterra, I (1210-1224)*. Firenze: Deputazione di Storia Patria per la Toscana.
Forgiarini, G. (ed.) 1996. *Lo statuto di Bergamo del 1353*. Spoleto: CISAM.
Fornarese, G. (ed.) 1971 (1st ed. 1905). *Statuta Vetera Civitatis Aqui (1276?)*. Bologna: Forni.
Frati, L. (ed.) 1869. *Gli statuti di Bologna dall'anno 1245 all'anno 1267*. Bologna: Regia Tipografia.
Fridh, Å. J. (ed.) 1973. Magni Aurelii Cassiodori *Variarum libri XII*. Turnholti: Brepols.
Frola, G. 1918. *Corpus statutorum Canavisii*. Torino: Tip. Salesiana.
Fugazza, E. (ed.) 2012. *Lo statuto di Piacenza del 1323*. Pavia: Pavia University Press.
Fumi, L. (ed.) 1874. *Gli statuti di Chianciano dell'anno MCCLXXXVII ora per la prima volta messi in luce*. Orvieto: Tosini.
Gaddoni, S. (ed.) 1932. *Statuti di Imola, sec. XIV*. I. Statuti della città (1334). Milano: Hoepli.
Genova. Biblioteca Universitaria. *Manoscritti*. B.VI.27: *Statuta et Conventiones Albisolae* 1389.
Ghignoli, A. (ed.) 1998. *I Brevi del Comune e del Popolo di Pisa dell'anno 1287*. Roma: ISIME.
Gloria, A. 1873. *Gli statuti del comune di Padova dal secolo XII all'anno 1285*. Padova: Sacchetto.
Gorni, G. 1970. Il «Liber Pergaminus» di Mosè de Brolo. *Studi medievali* s. 3, 11: 409-460.
Gualazzini, U. (ed.) 1952. *Statuta et ordinamenta comunis Cremonae facta et compilata currente anno Domini MCCCXXXIX*. Milano: Giuffrè.
Gualtieri, R. 1991. *Gli Statuti di Vernio*. Prato: Comune di Vernio.
Guasco, F. 1975. *Statuti di Masio*. Alessandria: Accademia degli Immobili.
Laderchi, C. (ed.) 1864. *Statuti di Ferrara dell'anno 1288*. Bologna: Tipografia Regia.

Lampertico, F. (ed.) 1886. *Statuti del comune di Vicenza. MCCLXIV*. Venezia: R. Deputazione veneta di Storia Patria.
Laudensium Statuta, seu jura municipalia. 1390, in De' Bosio 1855, appendice.
Liberali, G. (ed.) 1951. *Gli statuti del Comune di Treviso. II. Statuti degli anni 1231-33, 1260-63*. Venezia: Deputazione di Storia Patria per le Venezie.
Lucca. Archivio di Stato. *Statuti* 3, ms.
Maddalo, S. (ed.) 2000. De Balneis Puteolanis *di Pietro da Eboli. Biblioteca Angelica 1474, Facsimile e commentario*. Roma: Istituto Poligrafico e Zecca dello Stato.
Malvolti, A., G. Micheli, A. Prosperi, G., La Tosa and A. Zagli (eds) 1990. *Memorie sul Padule di Fucecchio (secoli XVI-XVII)*. Fucecchio: Ed. dell'Erba.
Manganelli, G. (ed.) 1936-57. *Statuti di Como del 1335. Volumen magnum*. Como: Presso la Società.
Marrocchi, M. (ed.) 2019. *Lo statuto duecentesco del Comune di Radicofani. Edizione del testo dal ms. D. 310 della Biblioteca Forteguerriana di Pistoia*. Bologna: Clueb.
Masé Dari, E. 1960. Lo statuto gonzaghesco (XV secolo) delle «Digagne» dell'Oltrepò mantovano. *Atti e memorie dell'Accademia Virgiliana di Mantova* n.s. 32: 19-68.
Mattiocco, E. (ed.) 2001. *Capitula civitatis Sulmonis*. Sulmona: Museo Civico.
Mendoza, R. 2022. *Roma nel Trecento. Gli Statuti del Comune di Roma del 1363*. Roma: Aracne.
Mezzetti, C. (ed.) 2016. *Le carte dell'archivio di Santa Maria di Pomposa (932-1050)*. Roma: Istituto Storico Italiano per il Medio Evo.
Milano, Biblioteca Ambrosiana, ms. B.19: *Statuta Civitatis Mediolanensis de anno MCCCXCVI*.
Montorsi, W. (ed.) 1955. *Statuta Ferrariae anno MCCLXXXVII*. Ferrara: Cassa di Risparmio di Ferrara.
Mor, C. G. (ed.) 1932. *Statuti della Valsesia del secolo XIV: Valsesia, Borgosesia, Crevola, Quarona*. Milano: Hoepli.
Morandi, U. (ed.) 1966. *Statuto del Comune di Montepulciano (1337)*. Firenze: Olschki.
Morandini, F. (ed.) 1958. *Statuti dell'arte dei legnaioli di Firenze (1301-1346)*. Firenze: Olschki.
Mordini, M. (ed.) 2019. *Statuta civitatis Grosseti (1421-1422)*. Siena: Accademia Senese degli Intronati.
Mosca, E. (ed.) 1958. *Gli antichi Statuti di Bra*. Torino: Deputazione Subalpina di Storia Patria.
Murgia, G. (ed.) 2016. Carta de Logu *d'Arborea. Edizione critica secondo l'*editio princeps *(BUC, Inc. 230)*. Milano: Angeli.
Nelli, R. and G. Pinto (eds) 2002. *Statuti pistoiesi del secolo XIII. Studi e testi*. Pistoia: Società Pistoiese di Storia Patria.
Nico Ottaviani, M. G. (ed.) 1991. *Statuto di Deruta in volgare dell'anno 1465*. Spoleto: CISAM (2nd ed.).
Nicolini, U. (ed.) 1969. *Reformationes Comunis Perusii quae extant anni MCCLXII*. Perugia: Deputazione di Storia Patria per l'Umbria.
Ninci, R. (ed.) 1999. *Statuta antiqua Communis Collis Vallis Else (1307-1407)*. Roma: ISIME.
Nogara B., R. Cessi and G. Bonelli (eds) 1927. *Statuti rurali bresciani del secolo XIV (Bovegno, Cimmo ed Orzinuovi)*. Milano: Hoepli.
Odorici, F. (ed.) 1876. *Statuti di Brescia del secolo XIII*. Torino: Bocca.
Onori, A. M. (ed.) 2000. *Lo statuto di Pescia del 1339*. Pistoia: Società Pistoiese di Storia Patria.
Orlando, E. (ed.) 2010. *Strade, traffici, viabilità in area veneta. Viaggio negli statuti comunali*. Roma: Viella.
Ortalli, G., G. Parolin and M. Pozza (eds) 1984. *Statuti di Cittadella del secolo XIV*. Roma: Jouvence.
Pasolini, P. D. (ed.) 1868 (repr. 1985). *Gli Statuti di Ravenna*. Bologna: Forni.
Pene Vidari, G. S. (ed.) 1969. *Gli statuti del comune di Ivrea*. Torino: Deputazione Subalpina di Storia Patria.

Pesce, A. 1914. *Statuti di Rossiglione*. Pinerolo: Società Storica Subalpina.
Piattoli, R. (ed.) 1936. *Lo Statuto dell'Arte dei padroni dei mulini sulla destra del fiume Bisenzio (1296)*. Prato: Bechi.
Pisa. Archivio di Stato. *Opera della Primaziale*. 16.
Pistoia, U. and D. Fusaro (eds) 2006. *Statuti di Feltre del secolo XIV nella trascrizione cinquecentesca, con il frammento del codice statutario del 1293*. Roma: Viella.
Pittarello, O. (ed.) 2017. *Statuti di Padova di età carrarese*. Roma: Viella.
Pitzorno, B. 1913. *Gli statuti civili di Venezia attribuiti ad Enrico Dandolo*. Perugia: Guerra.
Pozza, M. (ed.) 1984. *Statuti di Lendinara del 1321*. Roma: Jouvence.
Pucci, S. and Ch. M. De la Roncière (eds) 1995. *Una comunità della Valdelsa nel Medioevo: Poggibonsi e il suo statuto del 1332*. Poggibonsi: Lalli.
Ravani, S. (ed.) 2011. *Il Breve di Villa di Chiesa (Iglesias)*. Cagliari: Centro di Studi Filologici Sardi.
Rinaldi, E. (ed.) 1913. *Statuto di Forlì dell'anno MCCCLIX con le modificazioni del MCCCLXXIII*. Roma: Loescher.
Ronchini, A. (ed.) 1857. *Statuta Communis Parmae ab anno MCCLXVI. ad annum MCCCIV*. Parmae: Fiaccadori.
Rovigo. Accademia dei Concordi. Biblioteca. Ms. Silv. 480. *Statuta totius Policinij*. 1440.
Sacco, I. M. (ed.) 1932. *Statuti di Savigliano*. Torino: Gabetta.
Salem Elsheikh, M. (ed.) 2000. *Statuto del Comune e del Popolo di Perugia del 1342 in volgare*. Perugia: Deputazione di Storia Patria per l'Umbria.
Salem Elsheikh, M. (ed.) 2002. *Il Costituto del Comune di Siena volgarizzato nel MCCCIX-MCCCX*. Siena: Fondazione Monte dei Paschi di Siena.
Salimbene Parmigiano [de Adam] 1882. *Cronaca volgarizzata da Carlo Cantarelli*. Parma: Battei.
Salvestrini, F. (ed.) 1994. *Statuti del Comune di San Miniato al Tedesco (1337)*. Pisa: ETS.
Salvestrini, F. (ed.) 1998. *Statuti del comune di Santa Croce (Prima metà del secolo XIV-1422)*. Pisa: Pacini.
Samaritani, A. (ed.) 1958. *Statuta Pomposiae annis MCCXCV et MCCCXXXVIII-LXXXIII. Monumenti della Deputazione provinciale ferrarese di Storia Patria* 1 (Statuti)/4.
Sandri, G. (ed.) 1959. *Gli statuti veronesi del 1276 colle correzioni e le aggiunte fino al 1323*. Verona: Deputazione di Storia Patria per le Venezie (2nd ed.).
Santarelli, U. 1969. *Statuto dei comuni di Rincine e Fornace (1446)*. Firenze: Olschki.
Savino, G. and M. Soffici (eds) 2003. *Statuto di Monsummano 1331*. Pisa: Pacini.
Silva, A. (ed.) 1987. *Corpus inscriptionum medii aevi Liguriae*. III: *Genova. Centro storico*. Genova: Brigati Carucci.
Šoljić, A., Z. Šundrica and I. Veselić (eds) 2002. *Liber statutorum civitatis Ragusii compositus anno MCCLXXII*. Ragusii: Drzavni arhiv u Dubrovnik.
Statuta civilia Civitatis Papiae. 1393, in De' Bosio 1855, appendice.
Statuta civitatis Brixiae. 1557, in De' Bosio 1855, appendice.
Statuta Civitatis Cremonae accuratius quam antea excusa, et cum archetypo collata. Additis quamplurimis, quae omnia sequenti pagella indicantur. 1485. Brescia-Cremona: Boninum de Boninis de Ragusia.
Statuta civitatis Mutine ad iudices aquarum pertinentia, cum quibusdam additionibus valde necessariis ac indice copiosissimo edita. 1575. Modena: Gadaldini.
Statuta Communis Parmae digesta anno MCCLV. 1856. Parma: Fiaccadori.
Statuta et iura municipalia antiquae urbis & populi Civitatis Nucerii. 1567. Fulginei: per Augustinum Colaldum de Civitate Ducali.
Statuta Massae. Lucae: Busdraghi: 1591, repr. 1991. Massa: Provincia di Massa.

Statuta Populi et Communis Florentiæ, anno salutis MCCCCXV. 1777-83. Friburgi: Apud Michaelem Kluch [actually Florence: Stamperia Bonducciana].

Statuto della terra di Stroncone 1700. 1707. Terni: Salutii.

Stella, A., L. F. Farina and G. Balestreri (eds) 1992. *Gli statuti delle strade e delle acque del contado di Milano*. Milano: LED.

Strabo 1928. *The Geography of Strabo*. 5. transl. by H. L. Jones. London: Heinemann.

Tomassetti, F., V. Federici and P. Egidi (eds) 1910. *Statuti della Provincia Romana, Vicovaro, Cave, Roccantica, Ripi, Genazzano, Tivoli, Castel Fiorentino*. Roma: ISIME.

Trombetti Budriesi, A. L. and V. Braidi (eds) 1995. *Per l'edizione degli statuti del Comune di Bologna (secoli XIV-XV). I rubricari*. Bologna: La Fotocromo Emiliana.

Vaccari, R. (ed.) 2014. *Il «Chronicon Veronense» di Paride da Cerea e dei suoi continuatori*. Legnago: Fondazione Fioroni Musei.

Valori, R. 2006. Lo "Statuto delle gabelle di San Miniato al Tedesco" del 1364. Trascrizione e commento della fonte. *Bollettino dell'Accademia degli Euteleti* 73: 161-196.

Vicini, E. P. (ed.) 1929-32. *Respublica Mutinensis (1306-1307)*. Milano: Hoepli.

Vicini, E. P. (ed.) 1938. *Statuti dell'Arte dei navigatori di Modena, statuti e privilegi concessi alla Fabbrica di S. Geminiano di Modena; Le Pergamene del Monastero di S. Eufemia di Modena*. Reggio Emilia: Costi.

Vignoli, G. 2001. *Statuti del Vicariato del Podere Fiorentino. Palazzuolo 1406, libri* 5. Palazzuolo sul Senio: Oste Ghibellina.

Villani, Giovanni 1990. *Nuova cronica*, ed. G. Porta. Parma: Guanda.

Viola, F. 2018. *Montalcino nel Quattrocento. Lo statuto dei danni dati e degli straordinari (1452): edizione e note storiche*. Siena: Effigi.

Zaccarini, U. (ed.) 1998. *Statuto ravennate di Ostasio da Polenta (1327-1346)*. Bologna: Forni.

Zdekauer, L. (ed.) 1888. *Statutum Potestatis Comunis Pistorii (1296)*, in Nelli and Pinto (eds) 2002.

Zdekauer, L. (ed.) 1891. *Breve et ordinamenta Populi Pistorii (1284)*, in Nelli and Pinto (eds) 2002.

Zdekauer, L. and P. Sella (eds) 1910. *Statuti di Ascoli Piceno dell'anno .MCCCLXXVII*. Roma: Forzani.

Zucchini, M. 1962. Statuta Communis Ferrariae ad Offitium Argerum. *Rivista di Storia dell'Agricoltura* 2/2: 47-54.

Secondary sources

Abulafia, D. 1977. *The Two Italies. Economic relations between the Norman Kingdom of Sicily and the Northern Communes*. Cambridge: Cambridge University Press.

Acot, P. 2004. *Storia del clima. Dal Big Bang alle catastrofi climatiche*. Trad. it. Roma: Donzelli.

(L')acqua nei secoli altomedievali. 2008. Spoleto: Centro Italiano di Studi sull'Alto Medioevo.

Agnoletti, M. 1993. Gestione del bosco e segagione del legname nell'alta valle del Piave, in Caniato (ed.) 1993: 73-126.

Agnoletti, M. 1996. Aspetti tecnici ed economici del commercio del legname in Cadore (XIV-XVI secolo), in S. Cavaciocchi (ed.) *L'uomo e la foresta. Secc. XIII-XVIII*. Prato-Firenze: Le Monnier: 1025-1040.

Agnoletti, M. 1998. *Segherie e foreste nel Trentino. Dal Medioevo ai giorni nostri*. San Michele all'Adige: Museo Usi Gente Trentina.

Albertani, G. 2007. Igiene e decoro: Bologna secondo il registro del "notaio del fango" (1285). *Storia Urbana* 116: 19-36.

Alberth, J. 2000. *From the Brink of the Apocalypse: Confronting Famine, War, Plague, and Death in the Later Middle Ages*. London-New York: Routledge.

Albini, G. (ed.) 1998. *Le scritture del Comune. Amministrazione e memoria nelle città dei secoli XII e XIII*. Torino: Scriptorium.

Albini, G. and *et al.* (eds) 1998. *Bibliografia Statutaria Italiana, 1985-1995*. Roma: Biblioteca del Senato della Repubblica; Id. 2009. *1996-2005*; Id. 2017. *2006-2015*.

Albini, G., P. Grillo and B. A. Raviola (eds) 2022. *Il fuoco e l'acqua. Prevenzione e gestione dei disastri ambientali fra Medioevo e Età Moderna. Quaderni degli Studi di Storia Medioevale e di Diplomatica, Università di Milano* 7.

Aldrete, G. S. 2007. *Floods of the Tiber in Ancient Rome*. Baltimore: The Johns Hopkins University Press.

Alexandre, P. 1987. *Le climat en Europe au Moyen Âge. Contribution à l'histoire des variations climatiques de 1000 à 1425, d'après les sources narratives de l'Europe occidentale*. Paris: École des hautes études en sciences sociales.

Alexandre-Bidon, D. 1994. Pozzi e fontane nella città medievale. *Rassegna* 16, 57/1: 33-36.

Alfani, G., M. Di Tullio and L. Mocarelli (eds) *Storia economica e ambiente italiano (ca. 1400-1850)*. Milano: Angeli.

Ambrogi, A. 2005. Labra *di età romana in marmi bianchi e colorati*. Roma: «L'Erma» di Bretschneider.

Andenna, G. 1996. Il concetto geografico-politico di Lombardia nel Medioevo. *Vita e Pensiero* 79: 653-668.

Andenna, G. 2002. *Linea Ticino. Sull'unità culturale delle genti del fiume nel Medioevo*. Bellinzona: Humilibus consentientes.

Andenna, G. 2018. L'acqua come strumento per lo sviluppo dell'economia agricola nella Lombardia Occidentale tra XII e XIII secolo. Il caso della Corbelleta di Momo in diocesi di Novara, in D. Chamboduc de Saint Pulgent and M. Dejoux (eds) *La fabrique des sociétés médiévales méditerranéennes. Le Moyen Âge de François Menant*. Paris: Éditions de la Sorbonne: 83-95.

Andermann, K. and G. J. Schenk (eds) 2020. *Wasser. Ressource - Gefahr - Leben*. Ostfildern: Thorbecke.

Andreolli, B. 2008. Gestione e misurazione dell'acqua nell'alto medioevo, in *L'acqua nei secoli altomedievali*: 429-465.

Annoscia, G. M. 2007. *Fonti e strutture per la conoscenza del sistema idrico di Roma nel Medioevo*. Roma: Aracne.

Appuhn, K. R. 2009. *A Forest on the Sea. Environmental Expertise in Renaissance Venice*. Baltimore: The Johns Hopkins University Press.

Armiero, M. and S. Barca 2004. *Storia dell'ambiente. Una introduzione*. Roma: Carocci.

Arnold, E. F. 2017. Rivers of Risk and Redemption in Gregory of Tours' Writings. *Speculum* 92/1: 117-143.

Arnoux, M. 2008. Les moulins à eau en Europe occidentale (IXe-XIIe siècle). Aux origines d'une économie institutionnelle de l'énergie hydraulique, in *L'acqua nei secoli altomedievali*: 693-746.

Artifoni, E. 1985. I ribaldi: immagini e istituzioni della marginalità nel tardo medioevo piemontese, in *Piemonte medievale. Forme del potere e della società. Studi per Giovanni Tabacco*. Torino: Einaudi: 227-248.

Artizzu, F. 1961. Un inventario dei beni sardi dell'Opera di Santa Maria di Pisa (1339). *Archivio Storico Sardo* 27: 63-80.

Artizzu, F. 1974. *L'Opera di Santa Maria di Pisa e la Sardegna*. Padova: Cedam.

Artizzu, F. 1992. Disposizioni riguardanti l'edilizia nella legislazione statutaria della Sardegna medievale. *Archivio Storico Sardo* 37: 71-82.

Asche, R., G. Bettega and U. Pistoia 2010. *Un fiume di legno, fluitazione del legname dal Trentino a Venezia*. Ivrea: Priuli & Verlucca.

Ascheri, M. 1991. *Diritto medievale e moderno. Problemi del processo, della cultura e delle fonti giuridiche*. Rimini: Maggioli.

Ascheri, M. 1995. Leggi e statuti, in G. Cavallo, C. Leonardi and E. Menestò (eds) *Lo spazio letterario del Medioevo*. 1: *Il Medioevo latino*. III. *La ricezione del testo*. Roma: Salerno Ed.: 541-574.

Ascheri, M. 2001. Beyond the *Comune*. The Italian City-State and its Inheritance, in P. Linehan and J. L. Nelson (eds) *The Medieval World*. London-New York: Routledge: 451-468.

Ascheri, M. 2010. Statutory Law of Italian Cities from Middle Ages to Early Modern, in Drossbach (ed.): 201-216.

Ascheri, M. 2013. *The Laws of Late Medieval Italy (1000-1500)*. Leiden-Boston: Brill.

Ascheri, M. 2023. Tra Stato e autonomie nel medioevo italiano. *Le Carte e la Storia* 24/1: 21-29.

Astuti, G. 1958. Acque. Introduzione storica generale, in *Enciclopedia del diritto*. Milano: Giuffré. I: 346-387.

Autorità di Bacino, Fiume Arno. website: http://www.adbarno.it/cont/testo.php?id=11.

Bacchi, T. 1988. Il bosco e l'acqua. Uso dell'incolto e colonizzazione agraria nel territorio ferrarese (secoli XI-XIII), in B. Andreolli and M. Montanari (eds) *Il bosco nel Medioevo*. Bologna: Clueb: 185-198.

Bacchi, T. 2000. Statuti comunali e regolamentazione delle acque a Ferrara nel secolo XIII, in Montanari and Vasina (eds): 107-116.

Bacci, A. 1571. *De Thermis libri septem*. Venetiis: Valgrisium.

Bailey, M. 2021. *After the Black Death. Economy, society and the law in fourteenth-century England*. Oxford: Oxford University Press.

Baldaccini, R. 1947. *Monumenti fiorentini del Trecento. Il ponte Vecchio*. Firenze: Cya.

Balestracci, D. 1990. L'acqua a Siena nel Medioevo, in J-C. Maire Vigueur, A. Paravicini Bagliani (eds) Ars et Ratio. *Dalla torre di Babele al ponte di Rialto*. Palermo: Sellerio: 19-31.

Balestracci, D. 1992. La politica delle acque urbane nell'Italia comunale. *Mélanges de l'École française de Rome - Moyen Âge* 104/2: 431-479.

Balestracci, D. 1994. Systèmes d'hydraulique urbaine (Italie centrale, fin du Moyen Âge), in Crouzet-Pavan and Maire-Vigueur (eds): 115-122.

Balestracci, D. 2000. Die Bottini von Siena, in A. Hoffmann (ed.) *Die Wasserversorgung in der Renaissancezeit*. Mainz am Rhein: von Zabern: 199-205.

Balestracci, D. 2003. Il controllo delle acque nel territorio senese tra XIII e XV secolo, in É. Crouzet-Pavan (ed.) *Pouvoir et édilité. Les grands chantiers dans l'Italie communale et seigneuriale*. Roma: École française de Rome: 419-438.

Balestracci, D. 2011. Le Virtù in Piazza. Genesi e realizzazione della Fonte Gaia, in E. Toti and S. Dei (eds) *La Fonte Gaia di Jacopo della Quercia. Storia e restauro di un capolavoro dell'arte senese*. Firenze: Polistampa: 24-35.

Balestracci, D., A. Costantini and L. Vigni 2006. *La memoria dell'acqua. I Bottini di Siena*. Siena: Protagon.

Balestracci, D. and P. Pasini. 2001. *Pesca e pescatori. Dal tardo Medioevo alla prima Età Moderna*. Milano: Leonardo Arte.

Balestracci, D. and G. Piccinni. 1977. *Siena nel Trecento. Assetto urbano e strutture edilizie*. Firenze: CLUSF.

Ballut, Ch. and P. Fournier (eds) 2013. *Au fil de l'eau. Ressources, risques et gestion du Néolithique à nos jours*. Clermont-Ferrand: Presses Universitaires Blaise Pascal.

Balossino, S. 2015. *I podestà sulle sponde del Rodano. Arles e Avignone nei secoli XII e XIII*. Roma: Viella.

Balossino, S. 2022. *Le pont d'Avignon. Une société de bâtisseurs (XIIe-XVe siècle)*. Avignon: Éditions Universitaires.

Bannon, C. 2017. Fresh Water in Roman Law: Rights and Policy. *The Journal of Roman Studies* 107: 60-89.

Barbagli, A. 2017. Lo statuto di Foiano del 1387. Storia statutaria e istituzionale di un comune nella Valdichiana del XIV secolo, in Allegria (ed.) *Statuto del Comune di Foiano*: 13-38.

Barbanera, M. and O. Stefanucci. 2015. *Dare acqua ad Assisi. L'acquedotto del Sanguinone e il condotto di frate Elia*. Perugia: Deputazione di Storia Patria per l'Umbria.

Barbini, B. 1975. Dalle scoperte medievali a oggi, in *Viterbo e le sue acque termali*. Viterbo: Quatrini: 43-66.

Barbot, M. 2013a. Non tutti i conflitti vengono per nuocere. Usi, diritti e litigi sui canali lombardi fra XV e XX secolo (prime indagini), in Mocarelli (ed.): 35-56.

Barbot, M. 2013b. La costruzione giuridica di una civiltà. Il *diritto* e i *diritti* sulle terre e sulle acque in Lombardia fra norme, usi e conflitti tra il XIII e il XIX secolo, in L. Aiello, M. Bascapè and S. Rebora (eds) *Il paese dell'acqua. I Luoghi Pii Elemosinieri di Milano e le loro terre: un itinerario nel paesaggio dal medioevo ai nostri giorni*. Milano: NodoLibri: 256-269.

Bargagli Petrucci, F. 1906. *Le fonti di Siena e i loro acquedotti. Note storiche dalle origini fino al 1555*. Firenze: Olschki.

Baroffio, B. and M. Magrassi. 1977. Battesimo, in L. Pacomio (ed.) *Dizionario Teologico Interdisciplinare*. Torino: Marietti: I: 472-491.

Bärsch, J. 2017. Der Wasserritus der Taufe im Spiegel der mittelalterlichen Liturgiepraxis und -kommentare, in Gerlinde H.-R., Ch. Rohr, M. Stolz (eds) *Wasser in der mittelalterlichen Kultur*. Berlin: De Gruyter: 354-366.

Bartoli Langeli, A. 1985. La documentazione degli Stati italiani nei secoli XIII-XV: forme, organizzazione, personale, in *Culture et idéologie dans la genèse de l'État moderne*. Roma: École française de Rome: 35-55.

Bartoli Langeli, A. 1987. La formula d'onore. Un esperimento notarile per il Comune di Perugia. *Il pensiero politico. Rivista di storia delle idee politiche e sociali* 20/1: 121-135.

Bartoli Langeli, A. and N. Giové Marchioli. 1996. Le scritte incise della Fontana Maggiore, in C. Santini (ed.) *Il linguaggio figurativo della Fontana Maggiore di Perugia*. Perugia: Calzetti-Mariucci: 163-195.

Bartoli Langeli, A. and S. Merli. 2013. Un aspetto della committenza pubblica in ambito urbano: le fontane, in S. Maddalo and I. Lori Sanfilippo (eds) *Civiltà urbana e committenze artistiche al tempo del maestro di Offida (secoli XIV-XV)*. Roma: ISIME: 69-100.

Bartoli Langeli, A. and L. Zurli. 1996. *L'iscrizione in versi della Fontana Maggiore di Perugia*. Roma: Herder.

Basing, P. 1990. *Trades and Crafts in Medieval Manuscripts*. London: British Library.

Bassani, M., G. D'Acunto and F. Madricardo (eds) 2022. *Crossing the Water. The Venice Lagoon from Antiquity throughout the centuries*. Roma-Bristol CT: L'«Erma» di Bretschneider.

Bauch, M. 2019. Die Magdalenenflut 1342 am Schnittpunkt von Umwelt- und Infrastrukturgeschichte. Ein *compound event* als Taktgeber für mittelalterliche Infrastrukturentwicklung und Daseinsvorsorge. *NTM Zeitschrift für Geschichte der Wissenschaften, Technik und Medizin* 27/3: 273-309.

Bauch, M. 2020. Chronology and impact of a global moment in the 13th century. The Samalas eruption revisited, in A. Kiss and K. Pribyl (eds) *The Dance of Death in Late Medieval and Renaissance Europe. Environmental Stress, Mortality and Social Response*. London-NewYork: Routledge: 214-232.

Bayless, M. 2012. *Sin and Filth in Medieval Culture. The Devil in the Latrine*. London-New York: Routledge.

Bazzana, A. and P. Guichard 1981. Irrigation et société dans l'Espagne Orientale au Moyen Âge, in J. Métral and P. Sanlaville (eds) *L'homme et l'eau en Méditerranée et au Proche Orient*. I. Lyon: Maison de l'Orient et de la Méditerranée: 115-140.

Bebermeier, W., A.-S. Hennig and M. Mutz (eds) 2008. *Vom Wasser. Umweltgeschichtliche Perspektiven auf Konflikte, Risiken und Nutzungsformen*. Siegburg: BoD.

Becattini 2015. Dalla Selva alla Cupola. Il trasporto del legname dell'Opera di Santa Maria del Fiore e il suo impiego nel cantiere brunelleschiano, in M. Haines (ed.) *The Years of the Cupola. Studies*. Berlin-Firenze: Max-Planck-Institut für Wissenschaftsgeschichte: 7-53.

Bechmann, R. 1984. *Des arbres et des hommes. La forêt au moyen âge*. Paris: Flammarion.

Beggio, G. 1977. Navigazione, trasporto, mulini sul fiume: i tratti di una tipologia, in Borelli (ed.) II: 483-567.

Bellinazzi, A. 1993. La fluitazione del legname in Toscana, in Caniato (ed.): 209-226.

Benoît, P. 2006. Les ponts aqueducs dans la France médiévale, in D. James-Raoul and C. Thomasset (eds) *Les ponts au Moyen Âge*. Paris: PUPS: 77-90.

Benucci, F. 2015. Alluvioni e altre *ruine*. Padova e Verona in età presignorile nelle fonti annalistiche ed epigrafiche. *Città e Storia* 10: 23-39.

Benvenuti, A. 2009. Sotto la volta del cielo. Luoghi, simboli e immagini dell'identità cittadina, in *La costruzione della città comunale*: 243-256.

Bépoix, S. and H. Richard (eds) 2019. *La forêt au Moyen Âge*. Paris: Les Belles Lettres.

Berardi, M. R. 2005. *I monti d'oro. Identità urbana e conflitti territoriali nella storia dell'Aquila medievale*. Napoli: Liguori.

Bergier, J.-F. and G. Coppola (eds) 2007. *Vie di terra e d'acqua. Infrastrutture viarie e sistemi di relazioni in area alpina (secoli XIII-XVI)*. Bologna: Il Mulino.

Bériac-Lainé, F. 1998. À propos de la fin de la lèpre : XIIe-XVe siècles, in A. Paravicini Bagliani and F. Santi (eds) *The Regulation of Evil. Social and Cultural Attitudes to Epidemics in the Late Middle Ages*. Firenze: SISMEL: 159-173.

Bernardi, A., E. Fox and A. Adamoli 1988. *La civiltà dell'acqua. Le fontane del Trentino*. Trento: Provincia Autonoma.

Bernat i Roca, M. 1998. El mantenzment de la salubritat pública a Ciutat de Mallorca (segles XIV-XV). *Acta Historica et Archaeologica Mediaevalia* 19: 91-125.

Berti, C. and F. Landi (eds) 2019: *Disegni d'acqua. Acque e trasformazioni del territorio*. Firenze: Phasar.

Bertoncin, M., A. Pase and D. Quatrida 2014. La construction géo-historique du Delta du Po, in M. Franchomme, Ch. Labeur, D. Quatrida and R. Simonetti (eds) *Les zones humides méditerranéennes hier et aujourd'hui*. Padova: Padova University Press: 313-330.

Bertoni, L. 2022. Uso e commercio del legname nella Pavia di fine XIII secolo, in Grillo (ed.): 191-203.

Besta, E. 1899. *Il senato veneziano (origine, costituzione, attribuzioni e riti)*. Venezia: Società di Storia Veneta.

Besta, E. 1899. Intorno ad alcuni frammenti di un antico statuto di Castelsardo. *Archivio Giuridico Filippo Serafini* 62: 281-332.
Bevilacqua, P. 2001. *Demetra e Clio. Uomini e ambiente nella storia*. Roma: Donzelli.
Bianca, C. and F. Salvestrini (eds) 2017. *L'acqua nemica. Fiumi, inondazioni e città storiche dall'antichità al contemporaneo*. Spoleto: CISAM.
Bichsel, Ch. 2016. Water and the (Infra-)Structure of Political Rule: A Synthesis. *Water Alternatives* 9/2: 356-372.
Biosca i Bas, A. 2013. «Sine aqua salvari non valemus». El agua como purificación de creyentes y de infieles en las polémicas antiislámicas, in J. Martínez Gázquez and J. V. Tolan (eds) Ritus infidelium. *Miradas interconfesionales sobre las prácticas religiosas en la Edad Media*. Madrid: Casa de Velázquez: 29-44.
Biraben, J.-N. 1985. Epidémies, hygiène et santé publique au Moyen Âge, in *Colloque international d'Histoire de la médecine médiévale*. 1. Orléans: La Société: 74-82.
Biscaro, G. 1908. Gli antichi «Navigli» milanesi. *Archivio Storico Lombardo* 35/20: 285-326.
Blair, J. (ed.) 2014. *Waterways and Canal-Building in Medieval England*. Oxford: Oxford University Press.
Blattmann, M. 2001. Aderenza alla realtà, rilevanza pratica e impiego effettivo degli statuti tedeschi e italiani (secoli XII-XIV), in Rossetti (ed.)b: 117-132.
Blockmans, W. 2001. La normativa nelle città fiamminghe (secoli XI-XIII), in Rossetti (ed.)b: 67-77.
Bocchi, F. 1990. Regulation of the Urban Environment by the Italian Communes from the Twelfth to the Fourteenth Century. *Bulletin of the John Rylands Library* 72: 63-78.
Bocchi, F. 1995. Regolamenti urbanistici, spazi pubblici, disposizioni antinquinamento e per l'igiene nelle maggiori città della Sardegna medievale, in *La Corona d'Aragona in Italia (secc. XIII-XVIII)*. II/1. *Il «regnum Sardiniae et Corsicae» nell'espansione mediterranea della Corona d'Aragona*. Sassari: Carlo Delfino: 73-124.
Bocchi, F. 2009. La "modernizzazione" delle città medievali, in *La costruzione della città comunale*: 331-347.
Boisseuil, D. 2002. *Le thermalisme en Toscane à la fin du Moyen Âge. Les bains siennois de la fin du XIIIe siècle au début du XVIe siècle*. Roma: École française de Rome.
Boisseuil, D. 2003. Les sites thermaux toscans à la fin du Moyen Age, in Galetti and Racine (eds): 351-368.
Boisseuil, D. 2009. Les juristes et les eaux thermales dans la Toscane des XIIIe-XIVe siècles. *Mélanges de l'École française de Rome - Moyen Âge* 121/1: 155-167.
Boisseuil, D. 2010. Impiego e cultura delle acque termali in Italia nel Rinascimento (XIII-XVI secolo), in Calzona and Lamberini (eds) II: 491-505.
Boisseuil, D. 2018. Gestione delle acque termali alla fine del Medioevo in Italia e nel bacino del Mediterraneo occidentale, in *Water Management in Europe*: 101-116
Bologna, F. 1997. *La Fontana della Riviera all'Aquila, detta delle novantanove cannelle*. L'Aquila: Il Cicerone.
Bonfiglio Dosio, G. 1995. *Lo statuto come chiave d'accesso all'archivio comunale di antico regime: il caso di Cittadella*, in G. Citton, D. Mazzon and G. Bonfiglio Dosio (eds) *Statuti di Cittadella del XIV secolo*. Cittadella: Biblos: 9-55.
Boone, M. 2017. La représentation politique dans les villes flamandes du bas Moyen Âge: limites et possibilités des 'anciennes démocraties des Pays Bas', in J.-Ph. Genet, D. Le Page and O. Mattéoni (eds) *Consensus et représentation*. Paris-Rome: Éd. de la Sorbonne: 421-450.

Boone, M. and J. Haemers 2018. 'The Common Good': Governance, Discipline and Political Culture, in B. Blondé, M. Boone and A.-L. Van Bruaene (eds) *City and society in the Law Countries, 1100-1600*. Cambridge: Cambridge University Press: 93-127.

Borelli, G. (ed.) 1977. *Una città e il suo fiume: Verona e l'Adige*. Verona: Banca Popolare di Verona.

Borghero, F. and F. Salvestrini. 2023. Fuoco e acqua negli ordinamenti normativi della Sardegna bassomedievale. *Mélanges de l'École française de Rome - Moyen Âge* 135/1: 137-170.

Bortolami, S. 1988. Acque, mulini e folloni nella formazione del paesaggio urbano medievale (secoli XI-XIV): l'esempio di Padova, in Comba (ed.): 277-330.

Bortolami, S. 2003. Il Brenta medievale nella pianura veneta. Note per una storia politico-territoriale, in A. Bondesan, G. Caniato, D. Gasparini, F. Vallerani and M. Zanetti (eds) *Il Brenta*. Verona: Cierre: 215-225.

Bortolami, S. 2008. Il Bacchiglione nel Medioevo, in F. Selmin and C. Grandis (eds) *Il Bacchiglione*. Verona: Cierre: 141-157.

Bortoluzzi, D. 2022. Bologna e gli *Ordinamenta Bladi*, in Albini, Grillo and Raviola (eds): 81-91.

Boucheron, P. 1994. Usages et partage de l'eau à Milan et dans le Milanais (XIIIe-XVe siècles), in Crouzet-Pavan and Maire-Vigueur (eds): 123-138.

Boucheron, P. and N. Offenstadt 2011. Introduction générale: Une histoire de l'échange politique au Moyen Âge, in P. Boucheron and N. Offenstadt (eds) *L'espace public au Moyen Âge. Débats autour de Jürgen Habermas*. Paris: Puf: 1-21.

Braudel, F. (ed.) 1991. *Prato. Storia di una città*. 1. G. Cherubini (ed.) *Ascesa e declino del centro medievale. Dal Mille al 1494*. Firenze: Le Monnier.

Braunstein, Ph. 1988. De la montagne à Venise: les réseaux du bois au XVe siècle. *Mélanges de l'Ecole française de Rome* 100/2: 761-799.

Breda, N. 2005. Per un'antropologia dell'acqua, in N. Breda (ed.) *Antropologia dell'acqua. La Ricerca Folklorica* 51: 3-16.

Brogiolo, G. P. (ed.) 2017. *Este, l'Adige e i Colli Eugenei. Storie di paesaggi*. Firenze: SAP.

Broussais, R. 2018. Comparer les statuts urbains médiévaux. *Historia et Ius* 13: 22-28.

Brundage, J. A. 2008. *The Medieval Origins of the Legal Profession: Canonists, Civilians and Courts*. Chicago: University of Chicago Press.

Brunori Cianti, L. and G. Lazzi (eds) 2005. *Scarperia: la Firenze del contado. Immagini di vita quotidiana dagli statuti del XV secolo*. Firenze: Polistampa.

Bufanio, V. 2022a. L'eruzione del 1257 tra cronisti e vulcanologi, in Albini, Grillo and Raviola (eds): 19-31.

Bufanio, V. 2022b. Lo sfruttamento dei boschi per l'edilizia in Piemonte (inizio XIV secolo), in Grillo (ed.): 205-216.

Buonora, P. 2019. The Tiber river and hydraulic risk: models of interpretation in history, in Canzian and Novello (eds): 97-104.

Butters, S. B. 2010. Princely waters: an elemental look at the Medici dukes, in Calzona and Lamberini (eds) I: 389-411.

Cadinu, M. 2015 *Water-related architecture in Sardinia*. Wuppertal: Steinhäuser Verlag.

Cadinu, M. 2019. Aspetti internazionali dell'urbanistica giudicale e dell'edilizia nella Sassari medievale, in Mattone and Simbula (eds): 775-798.

Calasso, F. 1970. *Introduzione al diritto comune*. Milano: Giuffrè (2nd ed.).

Calzolari, M. 1990. La navigazione interna in Emilia Romagna tra l'VIII e il XIII secolo, in G. Adani (ed.) *Vie del commercio in Emilia, Romagna, Marche*. Milano: Pizzi: 115-124.

Calzona, A. and D. Lamberini (eds) 2010. *La civiltà delle acque tra Medioevo e Rinascimento*. Firenze: Olschki.

Cammarosano, P. 2021. Gli statuti italiani, in Lett (ed.): 51-72.
Campbell, B. M .S. 2016. *The Great Transition. Climate, Disease and Society in the Late-Medieval World.* Cambridge: Cambridge University Press.
Campbell, B. M. S. 2017. Global climates, the 1257 mega-eruption of Samalas Volcano, Indonesia, and the English food crisis of 1258. *Transactions of the Royal Historical Society* 6 s. 27: 87-121.
Campopiano, M. 2013. Rural communities, land clearence and water management in the Po Valley in the central and late Middle Ages. *Journal of Medieval History* 39/4: 377-393.
Campopiano, M. 2017, Cooperation and Private Enterprise in Water Management in Iraq: Continuity and Change between the Sasanian and Early Islamic Periods (Sixth to Tenth Centuries). *Environment and History* 23/3: 385-407.
Campopiano, M. 2018. Gestione ordinaria delle acque e rischi idrogeologici. L'amministrazione delle acque nella Pianura Padana tra esigenze energetiche, trasporti, irrigazione e rischi di inondazione (secoli XII-XV), in *Water Management in Europe*: 25-39.
Campopiano, M. 2023. Città e risorse idriche: l'acqua come risorsa e come minaccia nella Pianura Padana e nella Valle del Reno (secc. XIV-XVI), in E. Bini, D. Carnevale and D. Cecere (eds) *L'acqua: risorsa e minaccia. La gestione delle risorse idriche e delle inondazioni in Europa (XIV-XIX secolo).* Napoli: Federico II University Press: 21-39.
Campopiano, M. forthcoming. Water and Land in Mediterranean River Basins: Wetlands, Land Reclamation, and Water Management in Medieval Italian Societies (9th-12th Centuries), in *Thalassocracy. The Explanatory Power of the Mediterranean.* International Conference, University of Haifa 29-31 May 2023.
Campopiano, M. and F. Menant 2015. Agricolture irrigue: l'Italia padana, in *Paesaggi agrari d'Europa*: 291-322.
Cangelosi, E. 2021. L'eau bien commun, bien public. Une réflexion à partir de la Rome ancienne. https://hal.archives-ouvertes.fr/hal-03407473.
Caniato, G. 1993 (ed.) *La via del Fiume dalle Dolomiti a Venezia.* Verona: Cierre.
Caniato, G. 2007. L'arte dei *remèri* di Venezia: una singolare persistenza, in Caniato (ed.): 15-23.
Caniato, G. 2007 (ed.) *L'arte dei remèri, i 700 anni dello statuto dei costruttori di remi.* Verona: Cierre.
Caniato, G. and M. Dal Borgo (eds) 1988. *Dai monti alla laguna: produzione artigianale e artistica del Bellunese per la cantieristica veneziana.* Venezia: La Stamperia di Venezia.
Canning, J. 1996. *A History of Medieval Political Thought, 300-1450.* London-New York: Routledge.
Canning, J. (ed.) 2004. *Power, Violence, and Mass Death in Pre-Modern and Modern Times.* London-New York: Routledge.
Canzian, D. 2003. Castelli di passo e di fiume, in D. Gallo and F. Rossetto (eds) *Per terre e per acque. Vie di comunicazione nel Veneto dal medioevo alla prima età moderna.* Padova: Il Poligrafo: 165-201.
Canzian, D. 2012. Ambiente naturale e intervento umano tra Sile, Piave e Livenza nei secoli XI-XV, in Canzian and Simonetti (eds): 17-39.
Canzian, D. 2014. Acque, insediamenti e attività umane nella marca veronese-trevigiana (secoli X-XIV), in Lusso (ed.): 215-244.
Canzian, D. 2019. Studying the environmental history of Medieval Veneto: elements for an eco-systemic assessment (12th-13th centuries), in Canzian and Novello (eds): 13-28.
Canzian, D. 2022a. Acqua e igiene pubblica nelle città medievali, in Canzian and Valenzano (eds): 109-124.
Canzian, D. 2022b. I boschi della Repubblica di Venezia tra terraferma e laguna (XII-XIII secolo), in Grillo (ed.): 135-150.

Canzian, D. and P. Grillo 2019. Dalla parte della natura: il rapporto uomo-ambiente nella medievistica italiana recente. *Società e storia* 165: 471-484.

Canzian, D. and E. Novello (eds) 2019. *Ecosystem Services in Floodplains*. Padova: Padova University Press.

Canzian, D. and R. Simonetti (eds) 2012. *Acque e territorio nel Veneto medievale*. Roma: Viella.

Canzian, D. and Valenzano, G. (eds) 2022. *Acqua e terra nei paesaggi monastici. Gestione, cura e costruzione del suolo*. Padova: Padova University Press.

Capecchi, G. 2012. Florentia e le acque. Fonti, acquedotto e terme dell'antica città. *Vivens Homo* 23/1: 125-142.

Capellini, P. 1990. *Acqua e acquedotti nella storia di Bergamo*. Bergamo: Arnoldi.

Capogrossi Colognesi, L. and E. Gabba (eds) 2006. *Gli Statuti Municipali*. Pavia: Pavia University Press.

Caracciolo, A. 1988. *L'ambiente come storia. Sondaggi e proposte di storiografia dell'ambiente*. Bologna: Il Mulino.

Carlotti, M. and M. Saltamacchia (eds) 2012. Ad usum fabricae *L'infinito plasma l'opera. La costruzione del Duomo di Milano*. Milano: Concreo.

Carocci, S. 2018. La «crisi del Trecento» e le recenti teorie economiche, in D. Chamboduc de Saint Pulgent and M. Dejoux (eds) *La fabrique des sociétés médiévales méditerranéennes. Le Moyen Âge de François Menant*. Paris: Éditions de la Sorbonne: 129-139.

Carriero, L. 2013. Sistemi urbani di approvvigionamento idrico pubblico e privato. Il caso di Napoli nei secoli X-XII, in A. Luongo *et al.* (eds) *Medioevo in Formazione. I giovani storici e il futuro della ricerca*. Livorno: Debatte: 49-57.

Carriero, L. 2014. *Dark Earth*, rifiuti urbani e uso delle acque a Napoli tra X e XII secolo. *Società e storia* 145: 433-458.

Caruso, E. 2004. *Mulini e mugnai in Romagna e nell'Italia del Medioevo*. Cesena: Il Ponte Vecchio.

Casali, G. 1998. *San Gimignano. L'evoluzione della città tra XIV e XVI secolo*. Firenze: Olschki.

Casalini, D. 2014. *Fondamenti per un diritto delle acque dolci*. Torino: Giappichelli.

Cassi, L. and M. Tinacci Mossello (eds) forthcoming. *Le forme dell'acqua. Dalla cultura al governo e alla cura*. Firenze: Accademia di Scienze e Lettere "La Colombaria".

Castagnetti, A. 1974. Primi aspetti di politica annonaria nell'Italia comunale. La bonifica della 'palus communis Verone' (1194-1199). *Studi medievali* 3rd s. 13: 363-481.

Castagnetti, A. 1976. *La pieve rurale nell'Italia padana. Territorio, organizzazione patrimoniale e vicende della pieve veronese di San Pietro di 'Tillida' dall'alto medioevo al secolo XIII*. Roma: Herder.

Castagnetti, A. 1977. La pianura veronese nel Medioevo. La conquista del suolo e la regolamentazione delle acque, in Borelli (ed.) I: 33-138.

Castellaccio, A. 1990. Utilizzazione militare di alcune acque interne nella Sardegna catalano-aragonese, in *La Sardegna nel mondo mediterraneo*. 6. M. Brigaglia (ed.) *Per una storia dell'acqua in Sardegna*. Nuoro: Gallizzi: 83-116.

Castiglione, R. 2004. Le gabelle nella Toscana del XIV secolo. *Bollettino Storico Pisano* 73: 49-104.

Cavallar, O. 2008. The Wheels of Watermills and the Wheel of Fortune. A consilium of Donatus *Ricchi de Aldighieris*. *Rechtsgeschichte* 13: 80-116.

Cavallar, O. 2010. *Quod de Tibere dicetur*: fiumi, incrementi fluviali, mulini ad acqua e giuristi, in Calzona and Lamberini (eds) I: 91-120.

Cavallar, O. and J. Kirshner (eds) 2020. *Jurists and Jurisprudence in Medieval Italy: Texts and Contexts*. Toronto: University of Toronto Press.

Cavallo, S. and T. Storey. 2013. *Healthy Living in Late Renaissance Italy*. Oxford: Oxford University Press.

Cavallucci, F. 2019. *La Fontana Maggiore di Perugia. Diario di una comunità del XIII secolo*. Perugia: Morlacchi.
Cazzola, F. 2010. Il Po, in Matheus *et al.* (eds): 197-230.
Cazzola, F. 2021. *Uomini e fiumi. Per una storia idraulica ed agraria della bassa pianura del Po (1450-1620)*. Roma: Viella.
Cazzola, F. (ed.) 2000. *Acque di frontiera. Principi, comunità e governo del territorio nelle terre basse tra Enza e Reno (secoli XIII-XVIII)*. Bologna: Clueb.
Cengarle, F., G. Chittolini and G. M. Varanini (eds) 2005. *Poteri signorili e feudali nelle campagne dell'Italia settentrionale fra Tre e Quattrocento: fondamenti di legittimità e forme di esercizio*. Firenze: Firenze University Press.
Chambers, D. S. 1992. Spas in the Italian Renaissance, in M. A. Di Cesare (ed.) *Reconsidering the Renaissance*. Binghamton NY: Cambridge University Press: 3-28.
Chandelier, J. 2010. La naissance d'un savoir médical sur les bains thermaux : les traités de Gentile da Foligno (m. 1348) in D. Boisseuil and M. Nicoud (eds) *Séjourner au bain. Le thermalisme entre médecine et société (XIVe-XVIe siècle)*. Lyon: Presses Universitaires: 15-30.
Chandelier, J. 2013. Pietro d'Abano et les médecins: réception et reputation du *Conciliator* en Italie dans les premières années du XIVe siècle, in J.-P. Boudet, F. Collard and N. Weill-Parot (eds) *Médicine, astrologie et magie entre Moyen Âge et Renaissance: autour de Pietro d'Abano*. Firenze: SISMEL: 183-201.
Chelazzi, C. 1943-2022. Biblioteca del Senato della Repubblica, *Catalogo della raccolta di statuti*. Roma-Firenze: Olschki *et al.*
Cherubini, G. 1985. *L'Italia rurale del basso Medioevo*. Roma-Bari: Laterza.
Cherubini, G. 1986. Terme e società nell'Italia centro-settentrionale (secc. XIII-XV), in C. D. Fonseca (ed.) *La città termale e il suo territorio*. Galatina: Congedo: 21-37.
Cherubini, G. 1988. Lo sfruttamento dell'acqua negli statuti della Marca meridionale, in *Arti e manifatture nella Marca nei secoli XIII-XVI*. Macerata: Centro di studi storici maceratesi: 27-39.
Cherubini, G. 2003. *Città comunali di Toscana*. Bologna: Clueb.
Cherubini, G. 2009. *Le città europee del Medioevo*. Milano: Mondadori.
Chiappa Mauri, L. 1990. *Paesaggi rurali di Lombardia. Secoli XII-XV*. Roma-Bari: Laterza.
Chiappa Mauri, L. 1998. *I mulini ad acqua nel Milanese (secoli X-XV)*. Milano: Dante Alighieri (2nd ed.).
Chiappa Mauri, L. 2003a. Acque e mulini nella Lombardia medievale. Alcune riflessioni, in Galetti and Racine (eds): 233-268.
Chiappa Mauri, L. 2003b. Statuti rurali e autonomie locali in Lombardia (XIII-XIV secolo), in Chiappa Mauri (ed.): 227-268.
Chiappa Mauri, L. (ed.) 2003. *Contado e città in dialogo. Comuni urbani e comunità rurali nella Lombardia medievale*. Milano: Cisalpino.
Chiodi, G. 2008. Conflitti per l'uso delle acque nella Milano del XII secolo, in *L'acqua nei secoli altomedievali*: 505-582.
Chittolini, G. 2007. «Crisi» e «lunga durata» delle istituzioni comunali in alcuni dibattiti recenti, in L. Lacchè, C. Latini, P. Marchetti and M. Meccarelli (eds) *Penale Giustizia Potere. Metodi, Ricerche, Storiografie. Per ricordare Mario Sbriccoli*. Macerata: Eum: 125-154.
Chittolini, G. 2010. Urban Population, Urban Territories, Small Towns: Some Problems of the History of Urbanization in Northern and Central Italy (Thirteenth-Sixteenth Centuries), in P. Hoppenbrouwers, A. Janse and R. Stein (eds) *Power and Persuasion. Essays in the Art of State Building in Honour of W.P. Blockmans*. Turnhout: Brepols: 227-241.

Chittolini, G. and D. Willoweit (eds) 1991. *Statuti città territori in Italia e Germania tra Medioevo ed Età moderna*. Bologna: Il Mulino.

Ciciliot, F. 2007. Remolai liguri medievali, in Caniato (ed.): 107-109.

Ciconi, G. 1862. *Udine e sua provincia. Illustrazione*. Udine: Trombetti-Murero (2nd ed.).

Ciriacono, S. 2018a. Management of the lagoon and urban environment in 18th-century Venice. *Water History* 10: 141-161.

Ciriacono, S. 2018b. Per una storia dell'acqua "à part entière", in *Water Management in Europe*: 1-21.

Ciriacono, S. 2020. Gli usi dell'acqua. Per un approccio multidimensionale, in G. Bonini and R. Pazzagli (eds) *Paesaggi dell'acqua*. Quaderni della Scuola di Paesaggio *Emilio Sereni*. 16. Gattatico: Istituto Alcide Cervi: 73-83.

Città e servizi sociali nell'Italia dei secoli XII-XV. 1990. Pistoia: Centro Italiano di Studi di Storia e d'Arte.

Clark, R. J. 1989-90. Peter of Eboli *de Balneis Puteolanis* manuscripts from the Aragonese scriptorium in Naples. *Traditio* 45: 380-389.

Codignola, T. 2005. *La Massa Trabaria*. G. Cherubini (ed.). Firenze: Olschki (2nd ed.).

Cohn, S. K. Jr. 1992. *The Cult of Remembrance and the Black Death. Six Renaissance Cities in Central Italy*. Baltimore-London: Johns Hopkins University Press.

Cohn, S. K. Jr. 2002. The Black Death: End of a Paradigm. *The American Historical Review* 107/3: 703-738.

Coli, M. and Pranzini, G. 2023. *Firenze e le sue acque*. Firenze: Pontecorboli.

Comba, R. (ed.) 1988. *Paesaggi urbani dell'Italia padana nei secoli VIII-XIV*. Bologna: Cappelli.

Comba, R. (ed.) 1993. *Mulini da grano nel Piemonte medievale. Secoli XII-XV*. Cuneo: Società per gli studi storici della Provincia di Cuneo.

Connell, W. J. and A. Zorzi (eds) 2000. *Florentine Tuscany. Structures and Practices of Power*. Cambridge: Cambridge University Press.

Conte, E. 2002. Il diritto delle acque tra antico regime e codificazioni moderne, in E. Rook Basile and A. Germanò (eds) *Acqua Agricoltura Ambiente*. Milano: Giuffrè: 11-32.

Coomans, J. 2019. The king of dirt: public health and sanitation in late medieval Ghent. *Urban History* 46/1: 82-105.

Coppa S. 2017. *I volti dell'acqua: la fontana di Fontecchio*. L'Aquila: Arti Grafiche Aquilane.

Coppola, G. 1998. *Ponti medievali in legno*. Roma-Bari: Laterza (2nd ed.).

Corrà, L. 1993. La fluitazione sul Piave, in Cortellazzo (ed.): 73-93.

Cortellazzo, M. (ed.) 1993. *Cultura popolare del Veneto. La civiltà delle acque*. Milano: Amilcare Pizzi.

Cortese, M. E. 1997. *L'acqua, il grano, il ferro. Opifici idraulici medievali nel bacino Farma-Merse*. Firenze: All'Insegna del Giglio.

Cortonesi, A. 1995. Ruralia. *Economie e paesaggi nel medioevo italiano*. Roma: Il Calamo.

Cortonesi, A. 2022. *Il Medioevo degli alberi. Piante e paesaggi d'Italia (secoli XI-XV)*. Roma: Carocci.

Cortonesi, A. and M. Montanari (eds) 2001. *Medievistica italiana e storia agraria*. Bologna: Clueb.

Costa, E. 1919. *Le acque nel diritto romano*. Bologna: Zanichelli.

(La) costruzione della città comunale italiana (secoli XII-inizio XIV) 2009. Pistoia-Roma: Viella.

Covini, N. 2010. Strutture portuali e attraversamenti del Po: alcuni aspetti delle relazioni tra comunità, signori e stato ducale lombardo (secolo XV), in Calzona and Lamberini (eds) I: 243-259.

Cracco Ruggini, L. 2008. Terre e acque: città e campagne fra antichità e medioevo, in *L'acqua nei secoli altomedievali*: 95-120.
Cresti, C. 1982. *Le fontane di Firenze*. Firenze: Bonechi.
Crouzet-Pavan, É. 1999. *Venise triomphante. Les horizons d'un mythe*. Paris: Albin Michel.
Crouzet-Pavan, É. 2019. Uma citade medieval e o problema de água. O exemplo de Veneza. *Cadernos de Pós-Graduação em Arquitetura e Urbanismo, Universidade presbiteriana Mackenzie* 19/2: 52-67.
Crouzet-Pavan, É. and J.C. Maire-Vigueur (eds) 1994. *Water control in Western Europe, twelfth-sixteenth centuries*. Milano: Bocconi.
Curtis, D. R. and M. Campopiano 2013. Medieval land reclamation and the creation of new societies: comparing Holland and the Po Valley, c.800-c.1500. *Journal of Historical Geography* 30: 1-16.
Cutini Zazzerini, C. 1990. La normativa sulle acque: controllo e salvaguardia dei territori (secoli XIII-XIX), in Grohmann (ed.): 64-71.
D'Angelis, E. 2021. La conquista dell'Italia. La grande storia delle bonifiche e dei bonificatori dai palafitticoli ai Consorzi, in *La grande storia d'Italia raccontata dall'acqua. Dalle opere di difesa idraulica alla transazione ecologica*. Firenze: Polistampa: 17-263.
Damiani, G. 1994. *Ecologia degli ambienti acquatici*. Udine: Pellegrini.
Dani, A. 2003. *Usi civici nello Stato di Siena di età medicea*. Bologna: Monduzzi.
Dani, A. 2013. *Le risorse naturali come beni comuni*. Arcidosso: Effigi.
Dani, A. 2015. *Gli statuti dei Comuni della Repubblica di Siena (secoli XIII-XV). Profilo di una cultura comunitaria*. Siena: Il Leccio.
Dani, A. 2020. Risorse naturali e diritto tra Medioevo ed Età moderna, in C. Lorenzi and A. Dani (eds) *Risorse naturali. Riflessioni multidisciplinari*. Roma: UniversItalia: 25-52.
Day, J. 1984. Peuplement, cultures et régimes fonciers en Trexenta (Sardeigne), XIIIe-XIXe siècles, in Guarducci (ed.): 683-708.
De Francesco, D. 2017. *Il papato e l'approvvigionamento idrico e alimentare di Roma tra la tarda Antichità e l'alto Medioevo*. Roma: Quasar.
De Matteis, M.C. 1981. *Societas christiana* e funzionalità ideologica della città in Italia: linee di uno sviluppo, in R. Elze and G. Fasoli (eds) *Le città in Italia e in Germania nel Medioevo. Cultura, istituzioni, vita religiosa*. Bologna: Il Mulino: 13-49.
De Minicis, E. 2020. Relazione introduttiva, in De Minicis and Pastura (eds): 9-11.
De Minicis E. and G. Pastura (eds) 2020. *Il rupestre e l'acqua nel Medioevo. Religiosità, quotidianità, produttività*. Firenze: All'Insegna del Giglio.
De' Bosio, C. 1855. *Dei consorzi d'acque del Regno Lombardo-Veneto, della loro instituzione, organizzazione ed amministrazione. Trattato amministrativo-legale*. Verona: Vicentini e Franchini.
Degrassi, D. 2007. Dai monti al mare. Transiti e collegamenti tra le Alpi orientali e la costa dell'alto Adriatico (secoli XIII-XV), in Bergier and Coppola (eds): 161-187.
del Val Valdivieso, M. I. 2007. Naturaleza y sociedad. La actitud urbana ante los recursos hídricos en la Castilla del siglo XV, in Sabaté (ed.): 173-189.
Dell'Oro, A. 1962-63. Le *res communes omnium* dell'elenco di Marciano e il problema del loro fondamento giuridico. *Studi Urbinati* 31: 237-290.
Dell'Oro, G. 2022. Acque, inondazioni, disastri idrici: un dialogo aperto a varie discipline, in Albini, Grillo and Raviola (eds): 241-251.
Delort, R. and F. Walter 2001. *Histoire de l'environnement européen*. Paris: Puf.

Destefanis, E. and Garanzini (eds), F. forthcoming. *Da San Genuario all'Europa. Monasteri e acqua, monasteri in terre d'acqua.* Crescentino.

Di Benedetto, F. 1995. Uno splendido esempio di ingegneria medioevale, in E. Mattiocco (ed.) *Sulmona in età sveva.* Sulmona: Museo Civico: 55-57.

Di Gianfrancesco, M. 1975. Per una storia della navigazione padana dal Medioevo alla vigilia del Risorgimento. *Quaderni storici* 10/28: 199-226.

Di Lollo, G.C. 1996. Idrologia dell'Umbria, in Santini (ed.): 3-7.

Di Stefano, E. 2012. Un'area-problema: l'Appennino centrale. Linee di sviluppo e condizionamenti ambientali fra XIV e XVIII secolo, in Alfani, Di Tullio and Mocarelli (eds): 188-204.

Di Tullio, M. 2012. Tra ecologia ed economia: uomo e acqua nella pianura lombarda d'età moderna, in Alfani, Di Tullio and Mocarelli (eds): 283-299.

Di Tullio, M. and C. Lorenzini 2019. Natural resources, conflict and sustainability in Northern Italy in the early modern period, in Canzian and Novello (eds): 73-96.

Difesa del dottor Tommaso Perelli sopra l'operazione da lui proposta dell'addirizzamento del fiume Arno a Barbaricina in vicinanza di Pisa. 1826, in *Raccolta d'autori italiani che trattano del moto dell'acque.* X. Bologna: Marsigli (4th ed.): 92-128.

Dijkman, J., E. van Onacker, M. Hannaford, M. de Keyzer, D. R. Curtis, B. van Bavel and T. Soens (eds) 2020. *Disasters and History. The Vulnerability and Resilience of Past Societies.* Cambridge: Cambridge University Press.

Dilcher, G. 2001. Fondamenti costituzionali dei comuni italiani e tedeschi: un'analisi comparata, in Rossetti (ed.)b: 97-115.

Diosono, F. 2008. Il commercio del legname sul fiume Tevere, in F. Coarelli and H. Patterson (eds) Mercator Placidissimus. *The Tiber Valley in Antiquity. New research in the upper and middle river valley.* Roma: Quasar: 251-283.

Dockès, P. 1991. Formes et diffusion d'une innovation technique: le cas du moulin hydraulique, in Guarducci (ed.) 1991: 113-154.

Dondarini, R. 2003. Lo statuto comunale come strumento di trasmissione dell'immagine politica ed etica della città, in F. Bocchi and R. Smurra (eds) Imago urbis. *L'immagine della città nella storia d'Italia.* Roma: Viella: 271-284.

Dondarini, R. (ed.) 1995. *La libertà di decidere. Realtà e parvenze di autonomia nella normativa locale del Medioevo.* Cento: Assessorato alla Cultura.

Doren, A. (trad. it. 1940). *Le arti fiorentine.* Firenze: Le Monnier.

Dotti Messori, G. 2000. Norme statutarie, magistrature e istituzioni per il governo del territorio a Modena in età medievale, in Cazzola (ed.): 103-124.

Douglas, M. 1966. *Purity and Danger. An Analysis of Concepts of Pollution and Taboo.* London and New York: Routledge.

Drossbach, G. (ed.) 2009. *Von der Ordnung zur Norm: Statuten in Mittelalter und Früher Neuzeit.* Paderborn: Schöningh.

Duranti, T. 2023. *Ammalarsi e curarsi nel medioevo. Una storia sociale.* Roma: Carocci.

Dussaix, C. 1979. Les moulins à Reggio d'Émile aux XIIe et XIIIe siècles. *Mélanges de l'École française de Rome - Moyen Âge-Temps modernes* 91/1: 113-147.

Duvia, S. 2007. Infrastrutture al servizio della mobilità in una città tra terra e lago (Como, secoli XIV-XV), in Bergier and Coppola (eds): 211-223.

Edigati, D. and L. Tanzini (eds) 2022. *Il Comune dopo il Comune. Le istituzioni municipali in Toscana (secoli XV-XVIII).* Firenze: Olschki.

El Faïz, M. 2005. *Les Maîtres de l'eau. Histoire de l'hidraulique arabe.* Arles: Actes Sud.

Ermini Pani, L. 2008. Condurre, conservare e distribuire l'acqua, in *L'acqua nei secoli altomedievali*: 389-428.

Esposito, A. 2010. Il Tevere e Roma, in Matheus *et al.* (eds): 257-275.

Esposito, A. 2012. Le terme dei papi ovvero i bagni di Viterbo nel tardo Medioevo, in D. Boisseuil and H. Wulfram (eds) *Die Renaissance der Heilquellen in Italien und Europa von 1200 bis 1600. Geschichte, Kultur Und Vorstellungswelt*. Frankfurt/Main: Peter Lang: 13-43.

Esposito, A. 2017. Le alluvioni del Tevere a Roma tra Medioevo e Rinascimento, in Bianca and Salvestrini (eds): 157-173.

Fabbiani, G. 1959. *Appunti per una storia del commercio del legname in Cadore*. Belluno: Tip. Benedetta.

Fabbrici, G. 2000. Il governo delle acque negli statuti reggiani del XIII secolo. Note di una ricerca in corso, in Cazzola (ed.): 79-86.

Faini, E., P. Terenzi and A. Zorzi (eds) 2023. *Reti italiche. Spazi e relazioni politiche da Roma alle Alpi nei tempi di Dante (1260-1330)*. Roma: Viella.

Faleschini, M. 2018. Il larice. Trasporto e commercio del legname dalle Alpi al Tirreno in epoca romana: un esempio di sistema integrato. *Quaderni friulani di archeologia* 28/1: 157-169.

Falqui, E. and A. Prati 1937. *Dizionario di marina medievale e moderno*. Roma: Reale Accademia d'Italia.

Fantoni, G. 1990. *L'acqua a Milano. Uso e gestione nel basso medioevo (1385-1535)*. Bologna: Cappelli.

Fara, A. 2023. Il Tevere quale via di trasporto, luogo di produzione e spazio commerciale a Roma nel Medioevo, in L. Barelli, M. Gianandrea and S. Passigli (eds) 2023. Viae Urbis. *Le strade di Roma nel Medioevo*. Roma: Viella: 251-261.

Fasoli, G. 1972. Un fossile nel vocabolario istituzionale bolognese del Duecento, in *Studi storici in onore di Ottorino Bertolini*. Pisa: Pacini.

Fasoli, G. 1976. Edizione e studio degli statuti: problemi ed esigenze, in *Fonti medioevali e problematica storiografica*. Roma: ISIME: 173-190.

Fasoli, G. 1978. Navigazione fluviale. Porti e navi sul Po, in *La navigazione mediterranea nell'Alto Medioevo*. Spoleto: CISAM: 565-607.

Febvre, L. 1935, n.p. P. Schlotter (ed.) 1997. *Le Rhin. Histoire, mythes et réalités*. Paris: Perrin.

Federici Vescovini, G. 1989. Il pensiero scientifico del secolo XIV nella storiografia contemporanea. *Studi Storici* 30/2: 279-320.

Ferrari, V. and E. Uberti. 1979. *I fontanili del territorio cremasco. Sorgenti di acque perenni e loro uso in questa parte di Lombardia*. Crema: Amministrazione Provinciale.

Ferretti, E. 2016. *Acquedotti e fontane del Rinascimento in Toscana. Acqua, architettura e città al tempo di Cosimo I dei Medici*. Firenze: Olschki.

Figliuolo, B. 2022. Le vene e il cuore: i porti fluviali del Friuli storico e i loro rapporti con le economie-mondo veneziana e fiorentina, in B. Figliuolo (ed.) *Guardando a Venezia e oltre. Connettività locale, mercati intermedi e l'emporio dell''economia-mondo' veneziana (secoli XIII-XV)*. Udine: Forum: 57-110.

Finch, M. 1991. The cantharus and pigna at old St. Peter's. *Gesta* 30: 16-26.

Fiore, A. 1992. La pietrificazione dell'identità cittadina (Italia centro-settentrionale, 1050-1200), in *Construir para perdurar. Riqueza petrificada e identidad social. Siglos XI-XIV*. Navas de Tolosa: Gobierno de Navarra: 185-212.

Fiore, A. 2012. Giurare la consuetudine. Pratiche sociali e memoria del potere nelle campagne dell'Italia centro-settentrionale (secoli XI-XIII). *Reti Medievali Rivista* 13/2: 47-80 <retimedievali.it>.

Fiorentini, M. 2003. Struttura ed esercizio della servitù d'acqua nell'esperienza giuridica romana. *Quaderni del Dipartimento di Scienze Giuridiche, Università di Trieste* 8: 51-197.

Fiorentini, M. 2023. Paesaggi marittimi in età romana (I a.C. – III d.C.). Prassi sociali e riflessione giuridica, in I. G. Mastrorosa and É. Gavoille (eds) *Enjeux environnementaux et souci de la nature, de la Rome ancienne à la Renaissance*. Bordeaux: Ausonius: 137-152.

Fiumi, E. 2006. *Volterra e San Gimignano nel Medioevo. Raccolta di* studi. G. Pinto (ed.) Firenze: FirenzeLibri (2nd ed.).

(La) Fonte delle Fate a Poggibonsi. 1990. Quaderni del Centro di Studi Romei 3.

Foresti, F. and M. Tozzi Fontana (eds) 1999. *Imbarcazioni e navigazione del Po. Storia, pratiche, tecniche, lessico*. Bologna: Clueb.

Foschi, P. 2000. Il governo del territorio negli statuti trecenteschi di Bologna, in Cazzola (ed.): 165-180.

Foschi, P. 2013. Il governo del territorio montano fra XIII e XIV secolo: magistrature preposte, luoghi notevoli e qualche esempio, in *Città e montagna*. Capugnano-Porretta Terme-Pistoia. Gruppo di Studi Alta Valle del Reno: 89-118.

Foschi, P. (ed.) 2022. *Le dinamiche del confine fra Romagna, Toscana e Umbria. Società locali, circolazione di uomini e merci, scambi culturali (secoli XIII-XVI)*. Bologna: Pàtron.

Foucault, M. 1997. The Birth of Biopolitics, in P. Rabinow (ed.) *Michel Foucault. The Essential Works, 1954-1984*. New York: Penguin (2nd ed.): 73-79.

Fournier, P. and S. Lavaud (eds) 2012. *Eaux et conflits dans l'Europe médievale et moderne*. Flaran: Presses universitaires du Midi.

Franceschi, F. and I. Taddei 2012. *Le città italiane nel Medioevo, XII-XIV secolo*. Bologna: Il Mulino.

Francesconi, G. and F. Salvestrini 2006. La scrittura del confine nell'Italia comunale. Modelli e funzioni, in O. Merisalo and P. Pahta (eds) *Frontiers in the Middle Ages*. Louvain-la-Neuve: Brepols: 197-221.

Francovich, R. and C. Citter (eds) 2003. *Castel di Pietra e la diga sul Bruna. Tra poteri signorili e poteri cittadini*. Firenze: ed. in CD Rom.

Frank, Th. 2009. Rechtsgeschichtliche Anmerkungen zu spätmittelalterlichen Bruderschaftsstatuten in Deutschland und Italien, in Drossbach (ed.): 311-326.

Frati, M. 2017. L'assetto dell'Arno a monte e a valle di Firenze nel 1333: ecofatti, manufatti e misfatti intorno al «grande diluvio», in Bianca and Salvestrini (eds): 95-136.

Frati, M. 2017-18. Empoli area di ponte. L'attraversamento delle acque fino al 'diluvio' del 1333. *Bullettino Storico Empolese* 61-62: 167-188.

Fried, J. 1974. *Die Entstehung des Juristenstandes im 12. Jahrhundert. Zur sozialen Stellung und politischen Bedeutung gelehrter Juristen in Bologna und Modena*. Köln-Wien: Böhlau: 115-130.

Frugoni, C. 2019. *Paradiso vista Inferno. Buon governo e tirannide nel Medioevo di Ambrogio Lorenzetti*. Bologna: Il Mulino.

Fugazza, E. 2009. *Diritto istituzioni e giustizia in un comune dell'Italia padana. Piacenza e i suoi statuti (1135-1323)*. Padova: CEDAM.

Fumagalli, V. 1985. Il paesaggio si trasforma: colonizzazione e bonifica durante il Medioevo. L'esempio emiliano, in B. Andreolli, V. Fumagalli and M. Montanari. 1985. *Le campagne italiane prima e dopo il Mille. Una società in trasformazione*. Bologna: Clueb: 95-131.

Fumagalli, V. 2007. *Storie di Val Padana*. Bologna: Il Mulino (2nd ed.).

Furió, A. 2015. I paesaggi dell'acqua nella Spagna mediterranea: le *huertas* e l'agricoltura irrigua, in *Paesaggi agrari d'Europa*: 323-384.

Fusco, A. 2011-13. *La gestione dell'acqua nelle* civitates *dell'Italia romana. La documentazione epigrafica*. PhD dissertation. Università degli Studi di Palermo.
Gabiani, N. and F. Gabotto 1906. *Contributi alla storia di Asti nel Medio Evo*. Pinerolo: Società Storica Subalpina.
Galetti, P. 2000. La disciplina delle acque nelle normative statutarie del territorio piacentino, in Cazzola (ed.): 37-51.
Galetti, P. and P. Racine (eds) 2003. *I mulini nell'Europa medievale*. Bologna: Clueb.
Gamberini, A. 2003. *La città assediata. Poteri e identità politiche a Reggio in età viscontea*. Roma: Viella.
Gamberini, A. 2021. Urban Hierarchies in the Heart of the Po Valley (12th-15th century). Persistence and Change, in M. Asenjo González, É. Crouzet-Pavan and A. Zorzi (eds) *Urban Hierarchy. The Interaction between Towns and Cities in Europe in the Late Medieval and Early Modern Times*. Turnhout: Brepols: 73-88.
Gamberini, A. and I. Lazzarini (eds) 2014. *The Italian Renaissance State*. Cambridge: Cambridge University Press.
García Marsilla, J. V. 2015. Ordenando el lujo. Ideología y normativa suntuaria en las ciutades valencianas (siglos XIV y XV), in S. Broquet and J. V. García Marsilla (eds) *Mercados del lujo, mercados del'arte. El gusto de las élites mediterráneas en los siglos XIV y XV*. Valencia: Puv: 561-591.
García-Ballester, L. 1994. *Practical Medicine from Salerno to the Black Death*. Cambridge: Cambridge University Press.
Gardoni, G. 2010. Uomini e acque nel territorio mantovano (secoli X-XIII), in Calzona and Lamberini (eds) I: 143-176.
Garzella, G. (ed.) 1998. *Etruria, Tuscia, Toscana. L'identità di una regione attraverso i secoli*. II *(secoli V-XIV)*. Pisa: Pacini.
Gelli, B., 2014. La Piana di Rosia nel Basso Medioevo: gli statuti della Compagnia del Padule. *Miscellanea Storica della Valdelsa* 120/1: 39-58.
Geltner, G. 2014. Finding matter out of place: Bologna's *fango* "dirt" notary in the history of premodern public health, in R. Smurra and H. Houben (eds) *The far-sighted gaze of capital cities. Essays in honour of Francesca Bocchi*. Roma: Viella: 307-321.
Geltner, G. 2019. *Roads to Health. Infrastructure and Urban Wellbeing in Later Medieval Italy*. Philadelphia: University of Pennsylvania Press.
Geltner, G. and J. Coomans (eds) *The History of Public Health in Pre-Industrial Societies: A Bibliography*. https://premodernhealthscaping.hcommons.org/documents/ (access October 2023).
Génicot, L. 1977. *La loi*. Turnhout: Brepols.
Gentilcore, D. *et al.* (eds) forthcoming. *The Water Cultures of Europe and the Mediterranean, 1500-1900*. International Conference. Venice, 13-15 September 2023.
Giambastiani, C. (ed.) 1996. *I Bagni di Corsena e la Val di Lima Lucchese dalle origini al XVI secolo*. Lucca: S. Marco.
Ginatempo, M. and L. Sandri 1990. *L'Italia delle città. Il popolamento urbano tra Medioevo e Rinascimento (secoli XIII-XVI)*. Firenze: Le Lettere.
Glick, Th. F. 1970. *Irrigation and Society in Medieval Valencia*. Cambridge Mass: Harvard University Press.
Glick, Th. F. 1996. *Irrigation and Hydraulic Technology. Medieval Spain and Its Legacy*. New York-London: Routledge.
Goppelt, L. ύδωρ, in G. Kittel and G. Friedrich (dir.) F. Montanini, G. Scarpat and O. Soffritti (It. eds) 1984. *Grande lessico del Nuovo testamento*. XIV. Brescia: Marietti: 53-104.

Graziani, N. 1986. *Le terme di Montecatini dal Mille al Duemila*. Montecatini-Pisa: Thermae.

Greci, R. 1988. Il controllo della città: l'ufficio dei fanghi e strade a Bologna nel XIII secolo. *Storia della città* 47: 119-124.

Greci, R. 1990. Il problema dello smaltimento dei rifiuti nei centri urbani dell'Italia medievale, in *Città e servizi sociali nell'Italia dei secoli XII-XV*: 439-464.

Greci, R. 2010. Le città navigabili. I progetti dell'età comunale, in Calzona and Lamberini (eds) I: 177-196.

Greci, R. 2016. Porti fluviali e ponti in età medievale. Il Po e l'area padana. *Hortus Artium Mediaevalium* 22: 238-248.

Grifoni, S. 2016. *Lungo l'Arno. Paesaggi, storia e culture. Dal Falterona, fin là dove il tosco fiume ha foce*. Firenze: Aska.

Grillo, P. 2003. Comuni urbani e poteri rurali nel governo del territorio in Lombardia (XII-inizi XIV secolo). in Chiappa Mauri (ed.): 41-82.

Grillo, P. 2017. *Nascita di una cattedrale. 1386-1418: la fondazione del Duomo di Milano*. Milano: Mondadori.

Grillo, P. 2021a. La città e il vulcano. Il comune di Como e le conseguenze dell'eruzione del Samalas (1257-1260), in P. Guglielmotti and I. Lazzarini (eds) *«Fiere vicende dell'età di mezzo». Studi per Gian Maria Varanini*. Firenze: Firenze University Press: 129-145.

Grillo, P. 2021b. L'utilizzazione dello statuto. La normativa locale nella documentazione pubblica e privata delle città comunali italiane, in Lett (ed.): 205-216.

Grillo, P. 2022. Introduzione: fra storia umana e storia della natura, in Albini, Grillo and Raviola (eds): 3-15.

Grillo, P. (ed.) 2022. *Selve oscure e alberi strani. I boschi nell'Italia di Dante*. Roma: Viella.

Grillo, P. and F. Menant (eds) 2019. *La congiuntura del primo Trecento in Lombardia (1290-1360)*. Roma: École française de Rome.

Grmek, M. D. (ed.) 1997. *Histoire de la pensée médicale en Occident*. 1. *Antiquité et Moyen Âge*. Paris: Le Seuil.

Grohmann, A. 1996. La Fontana Maggiore: sintesi dei fermenti economici e sociali della città a metà del Duecento, in Santini (ed.): 49-72.

Grohmann, A. 1990 (ed.) *L'Umbria e le sue acque. Fiumi e torrenti di una regione italiana*. Perugia-Milano: Electa.

Grossi, P. 2000. *L'ordine giuridico medievale*. Roma-Bari: Laterza (2nd ed.).

Grossi, P. 2006. *La proprietà e le proprietà nell'officina dello storico*. Napoli: Editoriale Scientifica (2nd ed.).

Guarducci, A. 2021. *Le terme della Toscana dal Medioevo ad oggi. Storia e beni culturali*. I. Firenze: Aska.

Guarducci, A. (ed.) 1984. *Agricoltura e trasformazione dell'ambiente, secoli XIII-XVIII*. Firenze: Le Monnier.

Guarducci, A. (ed.) 1991 *Forme ed evoluzione del lavoro in Europa: XIII-XVIII secc*. Prato-Firenze: Le Monnier.

Guenzi, A. and M. Grandi 2010. Interpretazione e valorizzazione di un 'monumento idraulico' di Bologna. La chiusa del Rondone tra XII e XV secolo, in Calzona and Lamberini (eds) II: 473-489.

Guérin-Beauvois, M. and J.-M. Martin (eds) 2007. *Bains curatifs et bains hygiéniques en Italie de l'Antiquité au Moyen Âge*. Roma: Ecole française de Rome.

Guillerme, A. 1985. Puits, aqueducs et fontaines : l'alimentation en eau dans les villes du nord de la France Xe-XIIIe siècles. *L'eau au Moyen Age*. *Senefiance* 15: 185-200.

Guillerme, A. 2015. Histoire et évolution de la distribution de l'eau, in A. Euzen, Ch. Jeandel and R. Mosseri (eds) *L'eau à découvert*. Paris: CNRS: 34-35.
Guillet, S., Ch. Corona, M. Stoffel *et. al.* 2017. Climate response to the Samalas volcanic eruption in 1257 revealed by proxy records. *Nature Geoscience* 10/2: 123-128.
Gunzburg, D. 2013. The Perugia Fountain: An Encyclopaedia of Sky, Culture and Society, in N. Campion, and L. Greene (eds) *Sky and Symbol*. Ceredigion: Sophia Centre Press: 103-118.
Habermas, J. 1965. *Strukturwandel der Öffentlichkeit*. Berlin: Luchterhand.
Hardin, G. 1968. The Tragedy of the Commons. *Science* 162/3859: 1243-1248.
Hayward, H.A. 1981. La via dei remi. *La Canaviglia* 6/3: 83-86.
Hébert, M. 2021. Production, réception, médiation. Statuts et patrimoine documentaire dans les villes de Provence (XIIe-XVe siècle), in Lett (ed.): 135-160.
Hidiroglou, P. 2007. *Acqua divina. Miti, riti, simboli*. It transl. Roma: Edizioni Mediterranee.
Hoch, A. S. 2006. Duecento Fertility Imagery for Females at Massa Marittima's Public Fountain. *Zeitschrift für Kunstgeschichte* 69/4: 471-488.
Hoffmann, R. C. 2005. A Brief History of Aquatic Resource Use in Medieval Europe. *Helgoland Marine Research* 59/1: 22-30.
Hoffmann, R. C. 2007. Footprint Metaphor and Metabolic Realities. Environmental Impacts of Medieval European Cities, in Squatriti (ed.): 288-325.
Hoffmann, R. C. 2014. *An Environmental History of Medieval Europe*. Cambridge: Cambridge University Press.
Hughes, J. D. 1996. Medieval Florence and the Barriers to Growth. *Capitalism, Nature, Socialism* 7/1: 63-68.
Hyde, J. K. 1973. *Society and Politics in Medieval Italy. The Evolution of the Civil Life, 1000-1350*. London: MacMillan.
Ito, T., F. Scaroni and N. Matsuda (eds) 2017. *Along the water: urban natural crises between Italy and Japan*. Tokyo: Sayusha.
Janku, A., G. J. Schenk and F. Mauelshagen (eds) 2012. *Historical Disasters in Context. Science, Religion, and Politics*. New York-London: Routledge.
Kaijser, A. 2002. System Building from Below. Institutional Change in Dutch Water Control Systems. *Technology and Culture* 43/3: 521-548.
Keller, H. 1988. Oberitalienische Statuten als Zeugen und als Quellen für den Verschiftlichungsprozess im 12. und 13. Jahrhundert. *Frühmittelalterliche Studien* 22: 286-313.
Keller, H. 2001. Tradizione normativa e diritto statutario in "Lombardia" nell'età comunale, in Rossetti (ed.)b: 159-173.
Keller, H. 2014. Electoral Systems and Conceptions of Community in Italian Communes (Twelfth-Fourteenth Centuries). *Revue Française de Science Politique* (English Edition) 64/6: 29-51.
Keller, H. and J. W. Busch (eds) 1991. *Statutencodices des 13. Jahrhunderts als Zeugen Pragmatischer Schriftlichkeit. Die Handschriften von Como, Lodi, Novara, Pavia und Voghera*. München: Fink.
Kidd, M., L. Feris, T. Murombo and A. Iza (eds) 2014. *Water and the Law. Towards Sustainability*. Cheltenham: Elgar.
Kirshner, J. 2005. Baldo degli Ubaldi's contribution to the rule of law in Florence, in C. Frova, M. G. Nico Ottaviani and S. Zucchini (eds) *VI Centenario della morte di Baldo degli Ubaldi, 1400-2000*. Perugia: Università degli Studi: 313-364.
Klapisch-Zuber, Ch. 1987. La donna e la famiglia, in J. Le Goff (ed.) *L'uomo medievale*. Roma-Bari: Laterza: 321-349.

Kucher, M. P. 2005. *The Water Supply System of Siena, Italy. The Medieval Roots of the Modern Networked City*. London-New York: Routledge.

Küster, H. 2003. *Geschichte des Waldes. Von der Urzeit dis zur Gegenwart*. München: Beck.

Lago, L. 1983. *Le conoscenze sul ciclo dell'acqua nell'antichità classica e nell'evo medio. Per un problema di storia delle scienze geografiche*. Trieste: Lint.

Lanconelli, A. and R. L. De Palma (eds) 1992. *Terra, acque e lavoro nella Viterbo medievale*. Roma: ISIME.

Lapucci, C. 1993. *Il dizionario dei modi di dire della lingua italiana*. 1ª ed. Milano: Garzanti Vallardi.

Lauretano, P. 2001. *Atlante d'acqua. Conoscenze tradizionali per la lotta alla desertificazione*. Torino: Bollati Boringhieri.

Lazzerini, F. 2001. *Le comunità rurali della Lunigiana negli statuti dei secoli XII-XIV*. Firenze: Chiari.

Lefebvre, H. 1996. The Specificity of the City, in Id. *Writings on Cities*. E. Kofman and E. Lebas (eds). Oxford: Blackwell: 100-103.

Leguay, J.-P. 1999. *La pollution au Moyen Âge dans le royaume de France et dans les grands fiefs*. Paris: Gisserot.

Leguay, J.-P. 2002. *L'eau dans la ville au Moyen Âge*. Rennes: PUR.

Leguay, J.-P. 2007. La pollution de l'air et de l'eau, un fléau urbain méconnu à la fin du Moyen Âge en France. in Sabaté (ed.): 99-128.

Leicht, P. S. 1966. *Storia del diritto italiano. Il diritto privato. Parte seconda. Diritti reali e di successione*. Milano: Giuffrè.

Lerner, J. 1972. *Signorie di Romagna. La società romagnola e l'origine delle Signorie*. Bologna: Il Mulino.

Lett, D. (ed.) 2021. *Statuts, écritures et pratiques sociales dans les sociétés de l'Italie communale et du Midi de la France (XIIe-XVe siècle)*. Roma: École française de Rome.

Lewin, A. 1983. Note sulla fluitazione del legname nell'alto Tevere in epoca romana. *Rivista di Storia dell'Agricoltura* 23: 127-133.

Licciardello, P. 2015. *Un vescovo contro il Papato: il conflitto fra Guido Tarlati e Giovanni XXII (1312-1339)*. Arezzo: Società Storica Aretina.

Linton, J. 2010. *What is Water? The History of a Modern Abstraction*. Vancouver-Toronto: UBC Press.

Loschiavo, L. 2019. La storiografia statutaria degli ultimi trent'anni. Considerazioni brevi tra passato e futuro prossimo, in Mattone and Simbula (eds): 71-88.

Lüning, S., L. Schulte *et al.* 2019. The Medieval Climate Anomaly in the Mediterranean Region. *Paleoceanography and Paleoclimatology* 34/10: 1625-1649.

Luongo, A. 2019. *Una città dopo la peste. Impresa e mobilità sociale ad Arezzo nella seconda metà del Trecento*. Pisa: Pisa University Press.

Lusso, E. (ed.) 2014. *Attività economiche e sviluppi insediativi nell'Italia dei secoli XI-XV. Omaggio a Giuliano Pinto*. Cherasco: CISIM.

Luterbacher, J. 2001. The Late Maunder Minimum (1675-1715) – Climax of the 'Little Ice Age' in Europe, in Ph. D. Jones, A. E. J. Ogilvie, T. D. Davies and K. R. Briffa (eds) *History and Climate. Memories of the Future?*. New York: Kluwer: 29-54.

Luzzini, F. 2016. *L'itale terre a vagheggiare inteso*. La regolazione dell'Adige nel XVIII secolo: tra storia e scienza, in V. Rovigo (ed.) *Il fiume, le terre, l'immaginario. L'Adige come fenomeno storiografico complesso*. Rovereto: Accademia degli Agiati: 287-312.

Mack, Ch. R. 1992. The Bath Palace of Pope Nicholas V at Viterbo, in H. A. Million and S. S. Munshower (eds) *An Architectural Progress in the Renaissance and Baroque. Sejourns In and Out of Italy*. Philadelphia: Pennsylvania State University. I: 45-63.

Magnusson, R. J. 2001. *Water Technology in the Middle Ages. Cities, Monasteries, and Waterworks after the Roman Empire*. Baltimore: Johns Hopkins University Press.
Magnusson, R. and P. Squatriti. 2000. The Technologies of Water in Medieval Italy, in P. Squatriti (ed.) *Working with Water in Medieval Europe. Technology and Resource-Use*. Leiden-Boston-Köln: Brill: 217-266.
Maire Vigueur, J.-C. (ed.) 2000. *I Podestà dell'Italia comunale. Parte I, Reclutamento e circolazione degli ufficiali forestieri (fine XII sec.-metà XIV sec.)*. I. Roma: École française de Rome.
Maire Vigueur, J.-C. 2023. *Così belle, così vicine: viaggio insolito nelle città dell'Italia medievale*. Bologna: Il Mulino.
Malvolti, A. and G. Pinto (eds) 2003. *Incolti, fiumi, paludi. Utilizzazione delle risorse naturali nella Toscana medievale e moderna*. Firenze: Olschki.
Mancassola, N. 2012. Uomini e acque nella pianura reggiana durante il Medioevo (secoli IX-XIV), in Canzian and Simonetti (eds): 115-132.
Maneglier, H. 1991. *Histoire de l'eau*. Paris: Bourin.
Mann, M. E, Z. Zhang, S. Rutherford *et al.* 2009. Global Signatures and Dynamical Origins of the Little Ice Age and Medieval Climate Anomaly. *Science* 326: 1256-1260.
Manselli, R. 1974. Evangelismo e povertà, in O. Capitani (ed.) *La concezione della povertà nel Medioevo*. Bologna: Pàtron: 153-191.
Mantelli, F. and G. Temporelli 2007. *L'acqua nella storia*. Milano: Angeli.
Marrocchi, M. 2003. L'impaludamento della Val di Chiana in epoca medievale, in Malvolti and Pinto (eds): 73-93.
Martín-Bueno, M. and I. Reklaityte 2008. L'acqua nella Spagna del Medioevo: elemento primordiale per tre ambienti culturali diversi, in *L'acqua nei secoli altomedievali*: 201-242.
Mastrelli, C.A. 2008. Polimorfismo nel lessico dell'acqua, in *L'acqua nei secoli altomedievali*: 43-94.
Matheus, M., G. Piccinni, G. Pinto and G. M. Varanini (eds) 2010. *Le calamità ambientali nel tardo Medioevo europeo: realtà, percezioni, reazioni*. Firenze: Firenze University Press.
Mattone, A. and P. Simbula (eds) 2019. *I settecento anni degli Statuti di Sassari. Dal Comune alla città regia*. Milano: Angeli.
Mazzi, M. S. 1978. *Salute e società nel Medioevo*. Florence: La Nuova Italia.
McAnany, P. and N. Yoffee (eds) 2009. *Questioning Collapse. Human Resilience, Ecological Vulnerability, and the Aftermath of Empire*. Cambridge: Cambridge University Press.
McNeill, J. R. and P. Engelke 2016. *The Great Acceleration. An Environmental History of the Anthropocene since 1945*. Harvard: Harvard University Press.
Mecacci, E. 1993. Un frammento palinsesto del più antico constituto del Comune di Siena, in M. Ascheri (ed.) *Antica Legislazione della Repubblica di Siena*. Siena: Il Leccio: 67-119.
Melchiorre, M. 2023. Cerimonie di pietra. La riscoperta della romanità e la costruzione di un'identità civica (Feltre, secoli XVI-XVII), in Varanini (ed.): 85-102.
Melis, F. 1989 (1 ed. 1963). La frequenza alle terme nel basso Medioevo, in Id. *Industria e commercio nella Toscana medievale*. B. Dini (ed). Firenze: Le Monnier: 319-347.
Melville, G. 2009. Costruire e decostruire i simboli della comunicazione religiosa del medioevo, in G. Andenna (ed.) *Religiosità e civiltà. Le comunicazioni simboliche (secoli IX-XIII)*. Milano: Vita e Pensiero: 49-69.
Menant, F. 2005. *L'Italie des communes (1100-1350)*. Paris: Belin.
Menzinger, S. 2011. *Consilium sapientium*: Lawmen and the Italian Popular Communes, in L. Armstrong and J. Kirshner (eds) *The Politics of Law in Late Medieval and Renaissance Italy. Essays in honour of Lauro Martines*. Toronto: University of Toronto Press: 40-54.

Merli, S. 2000. *Fonti e fontane dell'Umbria*. Perugia: Quattremme.
Miglio, M. 1989. Catastrofi naturali, in Musca (ed.): 49-65.
Milani, G. 2009. *I comuni italiani. Secoli XII-XIV*. Roma-Bari: Laterza.
Milner, S. J. 2000. Rubrics and Requests: Statutory Division and Supra-Communal Clientage in Pistoia, in Connell and Zorzi (eds): 312-332.
Milskaïa, L. T. 1984. Certains aspects du développement de l'agriculture en Catalogne aux XIIe-XIIIe siècles et l'environnement, in Guarducci (ed.) 1984: 9-33.
Mocarelli, L. 2011. L'acqua: per la storia economica di una risorsa contesa. *Studi Storici Luigi Simeoni* 61: 81-93.
Mocarelli, L. (ed.) 2013. *Quando manca il pane. Origini e cause della scarsità delle risorse alimentari in età moderna e contemporanea*. Bologna: Il Mulino.
Moglia, M. 2022. Il signore e la carestia: Parma 1258-1259, in Albini, Grillo and Raviola (eds): 49-60.
Molà, L. 2010: La repubblica di Venezia tra acque dolci e acque salse: investimenti tecnologici a Lizzafusina nel Rinascimento, in Calzona and Lamberini (eds) II: 447-472.
Molfetta, D. 1998. *Gli opifici idraulici e la fluitazione del legname nell'alto Bût*. Paluzza: Comune di Paluzza (2nd ed.).
Molinari, A. 2016. La "congiuntura del Trecento" e le fonti materiali, Note introduttive. *Archeologia Medievale* 43: 9-16.
Monceaux, P. 1920. *Histoire littéraire de l'Afrique chrétienne depuis les origines jusqu'à l'invasion arabe*. V. Paris: Leroux.
Montanari, M. 2012. *Gusti del Medioevo. I prodotti, la cucina, la tavola*. Roma-Bari: Laterza.
Montanari, M. and A. Vasina (eds) 2000. *Per Vito Fumagalli. Terra, uomini, istituzioni medievali*. Bologna: Clueb.
Morgan, J. E. 2017. The micro-politics of water management in early modern England: regulation and representation in Commissions of Sewers. *Environment and History* 23/3: 409-430.
Morpurgo, P. 2000. *L'armonia della natura e l'ordine dei governi*. Firenze: SISMEL.
Morrison, S. S. 2008. *Excrement in the Late Middle Ages. Sacred Filth and Chaucer's Fecopoetics*. New York: Palgrave Macmillan.
Moscati, L. 1997. Le concessioni di acque tra Diritto comune e codificazione unitaria, in *I rapporti contrattuali con la pubblica amministrazione nell'esperienza storico-giuridica*. Napoli: Jovene: 319-348.
Mostert, E. 2020. Water and national identity in the Netherlands: the history of an idea. *Water History* 12: 311-329.
Muendel, J. 1984. The 'French' mill in medieval Tuscany. *Journal of Medieval History* 10: 215-247.
Muendel, J. 1991. Medieval Urban Renewal. The Communal Mills of the City of Florence, 1351-1382. *Journal of Urban History* 17/4: 363-389.
Mugnaini, U. 1999. *Approdi, scali e navigazione del fiume Arno nei secoli*. Pisa: Felici.
Musarra, A. 2021. *Medioevo marinaro. Prendere il mare nell'Italia medievale*. Bologna: Il Mulino.
Musca, G. (ed.) 1989. *Uomo e ambiente nel Mezzogiorno normanno-svevo*. Bari: Dedalo.
Mussini, M. 2010. Governo delle acque nel territorio reggiano fra Medioevo e Rinascimento, in Calzona and Lamberini (eds) I: 221-241.
Nada Patrone, A. M. 1989. Pelli e pellami, in Musca (ed.): 165-201.
Nanni, P. 2017. History of Italian Agriculture and Agricultural Landscapes in the late Middle Ages. *Rivista di storia dell'agricoltura* 57/2: 3-24.
Napione E. 2009. *Le Arche Scaligere di Verona*. Venezia: Marsilio.

Naso, I. 1982. *Medici e strutture sanitarie nella società tardo-medievale. Il Piemonte dei secoli XIV e XV*. Milano: Angeli.

Neuheuser, H. P. 2017. Das Wasser als Naturelement und Zeichen in der mittelalterlichen Liturgie, in G. Huber-Rebenich, Ch. Rohr and M. Stolz (eds): *Wasser in der mittelalterlichen Kultur. Gebrauch – Wahrnehmung – Symbolik*. Berlin-Boston: De Gruyter: 333-344.

Nico Ottaviani, M. G. 2008. *Statuti, territorio e acque nel Medioevo. Perugia e Marsciano Tevere e Nestóre*. Spoleto: CISAM.

Nico Ottaviani, M. G. 2023. Gli statuti nella lunga durata: tra efficacia normativa e forza simbolica, in G. M. Varanini (ed.) *Rituali civici e continuità istituzionale nelle città italiane in età moderna*. Roma: Viella: 265-281.

Nicoud, M. 2007. *Les regimes de santé au Moyen Âge. Naissance et diffusion d'une écriture médicale, XIIIe-XVe siècle*. Roma: École française de Rome.

Nicoud, M. 2022. Le acque termali dei medici e dei filosofi medievali, in M. Lenzi, O. L. Lizzini, P. Totaro and L. Valente (eds) *Fonti, flussi, onde. L'acqua tra realtà e metafora nel pensiero antico, medievale e moderno*. Firenze: SISMEL: 53-70.

Nigro, G. 1994. *Il tempo liberato. Festa e svago nella città di Francesco Datini*. Firenze: Nuova Cesat.

Nutton, V. 1981. Continuity or Rediscovery? The City Physician in Classical Antiquity and Mediaeval Italy, in A. W. Russell (ed.) *The Town and State Physician in Europe*. Wolfenbüttel: Herzog August Bibliothek: 9-46.

Occhi, K. 2021. La fluitazione del legname nel XVI secolo, in G. Beltramini, B. Guidi, F. Magani and V. Tiné (eds): *Palladio, Bassano e il ponte. Invenzione, storia, mito*. Genova: Sagep: 133-139.

Ohler, N. 2000. I mezzi di trasporto terrestri e marittimi, in S. Gensini (ed.) *Viaggiare nel Medioevo*. Pisa: Pacini: 91-120.

Orlando, E. 2011. Governo delle acque e navigazione interna. Il Veneto nel basso medioevo. *Reti Medievali rivista* 12/2: 251-293.

Orsini, B. 2006. *Via Emilia*, in F. Lenzi (ed.) *Regio VIII. Luoghi, uomini, percorsi dell'età romana in Emilia-Romagna*. San Giovanni in Persiceto: Aspasia: 544-563.

Ortalli, G. 1999. Lo statuto tra funzione normativa e valore politico, in E. Menestò (ed.) *Gli statuti delle città: l'esempio di Ascoli nel secolo XIV*. Spoleto: CISAM: 11-35.

Ortu, G. G. 2019. *La Sardegna dei giudici*. Nuoro: Il Maestrale (2nd ed.).

Ostrom, E. 2002. Common-pool resources and institutions: Toward a revised theory, in B. L. Gardner and G. C. Rausser (eds) *Handbook of Agricultural Economics*. 2A: *Agriculture and Its External Linkages*. North Holland: Elsevier: 1315-1339.

Paesaggi agrari d'Europa (secoli XIII-XV). 2015. Roma: Viella.

Pagnoni, F. 2022. Disastri artificiali: alcune note su acqua e operazioni militari nel medioevo, in Albini, Grillo and Raviola (eds): 141-154.

Palermo, L. 1979. *Il porto di Roma nel XIV e XV secolo. Strutture socio-economiche e statuti*. Roma: Istituto Nazionale di Studi Romani.

Panero, F. and G. Pinto (eds) 2023. *Insediamenti, economia e società in aree di montagna. Appennino settentrionale – Alpi occidentali (secoli XII-XVI)*. Cherasco (CN), Centro Internazionale di Studi sugli Insediamenti Medievali.

Paolini, C. *et al.* 2016. *Di Pietra e d'Oro. Il Ponte Vecchio di Firenze Sette Secoli di Storia e di Arte*. Firenze: Maria Cristina de Montemayor.

Papaccio, G. 2008. I mulini del Comune di Firenze: uso e gestione nella città trecentesca, in C. Travaglini (ed.) *La città e il fiume, secoli XIII-XIX*. Roma: École française de Rome: 61-79.

Parente, M. 2000. Gli statuti e le acque a Parma nel Medioevo, in Cazzola (ed.): 53-64.

Park, K. 1985. *Doctors and Medicine in Early Renaissance Florence*. Princeton: Princeton Legacy Library.
Pasa, M. 1999a. Le acque un filo di storia, in Pasa (ed.): 53-57.
Pasa, M. 1999b. Lo scenario della storia: il Medioevo e la ricostruzione del paesaggio, in Pasa (ed.): 59-100.
Pasa, M. (ed.) 1999. *Acqua terra e uomini tra Lessinia e Adige*. Verona: Arti grafiche AZ.
Pasquali, G. 1995. *Contadini e signori della Bassa. Insediamenti e «deserta» del Ravennate e del Ferrarese nel Medioevo*. Bologna: Clueb.
Patitucci Uggeri, S. 2002. La viabilità di terra e d'acqua nell'Italia medievale, in S. Patitucci Uggeri (ed.) *La viabilità medievale in Italia. Contributo alla carta archeologica medievale*. Firenze: All'Insegna del Giglio: 1-72.
Pavoni, R. 1992. *Liguria medievale da provincia romana a stato regionale*. Genova: ECIG: 1992.
Pecorella, C. 1962. Note sull'ordinamento della navigazione padana nei secoli XIV-XV. *Archivio Storico Lombardo* 86, s. 9/2: 62-71.
Pene Vidari, G. S. 1999. *Introduzione*, in Chelazzi. VIII, *T-U*. Firenze: Olschki: XI-XCVI.
Perazzi, P., G. Millemaci and C. Taddei 2010. Pt 24-Pistoia, Piazza della Sala, in P. Perazzi (ed.) *Carta archeologica della provincia di Pistoia*. Firenze: Istituto Geografico Militare: 368-370.
Perco, D. (ed.) 1988. *Zattere, zattieri e menadàs. La fluitazione del legname lungo il Piave*. Feltre: Castaldi.
Pertile, A. 1892. Storia del diritto penale, in Id. *Storia del diritto italiano dalla caduta dell'Impero romano alla codificazione*. Torino: Utet: t. 5.
Pesci, G., C. Ugolini and G. Venturi (eds) 1994. *Bologna d'acqua. L'energia idraulica nella storia della città*. Bologna: Compositori.
Pesci, G. and C. Ugolini (eds) 1997. *Acque nascoste. Antichi manufatti e nuovi recuperi lungo i corsi d'acqua della città di Bologna*. Bologna: Compositori.
(La) peste nera: dati di una realtà ed elementi di una interpretazione. 1994. Spoleto: CISAM.
Petaros, A., A. Skorobonja, T. Culina, A. Bosnar, V. Frkovic and J. Azman. 2013. Public Health Problems in the Medieval Statutes of Croatian Adriatic Coastal Towns: From Public Morality to Public Health. *Journal of Religion and Health* 52: 531-37.
Petracco, F. 2010. Il divertimento delle acque. Irrigazione e bonifica tra Cinque e Seicento nella provincia cremonese: il caso del Diversivo Magio, infrastruttura privata di utilità pubblica, in Calzona and Lamberini (eds) I: 261-271.
Petti Balbi, G. 1990. Istituzioni cittadine e servizi scolastici nell'Italia centro-settentrionale tra XIII e XV secolo, in *Città e servizi sociali nell'Italia dei secoli XII-XV*: 21-48.
Pibiri, E. (ed.) 2018. *L'eau à la bouche. Boire et manger au Moyen Âge*. Chillon: Fondation du Château de Chillon.
Piccinni, G. 2002. La campagna e le città (secoli XII-XV), in A. Cortonesi, G. Pasquali and G. Piccinni (eds) *Uomini e campagne nell'Italia medievale*. Roma-Bari: Laterza: 123-189.
Piccinni, G. 2022. *Operazione Buon Governo. Un laboratorio di comunicazione politica nell'Italia del Trecento*. Torino: Einaudi.
Piergiovanni, V. 1980. *Gli statuti civili e criminali di Genova nel Medioevo. La tradizione manoscritta e le edizioni*. Genova: ECIG.
Piergiovanni, V. 1989. Statuti e riformagioni. *Atti della Società Ligure di Storia Patria* n.s. 29/2: 81-98.
Pierotti, P. 2005. L'agro Pisano tra acque e terre emerse, in *Il Fiume Morto. Il territorio, la storia, i progetti*. Pisa: Pacini: 17-53.

Pini, A. I. 1981. Dal comune città-stato al comune ente amministrativo, in G. Calasso (ed.) *Storia d'Italia*. 4. Torino: Utet: 449-587.

Pini, A. I. 1987. Energia e industria tra Sàvena e Reno: i mulini idraulici bolognesi tra XI e XV secolo, in *Tecnica e società nell'Italia dei secoli XII-XVI*. Pistoia-Roma: Viella: 1-22.

Pini, A. I. 1993. *Campagne bolognesi. Le radici agrarie di una metropoli medievale*. Firenze: Le Lettere.

Pinna, M. (ed.) 1929. Le Ordinazioni dei Consiglieri del Castello di Cagliari del Secolo XIV. *Archivio Storico Sardo* 17: III-XXV, 1-272.

Piovan, S. E. and M. E. Hodgson. 2019. Military-engineered flood as defense from the enemy: a brief review, and case study from WWI in Northern Italy, in Canzian and Novello (eds): 105-115.

Pirani, F. 2014. Città, insediamenti costieri e strutture portuali nel medio Adriatico, in Lusso (ed.): 187-213.

Piscitelli, T. Forthcoming. Il complesso rapporto dei cristiani dei primi secoli con l'acqua: simbolo di vita e rigenerazione o causa di corruzione, in Fluxit abunda tuis aqua potibus atque lavacris: *uso e simbologia dell'acqua fra tarda antichità e medioevo*. Convegno internazionale di studi, Cimitile – Santa Maria Capua Vetere (NA), June 16-17 2022.

Polonio, V. 2003. Da provincia a signora del mare. Secoli VI-XIII, in D. Puncuh (ed.) *Storia di Genova. Mediterraneo, Europa, Atlantico*. Genova: Società Ligure di Storia Patria: 111-231.

Pomeranz, K. 2000. *The Great Divergence. China, Europe and the Making of the Modern World Economy*. Princeton: Princeton University Press.

Pradi, A. 2011. L'acqua come bene giuridico, in Santucci, Simonati and Cortese (eds): 27-42.

Premuda, L. 1988-90. Il termalismo euganeo, aspetti storici. *Acta Medicae Historiae Patavina* 35-36: 39-58.

Prodi, R. and G. Zaccaria 2019. *L'acqua: armonie, disarmonie, conflitti*. Padova: Padova University Press.

Prosperi, A. (ed.) 1995. *Il Padule di Fucecchio. La lunga storia di un ambiente «naturale»*. Roma: Storia e Letteratura.

Public.wmo.int/en/our-mandate/water.

Pucci, B. 2017. *Fra cielo e acqua. Le romite del ponte alle Grazie (Rubaconte). Una storia fiorentina dal '300 al '400*. Firenze: Pagnini.

Quasten, J. 1980. *Patrologia*. Genova: Marietti.

Quertier, C. 2022. *Guerres et richesses d'une nation. Les Florentins à Pise au XIVe siècle*. Roma: École française de Rome.

Racine, P. 1986. Poteri medievali e percorsi fluviali nell'Italia padana. *Quaderni storici* n.s. 61: 9-32.

Racine, P. 2001. Dal "Breve" agli Statuti: le tradizioni normative di Parma e Piacenza (XII-XIV secolo), in Rossetti (ed.)b: 291-303.

Raggio, O. 1995. Norme e pratiche. Gli statuti campestri come fonti per la storia locale. *Quaderni storici* 88/1: 155-194.

Rampp, B., M. Endress and L. Clemens (eds) 2020. *Strategies, Dispositions and Resources of Social Resilience. A Dialogue between Medieval Studies and Sociology*. Wiesbaden: Springer.

Rao, R. 2015. *I paesaggi dell'Italia medievale*. Roma: Carocci.

Rao, R. 2016. Abitare, costruire e gestire uno spazio fluviale: signori, villaggi e beni comuni lungo la Sesia tra Medioevo ed età moderna, in R. Rao (ed.) *I paesaggi fluviali della Sesia fra storia e archeologia. Territori, insediamenti, rappresentazioni*. Firenze: All'Insegna del Giglio: 13-29.

Rao, R. 2022. *Risk societies* e resilienza ambientale: borghi nuovi, inondazioni e abbandoni sul Po nel medioevo e nella prima età moderna, in Albini, Grillo and Raviola (eds): 111-121.

Raveggi, L. and L. Tanzini (eds) 2001. *Bibliografia delle edizioni di statuti toscani, secoli XII-metà XVI*. Firenze: Olschki.

Ravegnani, G. 2020. *Venezia prima di Venezia. Mito e fondazione della città lagunare*. Roma: Salerno Ed.

Raviola, B. A. 2006. La strada liquida. Costruire un libro sul Po in età moderna. *Rivista storica italiana* 118/3: 1041-1078.

Raviola, B. A. 2011. «Terra nullius». Ghiare, siti alluvionali e incolti nella piana del Po di età moderna, in G. Alfani and R. Rao (eds) *La gestione delle risorse collettive. Italia settentrionale, secoli XII-XVIII*. Milano: Angeli: 157-173.

Rawcliffe, C. 2013. *Urban Bodies. Communal Health in Late Medieval English Towns and Cities*. Woodbridge: Boydell & Brewer.

Re, E. 1920. Maestri di strada. *Archivio della Società Romana di Storia Patria* 43: 5-102.

Redi, F. 1991. *Pisa com'era: archeologia, urbanistica e strutture materiali (secoli V-XIV)*. Napoli: Liguori.

Riccetti, L. 1992. *La città costruita. Lavori pubblici e immagine in Orvieto medievale*. Firenze: Le Lettere.

Riccetti, L. 1994. «Per havere dell'acqua buona per bevere». Orvieto: città e cantiere del duomo, secoli XIV-XV. *Nuova rivista storica* 78/2: 241-292.

Ricci, F. 2017. Taglio del bosco, dilavamento delle acque e inondazioni nel bacino dell'Arno durante la seconda metà del Cinquecento, in Bianca and Salvestrini (eds): 205-239.

Ricciardelli, F. and M. Fantoni (eds) 2020. *Republicanism. A Theoretical and Historical Perspective*. Roma: Viella.

(La) ricerca del benessere individuale e sociale. Ingredienti materiali e immateriali. 2011. Roma: Viella.

Righetti, M. 1959. *Manuale di storia liturgica*. Milano: Ancora (2nd ed.).

Righetti, M. and A. M. D'Achille (eds) 2022. *Roma medievale. Il volto perduto della città*. Roma: De Luca.

Rinaldi, R. 2000. La normativa bolognese del '200: tra la città e il suo contado, in Cazzola (ed.): 139-163.

Rippe, G. 2003. *Padoue et son contado (Xe -XIIIe siècle). Société et pouvoirs*. Roma: École française de Rome.

Rizzi, A. 1982. *Vere da pozzo di Venezia*. Verona: Cierre.

Rohr, Ch. 2021. Disaster or everyday risk? Perceiving, managing and commemorating floods in medieval central Europe, in Ch. M. Gerrard, P. Forlin and P. J. Brown (eds) *Waiting for the End of the World? New perspectives on natural disasters in medieval Europe*. London-New York: Routledge: 201-217.

Romagnoli, G. 2020. L'acquedotto medievale delle Pietrare e l'approvvigionamento idrico di Viterbo in età comunale, in De Minicis and Pastura (eds): 153-161.

Romalli, G. 2006. L'acquedotto medievale di Perugia e l'adduzione idrica nelle realtà comunali centroitaliane, in V. Franchetti Pardo (ed.) *Arnolfo di Cambio e la sua opera. Costruire, scolpire, dipingere, decorare*. Roma: Viella: 317-330.

Romanoni, F. 2008. Guerra e navi sui fiumi dell'Italia settentrionale (secoli XII-XIV). *Archivio Storico Lombardo* 134: 11-46.

Romanoni, F. 2023. *La guerra d'acqua dolce. Navi e conflitti medievali nell'Italia settentrionale*. Bologna: Clueb.

Rombai, L. 1993. L'ambiente, il fiume, gli uomini: per un itinerario di geografia umana dell'Arno, in *Un fiume: l'Arno*. Firenze: Comune di Firenze: 55-93.
Rossetti, G. (ed.) 2001a. *Legislazione e prassi istituzionale a Pisa (secoli XI-XIII). Una tradizione normativa esemplare*. Napoli: Liguori.
Rossetti, G. (ed.) 2001b. *Legislazione e prassi istituzionale nell'Europa medievale. Tradizioni normative, ordinamenti, circolazione mercantile (secoli XI-XV)*. Napoli: Liguori.
Rossiaud, J. 2005. Les ports fluviaux au Moyen Âge (France, Italie), in P. Boucheron (ed.) *Ports maritimes et ports fluviaux au Moyen Âge*. Paris: Éditions de la Sorbonne: 9-19.
Rosso, P. 2018. *La scuola nel Medioevo. Secoli VI-XV*. Roma: Carocci.
Roveda, E. 2012. *Uomini, terre e acque. Studi sull'agricoltura della "Bassa lombarda" tra XV e XVII secolo*. Milano: Angeli.
Roversi Monaco, F. 2000. L'uomo e l'ambiente nel Medioevo: la legislazione sulle acque a Ravenna tra XII e XV secolo, in Montanari and Vasina (eds): 77-106.
Saba, A. F. 2013. L'allocazione delle acque dolci fra teoria e storia, in Mocarelli (ed.): 57-73.
Sabaté, F. (ed.) 2007. *Natura i desenvolupament. El medi ambient a l'edat mitjana*. Lleida: Pagès.
Sabbionesi, L. 2019. Pro maiore sanitate hominum civitatis ... et borgorum. *Lo smaltimento dei rifiuti nelle città medievali dell'Emilia Romagna*. Firenze: All'Insegna del Giglio.
Saggioro F. 2012. Paesaggi in equilibrio: uomo e acqua nella pianura Padana centrale tra IV e IX secolo. *Antiquité Tardive* 20: 47-67.
Saggioro, F. and G. M. Varanini. 2012. Insediamento umano, terra e acque nella pianura veronese (IX-XIV secolo): archeologia e fonti scritte, in Canzian and Simonetti (eds): 95-114.
Salvestrini, F. 1992. San Miniato al Tedesco. Le risorse economiche di una città minore della Toscana fra XIV e XV secolo. *Rivista di Storia dell'Agricoltura* 32/1: 95-141.
Salvestrini, F. 2000. Law, Forest Resources and Management of Territory in the Late Middle Ages: Woodlands in Tuscan Municipal Statutes, in M. Agnoletti and S. Anderson (eds) *Forest History: International Studies on Socio-economic and Forest Ecosystem Change*. Wallingford-New York: Cabi Publishing: 279-288.
Salvestrini, F. 2003. Gli statuti delle 'quasi città' toscane (secoli XIII-XV), in R. Dondarini, G. M. Varanini, and M. Venticelli (eds) *Signori, regimi signorili e statuti nel tardo medioevo*. Bologna: Pàtron: 217-242.
Salvestrini, F. 2005. *Libera città su fiume regale. Firenze e l'Arno dall'Antichità al Quattrocento*. Firenze: Nardini.
Salvestrini, F. 2007. Manifattura e attività creditizia in Valdelsa fra XIII e XV secolo, in I. Moretti and S. Soldani (eds) *I centri della Valdelsa dal Medioevo ad oggi*. Firenze: Polistampa: 119-151.
Salvestrini, F. 2008. Disciplina caritatis. *Il monachesimo vallombrosano tra medioevo e prima età moderna*. Roma: Viella.
Salvestrini, F. 2009a. Navigazione, trasporti e fluitazione del legname sulle acque interne della Toscana fra Medioevo e prima Età moderna (secoli XIII-XVI). *Bollettino Storico Pisano* 78: 1-42.
Salvestrini, F. 2009b. Statuti e *cartae libertatum* di emanazione signorile nella Toscana dei secoli XIII e XIV. *Società e storia* 124: 197-229.
Salvestrini, F. 2010a. L'Arno e l'alluvione fiorentina del 1333, in Matheus *et al.* (eds): 231-256.
Salvestrini, F. 2010b. Navigazione e trasporti sulle acque interne della Toscana medievale e protomoderna (secoli XIII-XVI), in Calzona and Lamberini (eds) I: 197-220.
Salvestrini, F. 2012. Tra "civiltà" e "natura". La presenza del fiume nei contesti urbani, il caso toscano fra Medioevo e prima Età Moderna, in Canzian and Simonetti (eds): 133-145.

Salvestrini, F. 2013a. Erudizione storica e tradizioni normative. La stampa degli Statuti medievali toscani tra età moderna e contemporanea, in O. Muzzi and F. Ciappi (eds) *Studi in onore di Sergio Gensini*. Firenze: Polistampa: 237-278.

Salvestrini, F. 2013b. Les inondations de l'Arno à Florence du XIVe au XVIe siècle: risques, catastrophes, perceptions, in Ch. Ballut and P. Fournier (eds) *Au fil de l'eau. Ressources, risques et gestion du Néolithique à nos jours*. Clermont-Ferrand: Presses Universitaires Blaise Pascal: 325-334.

Salvestrini, F. 2014. «Recipiantur in choro [...] qualiter benigne et caritative tractantur». Per una storia delle relazioni fra Camaldolesi e Vallombrosani (XI-XV secolo), in C. Caby and P. Licciardello (eds) *Camaldoli e l'Ordine Camaldolese dalle origini alla fine del XV secolo*. Cesena: Centro Storico Benedettino Italiano: 53-96.

Salvestrini, F. 2015a. The Arno floods in Florence history, in F. Giovannelli and G. Sabella (eds) *The Colors of the Flood. Past, present and future through the unpublished color pictures by Joe Blaustein*. Empoli-Firenze: AB Edizioni: 70-88.

Salvestrini, F. 2015b. The Construction of the Urban Identity in Late Medieval Italy the Case of Tuscany (Thirteenth to Fourteenth Century). *Review of History and Political Science* 3/1: 47-59 <rhpsnet.com/journals/rhps/Vol_3_No_1_June_2015/5.pdf>.

Salvestrini, F. 2016. Firenze e l'Arno tra antichità ed età moderna, in L. Maccabruni and C. Zarrilli (eds) *Arno. Fonte di prosperità, fonte di distruzione. Storia del fiume e del territorio nelle carte d'archivio*. Firenze: Polistampa: 17-20.

Salvestrini, F. 2017a. Le inondazioni a Firenze e nella valle dell'Arno dal XII al XVI secolo, *in Bianca and Salvestrini (eds):* 31-60.

Salvestrini, F. 2017b. Urban society and environmental disasters. River floods in Medieval and Early Modern Tuscany, in Ito, Matsuda and Scaroni (eds): 97-107.

Salvestrini, F. 2019. Struttura, normazione e stratificazione testuale negli statuti di alcune città comunali italiane del XIII e XIV secolo, in D. Lett (ed.) *Les statuts communaux vus de l'intérieur dans les sociétés méditérranéennes de l'Occident (XIIe-XVe siècle). Statuts, écritures et pratiques sociales - III*. Paris: Éditions de la Sorbonne: 19-35.

Salvestrini, F. 2023a. «Patrïa degna di trïumfal fama». Il contesto storico-politico e la matrice culturale degli Statuti fiorentini del 1355, in Bambi, Salvestrini and Tanzini (eds) I: 3-78.

Salvestrini, F. 2023b. La festa di san Giovanni a Firenze tra medioevo e prima età moderna, in Varanini (ed.): 171-211.

Salvestrini, F. 2023c. Notariato e ordini monastici nella Toscana del primo Rinascimento. Considerazioni introduttive e approfondimenti documentari (secoli XIV e XV), in L. Tanzini (ed) *Notai e Chiesa nell'Italia bassomedievale. Casi di studio*. Roma: Aracne: 15-29.

Salvestrini, F. forthcoming a. Celebrations and Epitaphs of a Municipal Tradition. Reflections on the Fourteenth-Century Vulgarization and Sixteenth-Century Printing of Tuscan Communal Statutes. *Imago Temporis. Medium Aevum*.

Salvestrini, F. forthcoming b. The Use of the Vernacular: Language, Law, and Political Culture in Fourteenth-Century Italy, in M. A. Bilotta, M. Metelo de Seixas, S. Faccin, T. Leonardi (eds) *The Illuminated Legal Manuscript from the Middle Ages to the Digital Age. Forms, Iconographies, Materials, Uses and Cataloguing*, 1st International Conference of Ius Illuminatum - Oficina de investigação. Turnhout: Brepols.

Salvestrini, F. and L. Tanzini 2015. La lingua della legge. I volgarizzamenti di statuti nell'Italia del Basso Medioevo, in I. Lori Sanfilippo and G. Pinto (eds) *Comunicare nel medioevo. La conoscenza e l'uso delle lingue nei secoli XII-XV*. Roma: ISIME: 250-301.

Santarelli, U. 1993. Lo statuto «redivivo». *Archivio storico italiano* 151/2: 519-526.
Santucci G., A. Simonati and F. Cortese (eds) 2011. *L'acqua e il diritto. Quaderni del Dipartimento di Scienze Giuridiche, Università di Trento* 99.
Saragosa, C. 2005. *L'insediamento umano. Ecologia e sostenibilità*. Roma: Donzelli.
Sassu, P. 1985. Tra terra e acqua, un paese, in C. Zavattini (ed.) *La civiltà delle acque. Dall'acqua la vita e la morte - Sant'Alberto di Ravenna*. Bologna: Cappelli: 109-252.
Scaramellini, G. 2007. Vie di terra e d'acqua fra Lario e val di Reno nel medioevo. Nodi problematici e soluzioni pratiche sulle direttrici transalpine del Settimo e dello Spluga, in Bergier and Coppola (eds): 11-64.
Scavizzi, P. C. 1991. *Navigazione e regolazione fluviale nello Stato della Chiesa fra XVI e XVIII secolo (il caso del Tevere)*. Roma: Edilstampa.
Scharf, G. P. (ed.) 2022. *I rapporti fra città e campagna allo specchio della normativa statutaria. Un confronto fra lo Stato della Chiesa, la Toscana e l'Abruzzo (secoli XII-XVI)*. Napoli: Federico II University Press.
Schenk, G. J. 2007. "...prima ci fu la cagione de la mala provedenza de' Fiorentini..." Disaster and 'Life World'-Reaction in the Commune of Florence to the Flood of November 1333. *The Medieval History Journal* 10: 355-386.
Schenk, G. J. 2008. Der Mensch zwischen Natur und Kultur Auf der Suche nach einer Umweltgeschichtsschreibung in der deutschsprachigen Mediävistik - eine Skizze, in F. Duceppe-Lamarre and J. I. Engels (eds) *Umwelt und Herrschaft in der Geschichte*. Oldenbourg: Oldenbourg Wissenschaftsverlag: 27-51.
Schenk, G. J. 2012. Politik der Katastrophe? Wechselwirkungen zwischen gesellschaftlichen Strukturen und dem Umgang mit Naturrisiken am Beispiel von Florenz und Straßburg in der Reinassance, in U. Wagner (ed.) *Stadt und Stadtverderben*. Ostfildern: Thorbecke: 33-76.
Schenk, G. J. 2017. Friend or Foe? Negotiating the Future on the example of Dealing with the rivers Arno and Rhine in the Renaissance (ca. 1300-1600), in Bianca and Salvestrini (eds): 137-156.
Schenk, G. J. (ed.) 2017. *Historical Disaster Experiences. Towards a Comparative and Transcultural History of Disasters Across Asia and Europe*. Cham: Springer.
Schiavini, J. 1977. La politica cremonese delle acque nella seconda metà del '300. *Studi di Storia Medioevale e di Diplomatica, Università di Milano* 2: 195-227.
Schiavon, A. 2011. Acqua e diritto romano: "invenzione" di un modello?, in Santucci, Simonati and Cortese (eds): 117-181.
Schulze, U. 1994. *Brunnen im Mittelalter. Politische Ikonographie der Kommunen in Italien*. Frankfurt: Lang.
Seche, G. 2021. La diffusione delle *Cartas de Logu*. Secoli XIV-XVI, in G. Mele (ed.) *Elianora de Arbaree. Sa juighissa*. Oristano: S'Alvure: 133-169.
Settia, A. A. 1998. Il fiume in guerra. L'Adda come ostacolo militare (secoli V-XIV), in C. Tartari (ed.) *La storia di Vaprio d'Adda. II. Il Medioevo*. Vaprio d'Adda: Comune di Vaprio d'Adda: 155-180.
Settia, A. A. 2008. L'acqua come difesa: la penisola italica, in *L'acqua nei secoli altomedievali*: 357-388.
Silvestrelli, M. R. 1996. *«Super aquis habendis in civitate»*. L'acquedotto di Montepacciano e la Fontana Maggiore, in Santini (ed.): 73-161.
Simonetti, R. 2009. *Da Padova a Venezia nel medioevo. Terre mobili, confini, conflitti*. Roma: Viella.
Simonetti, R. 2012a. Il delta lagunare del fiume Brenta tra gestione del rischio idraulico e sfruttamento delle risorse naturali (secoli XII-XIV), in Canzian and Simonetti (eds): 59-81.

Simonetti, R. 2012b. Cultura umanistica e cultura scientifica in Leon Battista Alberti e Michele Savonarola, in S. Collodo and R. Simonetti (eds) *Filosofia naturale e scienze dell'esperienza fra Medioevo e Umanesimo. Studi su Marsilio da Padova, Leon Battista Alberti, Michele Savonarola.* Padova: Università degli Studi-Antilia: 239-430.

Simonetti, R. 2014. Governo delle acque e circolazione delle conoscenze tecniche nell'Italia comunale, in Z. Murat and S. Zonno (eds) *Medioevo veneto, Medioevo europeo. Identità e alterità.* Padova: Padova University Press: 11-25.

Simonetti, R. 2019. Environnement et services écosystémiques dans le *Polesine.* Le cas d'étude de Costa di Rovigo (XIIe-XVIe siècles), in Canzian and Novello (eds): 29-40.

Simonetti, R. 2022. Acque e dissesto idrogeologico nel Padovano (secc. XII-XIV), in Albini, Grillo and Raviola (eds): 157-177.

Sini, F. 2008. Persone e cose: *res communes omnium.* Prospettive sistematiche tra diritto romano e tradizione romanistica. *Diritto@Storia* 7. https://www.dirittoestoria.it/7/Tradizione-Romana/Sini-Persone-cose-res-communes-omnium.htm.

Siniscalco, P. 2009. In spirito e in acqua. Il pensiero degli scrittori cristiani antichi sul battesimo, in I. Folletti and S. Romano (eds) Fons Vitae. *Baptême, Baptistères et Rites d'initiation (IIe-VIe siècle).* Roma: Viella: 9-25.

Skinner, P. 1997. *Health and Medicine in Early Medieval Southern Italy.* Leiden: Brill.

Smith, J. L. 2018. Medieval Water Energies: Philosophical, Hydro-Social, and Intellectual. *Open Library of Humanities* 4/2, https://doi.org/10.16995/0lh.228: 1-27.

Soens, T. 2020. Resilience in Historical Disaster Studies: Pitfalls and Opportunities, in M. Endress, L. Clemens and B. Rampp (eds) *Strategies, Dispositions and Resources of Social Resilience. A Dialogue between Medieval Studies and Sociology.* Wiesbaden: Springer: 253-274.

Soranzo, G. 1964. *L'antico navigabile Po di Primaro nella vita economica e politica del Delta Padano.* Milano: Giuffrè.

Sorcinelli, P. 1998. *Storia sociale dell'acqua. Riti e culture.* Milano: Mondadori.

Sorcinelli, P. 1999. L'acqua, l'ambiente, gli uomini, in A. Varni (ed.) *Storia dell'ambiente in Italia tra Ottocento e Novecento.* Bologna: Il Mulino.

Spanò, G. 2014. *Alcune servitù in materia di acque.* Vicalvi: Key.

Sperandio, B. 2005. Relazione di restauro della Fontana Orsini, in V. Garibaldi and B. Toscano (eds) *Arnolfo di Cambio, una rinascita nell'Umbria medievale.* Milano: Silvana: 238.

Squatriti, P. 1998. *Water and society in early medieval Italy, AD 400-1000.* Cambridge: Cambridge University Press.

Squatriti, P. 2008. I pericoli dell'acqua nell'Alto Medioevo italiano, in *L'acqua nei secoli altomedievali*: 583-618.

Squatriti, P. (ed.) 2007. *Natures Past. The Environment and Human History.* Ann Arbor: The University of Michigan Press.

Stella, A. 2022. *Ai margini del contado. Terra, signoria ed élites locali a Sabbion e nel territorio di Cologna Veneta (secoli XII-XIII).* Firenze: Firenze University Press.

Sterpos, D. 1961. *Comunicazioni stradali attraverso i tempi. Bologna-Firenze.* Novara: De Agostini.

Storti Storchi, C. 1991. Appunti in tema di «potestas condendi statuta», in Chittolini and Willoweit (eds): 319-343.

Strang, V. 2004. *The Meaning of Water.* London-New York: Routledge.

Ström, F. 1942. *On the Sacral Origin of the Germanic Death Penalties.* Lund: H. Ohlssons.

Sydow, J. 2000. Le vie d'acqua, in S. Cavaciocchi (ed.) *Le acque interne, secc. XII-XVIII.* Istituto Internazionale di Storia Economica "F. Datini", Prato. Atti delle 'Settimane di Studi' e altri convegni in CD-rom.

Szabó, Th. 1986. Il controllo dello spazio e la genesi della rete viaria comunale nel Medioevo, in G. Rossetti (ed.) *Spazio, società, potere nell'Italia dei Comuni*. Napoli: Liguori: 27-36.
Szabó, Th. 2001. La legislazione statutaria tedesca, in Rossetti (ed.)b: 79-96.
Sznura, F. 2010. Veleni e *nobilissimi pesci*. Appunti sulla legislazione fiorentina in tema di pesca nelle acque interne (secolo XV), in Sznura (ed.): 270-282.
Sznura, F. (ed.) 2010. *Fiumi e laghi toscani fra passato e presente. Pesca, memorie, regole*. Firenze: Aska.
Szulman, E. 2014. *La navigation intérieure sous l'Ancien Régime*. Rennes: Presses de l'Université de Rennes.
Taddei, I. 1996. Gioco d'azzardo, ribaldi e baratteria nelle città della Toscana tardo-medievale. *Quaderni storici* 31, 92/2: 335-362.
Takada, K. (ed.) 2020. *Politica ed economia in area di fiume nell'età medievale. Veneto, Toscana e Kinai*. Padova-Kobe: University of Kobe.
Taleb, N. N. 2012. *Antifragile. Things that Gain from Disorder*. London: Penguin.
Tangheroni, M. 1996. *Commercio e navigazione nel Medioevo*. Roma-Bari: Laterza.
Tangheroni, M. 2001. Normativa marittima pisana. Osservazioni e confronti, in Rossetti (ed.) a: 163-180.
Tangheroni, M. (ed.) 2003. *Pisa e il Mediterraneo: uomini, merci, idee dagli Etruschi ai Medici*. Milano: Skira.
Tanzini, L. 2001. Tradizione e innovazione nella rubrica *De origine iuris* dello Statuto fiorentino del 1409. *Archivio Storico Italiano* 159/4: 765-796.
Tanzini, L. 2009. Le magistrature sulle acque nelle città comunali toscane. *Nuova rivista storica* 93: 161-187.
Tanzini, L. 2013. Delibere e verbali. Per una storia documentaria dei consigli nell'Italia comunale. *Reti Medievali Rivista* 14/1: 43-79.
Tanzini, L. 2014. *A consiglio. La vita politica nell'Italia dei comuni*. Roma-Bari: Laterza.
Tanzini, L. 2021a. Dentro e fuori dagli statuti. Il paesaggio documentario delle fonti normative dell'Italia bassomedievale, in Lett (ed.): 161-182.
Tanzini, L. 2021b. La vie politique et les formes de l'écrit de gouvernement dans les villes italiennes du Moyen Âge. Entre ritualisation et conflit, in F. Otchakovsky-Laurens and L. Verdon (eds) *La voix des assemblées. Démocratie urbaine et registres de délibération. Méditerranée-Europe XIIIe-XVIIe siècle*. Aix-en-Provence-Marseille: Presses Universitaires de Provence: 201-217.
Tanzini, L. 2021c. The language of change in the public sources from communal Italy (13th/14th centuries), in E. Poddighe and T. Pontillo (eds) *Resisting and justifying changes. How to make the new acceptable in the Ancient, Medieval and Early Modern world*. Pisa: Pisa University Press: 565-588.
Tanzini, L. 2021d. Volgarizzare i documenti, volgarizzare gli statuti nella Toscana tra Due e Trecento, in S. Bischetti, M. Lodone, C. Lorenzi and A. Montefusco (eds) *Toscana bilingue (1260 ca.-1430 ca.). Per una storia sociale del tradurre medievale*. Berlin-Boston: De Gruyter: 151-166.
TeBrake, W. H. 2002. Taming the Waterwolf: Hydraulic Engineering and Water Management in the Netherlands During the Middle Ages. *Technology and Culture* 43/3: 475-499.
Tedesco, A. 2023. Gli statuti di Brescia di Tommaso Ferrando: nuova indagine sulla stampa e la ricezione della prima edizione del *corpus* statutario bresciano, in D. Martini and M. Francalanci (eds) *Con la penna e con il torchio. Scritture politiche e normative di prìncipi e città nell'Italia centro-settentrionale della prima Età moderna. Annuario dell'Archivio di Stato di Milano* 2021-23: 135-157.

Terenzi, P. 2016. *L'Aquila nel Regno. I rapporti politici fra città e monarchia nel Mezzogiorno tardomedievale*. Bologna: Il Mulino.

Terenzi, P. 2019. Evoluzione politica e dialettica normativa nel Regno di Napoli: statuti, consuetudini, privilegi (secoli XIII-XV). *Archivio Storico Italiano* 177/1: 95-125.

Terenzi, P. 2022. Statuti e norme sul territorio nelle città e terre del regno di Napoli (secoli XIII-XV), in Scharf (ed.): 137-170.

Teti, V. (ed.) 2003. *Storia dell'Acqua. Mondi materiali e universi simbolici*. Roma: Donzelli.

Tevere *(Il): sistema idraulico e asse produttivo (XV-XIX secolo). Mélanges de l'Ecole française de Rome. Italie et Méditerranée* 118/1. 2006.

Tigler, G. 2005. Venezia e le fontane di Perugia, in *Der unbestechliche Blick. Festschrift zu Ehren von Wolfgang Wolters*. Trier: Porta Alba: 17-24.

Tognana, F. 2019. Landscape planning and integrated economy in Medieval Italy: the case study of the Adige plain and the Este marketplace, in Canzian and Novello (eds): 41-46.

Tognetti, S. 2008. Produzioni, traffici e mercati (secoli XIII-XIV), in A. Malvolti and G. Pinto (eds) *Il Valdarno inferiore terra di confine nel Medioevo (Secoli XI-XV)*. Firenze: Olschki: 127-150.

Tonutti, S. 2007. *Acqua e antropologia*. Bologna: EMI.

Tosi Brandi, E. 2007. Igiene e decoro. Bologna e Rimini tra XIII e XIV secolo. *Storia Urbana* 116: 7-18.

Tosti, M., Tosti M. and Tosti M. 2002. La Grande diga di Fratta perugina. *L'Ingegnere Umbro* 43. https://www.medioevoinumbria.it/home/la-grande-diga-di-fratta-perugina-umbertide/.

Toubert, P. 1960. Les statuts communaux et l'histoire des campagnes lombardes au XIVe siècle. *Mélanges d'archéologie et d'histoire, École française de Rome* 72: 397-508.

Traina, G. 1992. *Ambiente e paesaggi di Roma antica*. Roma: La Nuova Italia Scientifica.

Traniello, L. (ed.) 1988. *Rovigo. Ritratto di una città*. Rovigo: Minelliana.

Treggiari, F. 2012. Bene comune: la città medievale, in M. R. Marella and S. Rodotà (eds) *Oltre il pubblico e il privato. Per un diritto dei beni comuni*. Verona: Ombre corte: 222-229.

Triglia, A., C. Iadanza, B. Lastoria, M. Bussettini and A. Barbano 2021. *Dissesto idrogeologico in Italia: pericolosità e indicatori di rischio*. Roma: ISPRA. Rapporti, 356: 35-57.

Trillo San José, C. 2002. Agricoltura irrigua e struttura sociale dell'Andalusia musulmana. *Quaderni medievali* 54: 87-129.

Vaini, M. 2000. Il controllo delle terre e delle acque nel Mantovano fra Duecento e Trecento. Vicende, istituzioni, statuti (1317), in Cazzola (ed.): 65-77.

Valente, F. 1982. *Isernia. Origine e crescita di una città*. Campobasso: ENNE.

Vallerani, F. 1993. Geografia storica delle acque venete, in Cortellazzo (ed.): 9-28.

Vallerani, M. 1987. Il *Liber terminationum* del comune di Perugia. *Mélanges de l'École Française de Rome, Moyen Âge, Temps Modernes* 99/2: 649-699.

Vallerani, M. 1992. Le comunanze di Perugia nel Chiugi. Storia di un possesso cittadino tra XII e XIV secolo. *Quaderni storici* 27: 625-652.

Vallocchia, F. 2011-12. 'Aqua publica' e 'aqua profluens'. *Diritto@Storia* 10. https://www.dirittoestoria.it/10/Tradizione-Romana/Vallocchia-Aqua-publica-aqua-profluens.htm#_3.3._%E2%80%93_C).

van Dam, P. 2010. Rabbits Swimming Across Borders: Micro-Environmental Infrastructures and Macro-Environmental Change in Early Modern Holland, in B. G. Scott (ed.) *Economies and Ecologies in Medieval and Early Modern Europe. Sudies in Environmental History for Richard C. Hoffmann*. Leiden-Boston: Brill: 63-92.

van Dam, P. 2017. An Amphibious Culture. Coping with floods in the Netherlands, in P. Coates, D. Moon and P. Warde (eds) *Local Places, Global Processes. Histories of Environmental Change in Britain and Beyond*. Oxford: Windgather Press: 78-93.

van der Linden, H. 1984. L'influence de l'eau sur les institutions rurales hollandaises, in Guarducci (ed.) 1984: 665-682.

Van Dülmen, R. 1990. *Theatre of Horror. Crime and Punishment in Early Modern Germany*. Cambridge Mass.: Polity Press.

Vannini, G. and C. Cosi. 2004. L'Arno e la sua valle nel Medioevo, in S. Grifoni and L. Rombai (eds) *Adottare l'Arno e i suoi paesaggi*. Firenze: CET: 101-115.

Vannucchi, E. 2009. *Quod nullus possit extrahere aquam*. La disciplina delle acque negli statuti medievali della Valdinievole, in E. Vannucchi (ed.) *Le acque, le terre, le genti. Appunti per una storia dell'acqua nel territorio pistoiese*. Firenze: Edifir: 9-20.

Varanini, G. M. 1988. Energia idraulica e attività economiche nella Verona comunale: l'Adige, il Fiumicello, il Fibbio (secoli XII-XIII), in Comba (ed.) 1988: 331-372.

Varanini, G. M. 2009. Appunti sul sistema stradale nel Veneto tardomedievale. Secoli XII-XV, in Th. Szabó (ed.) *Die Welt Europäischen Straßen von der Antike bis in die Frühe Neuzeit*. Köln-Weimar-Wien: Böhlau: 97-117.

Varanini, G. M. (ed.) 2023. *Rituali civici e continuità istituzionale nelle città italiane in età moderna*. Roma: Viella. Online ed. Rituali civici e continuità istituzionale nelle città italiane in età moderna (viella.it).

Verdon, J. 2002. *Boire au Moyen Âge*. Paris: Perrin.

Vergani, R. 2010. Problemi d'acque e scavo di canali nell'alta pianura veneta dei secoli XIV-XVI, in Calzona and Lamberini (eds) II: 507-526.

Vigarello, G. 1987. *Lo sporco e il pulito. L'igiene del corpo dal Medio Evo a oggi*. It. transl. Venezia: Marsilio.

Vigarello, G. 1996. *Il sano e il malato. Storia della cura del corpo dal Medioevo a oggi*. It. transl. Venezia: Marsilio.

Visentin, L. 2016. *Alle fonti del Medio Evo. Fontane medievali dal XIII al XIV secolo in Italia*. Arezzo: Helicon.

Water Management in Europe (12th-18th Centuries) 2018. Prato-Firenze: Firenze University Press.

Water Meteorological Organization. Public.wmo.int/en/our-mandate/water.

Wickham, Ch. 2015. *Sleepwalking into a New World: The Emergence of Italian City Communes in the Twelfth Century*. Princeton: Princeton University Press.

Williams, M. 2006. *Deforesting the Earth. From Prehistory to Global Crisis. An Abridgment*. Chicago: The University of Chicago Press.

Wirozumsky, J. 1986. Les communications fluviales en Pologne du XIIe au XVIIIe siècles (Aspects économiques et techniques), in A. Vannini Marx (ed.) *Trasporti e sviluppo economico, secoli XIII-XVIII*. Firenze: Le Monnier: 164-177.

Wittfogel, K. A. 1957. *Oriental Despotism. A Comparative Study of Total Power*. Yale: Yale University Press.

Worster, D. 1985. *Rivers of Empire. Water, Aridity and the American West*. Oxford: Oxford University Press.

Zagli, A. (ed.) 2003. *Uomini del Padule. Lavoro, vita, tradizioni nel Padule di Fucecchio dal Medioevo a oggi*. Firenze: Polistampa.

Zaneri, T. and G. Geltner. 2020. The Dynamics of Healthscaping: Mapping Communal Hygiene in Bologna, 1287-1383. *Urban History* 47: 1-26.

Zanoboni, M. P. 2009. Il commercio del legname. *Rassegna di studi e di notizie* 39: 115-132.
Zanotti, A. 2000. *Il sistema delle acque a Bologna dal XIII al XIX secolo*. Bologna: Compositori.
Ziegler, P. 1982. *The Black Death*. London: Penguin (3rd ed.).
Zimolo, G. C. 1939. Cremona nella storia della navigazione interna, in *Atti e memorie del terzo Congresso storico lombardo*. Milano: R. Deputazione di Storia patria per la Lombardia: 221-266.
Zorzi, A. 1994. Rituali di violenza, cerimoniali penali, rappresentazioni della giustizia nelle città italiane centro-settentrionali (secoli XIII-XV), in *Le forme della propaganda politica nel Due e nel Trecento*. Roma: École française de Rome: 395-425.
Zorzi, A. 2010a. L'acqua e i rituali giudiziari nel tardo Medioevo, in Calzona and Lamberini (eds) I: 121-142.
Zorzi, A. 2010b. Scrivere le regole: l'Italia degli statuti, in S. Luzzato and G. Pedullà (eds). *Atlante della letteratura italiana*. I. A. De Vincentiis (dir.) *Dalle origini al Rinascimento*. Torino: Einaudi: 48-54.
Zorzi, A. 2011. L'angoscia delle repubbliche. Il "timor" nell'Italia comunale degli anni Trenta del Trecento, in A. Gamberini, J.-Ph. Genet and A. Zorzi (eds) *The Languages of Political Society. Western Europe, 14th-17th Centuries*. Roma: Viella: 287-324.
Zorzi, A. 2013a. Fonti normative e statutarie nei secoli XII-XIV. *Archivio storico italiano* 171/3: 415-541.
Zorzi, A. 2013b. Ripensando i vicariati imperiali e apostolici, in P. Grillo (ed.) *Signorie italiane e modelli monarchici. Secoli XIII-XIV*. Roma: Viella: 19-43.
Zorzi, A. (ed.) 2008. *La civiltà comunale italiana nella storiografia internazionale*. Firenze: Firenze University Press.
Zorzi, A. (ed.) 2013. *Tiranni e tirannide nel Trecento italiano*. Roma: Viella.
Zorzi, A. (ed.) 2020. *La libertà nelle città comunali e signorili italiane*. Roma: Viella.
Zucchini, M. 1965. Dai "Lavorieri del Po" ai Consorzi di Bonifica. *Rivista di Storia dell'Agricoltura* 5/3: 260-289.
Zupko, R. E. and R. A. Laures. 1996. *Straws in the Wind. Medieval Urban Environmental Law. The Case of Northern Italy*. London-New York: Routledge.

Figures

Figure 1. Rome, Aqua Virgo pipeline, I c. b.C., refurbished during the Middle Ages. ©2023 Francesco Salvestrini.

Figure 2. Rome, Aqua Virgo pipeline. ©2023 Francesco Salvestrini.

Figure 3. Siena Fountain of Pescaia, 13th c. ©2023 Francesco Salvestrini.

Figure 4. Siena, Fonte Branda, 13th c. ©2023 Francesco Salvestrini.

Figure 5. L'Aquila, Fontana della Riviera, 13th c. ©2023 Francesco Salvestrini.

Figure 6. Perugia, Fontana Maggiore, 13th c. ©2023 Francesco Salvestrini.

Figure 7. Massa Marittima (GR), Fonte dell'Abbondanza, 13th-14th c. ©2023 Francesco Salvestrini.

Figure 8. Massa Marittima (GR), Fonte dell'Abbondanza, Fertility Tree fresco. ©2023 Francesco Salvestrini.

Figure 9. Sassari, Fontana del Rosello, 17th c. ©2023 Francesco Salvestrini.

Figure 10. San Gimigano (SI), Piazza della Cisterna, 13th-14th c. ©2023 Francesco Salvestrini.

Figure 11. San Gimignano (SI), Piazza della Cisterna. ©2023 Francesco Salvestrini.

Figure 12. Pistoia, Piazza della Sala and Pozzo del Leoncino, 13th-16th c. ©2023 Francesco Salvestrini.

Figure 13. Stroncone (TR), Fontana Vecchia, 14th c. ©2023 Francesco Salvestrini.

Figure 14. Stroncone (TR), Fontana delle Tre Tazze, 16th c. ©2023 Francesco Salvestrini.

Figure 15. Fontecchio (AQ), 14th c. Fountain. ©2023 Francesco Salvestrini.

Figure 16. San Gimignano (SI), Medieval 'Fonti', 13th c. ©2023 Francesco Salvestrini.

Figure 17. San Gimignano (SI), Medieval 'Fonti'. ©2023 Francesco Salvestrini.

Figure 18. Poggibonsi (SI) Fonte delle Fate. ©2023 Francesco Salvestrini.

Figure 19. Volterra (PI), Fonti di Docciola, 13th c. ©2023 Francesco Salvestrini.

Figure 20. Volterra (PI), Fonte San Felice, 14th c. ©2023 Francesco Salvestrini.

Figure 21. Todi (PG), Fonte di Scannabecco, 13th c. ©2023 Francesco Salvestrini.

Figure 22. Gagliano Aterno (AQ), Fountain, 14th c. ©2023 Francesco Salvestrini.

Figure 23. Isernia, Fontana della Fraterna, 13th-20th c. ©2023 Francesco Salvestrini.

Figure 24. Viterbo, Fontana Grande or 'del Sepale', 13th c. ©2023 Francesco Salvestrini.

Figure 25. Spoleto (PG) Ponte delle Torri, 14th c. ©2023 Francesco Salvestrini.

Figure 26. Spoleto (PG), Ponte delle Torri. ©2023 Francesco Salvestrini.

Figure 27. Sulmona (AQ), Acquedotto Svevo, 13th c. ©2023 Francesco Salvestrini.

Figure 28. Sulmona AQ), Fontana Del Vecchio, 15th c. ©2023 Francesco Salvestrini.

Figure 29. Orvieto (TR), Antonio da Sangallo il Giovane, Pozzo di San Patrizio, 16th c. ©2023 Francesco Salvestrini.

Figure 30. Verona, Ponte Scaligero or 'di Castelvecchio', 14th c. ©2023 Francesco Salvestrini.

Figure 31. Bernardo Bellotto (1721-80), Verona, Ponte delle Navi, 14th-19th c., private collection. All right reserved.

Figure 32. Bassano del Grappa (VI), Ponte Vecchio, 13th-16th c. ©2023 Francesco Salvestrini.

Figure 33. Venezia, Ponte Chiodo. ©2023 Francesco Salvestrini.

Figure 34. Pavia, Ponte Coperto, 14th c. ©2023 Francesco Salvestrini.

Figure 35. Pavia, Ponte Coperto, post-World War II reconstruction. ©2023 Francesco Salvestrini.

Figure 36. Anonymous, 17th c., Alessandria, 'Ponte Coperto' over the Tanaro river (14th-15th c.), Alessandria, Sale d'Arte Comunali. All right reserved.

Figure 37. Pesaro, Ponte di Fermignano, 14th c. ©2023 Francesco Salvestrini.

Figure 38. Firenze, Ponte Vecchio, 14th c. ©2023 Francesco Salvestrini.

Figure 39. Firenze, Ponte Santa Trinita, 13th-16th c., before the 20th c. reconstruction.
©2023 Francesco Salvestrini.

Figure 40. Verona, Fontana 'Madonna Verona', 14th c., from reclaimed Roman materials.
©2023 Francesco Salvestrini.

Figure 41. Ludovico degli Uberti (from), View of Florence known as 'della Catena', 15th c. Original in Berlin, Kupferstichkabinett. All right reserved.

Figure 42. Caspar van Wittel (1652-53-1736), Verona, View of the Adige near the Church of San Giorgio in Braida, Verona, Casa Museo Palazzo Maffei. All right reserved.

Figure 43. Giuseppe Zocchi (1711-67), Firenze, View of the Arno from Porta San Niccolò, engraving. ©2023 Francesco Salvestrini.

Figure 44. Giuseppe Zocchi (1711-67), Firenze, View of the Arno from Porta San Niccolò, detail.

Figure 45. Firenze, 'pescaia' Santa Rosa. ©2023 Francesco Salvestrini.

Figure 46. Philippe Galle (1537-1612), from Jan Van der Straet (1523-1605), 'La pesca nell'Arno', engraving. ©2023 Francesco Salvestrini.

Figure 47. Bernardo Bellotto (1721-80), Firenze, 'Piazza delle Travi', private collection. All right reserved.

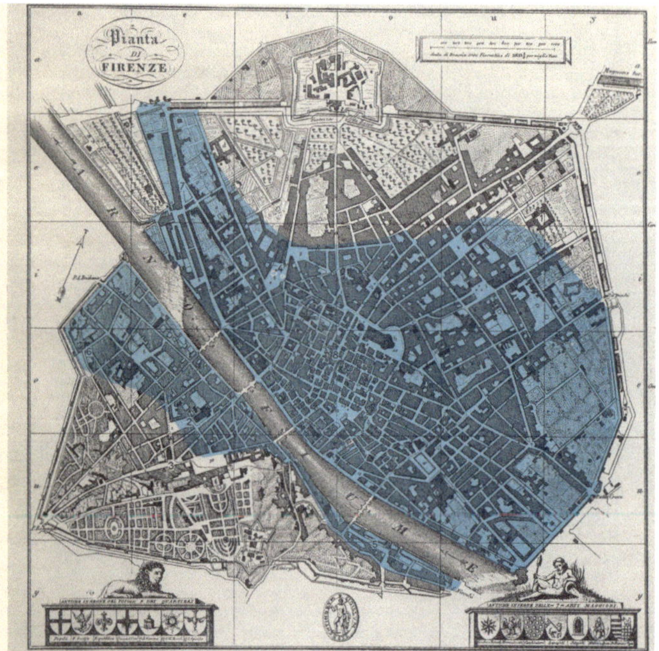

Figure 48. Approximate extent of flooded areas during the floods of medieval and modern Florence. ©2023 Francesco Salvestrini.

Figure 49. Florence floods (S = serious event)
©2023 Francesco Salvestrini.

12th century
??-11-1177

13th century
??-??-1200/01
??-10-1261
01-10-1269 S
15-12-1282
02-04-1284
05-12-1288

14th century
??-??-1302/03
??-01-1305
04-11-1333 S
05-12-1334
06-11-1345
??-11-1362
01-11-1368
21-07-1378
20-10-1380

15th century
??-05-1406
??-12-1434
18-10-1456
16-01-1465
19-01-1490
10-06-1491

16th century
24-08-1508
08-01-1515
28-08-1520
15-12-1532
??-??-1538
06-11-1543
15-11-1544
13-08-1547 S
08-11-1550
13-09-1557 S
31-10-1589 S

17th century
??-01-1621
09-11-1641
06-11-1646
??-01-1651
04-11-1660
11-05-1674
11-10-1676
19-02-1677
18-05-1680
20-04-1683
26-01-1687
08-12-1688
02-06-1695
??-01-1698

18th century
11-10-1705
28-02-1709
22-10-1714
06-09-1715
??-11-1719
03-12-1740 S
19-10-1745
01-12-1758 S
15-11-1761

19th century
03-11-1844 S
06-11-1864

20th century
04-11-1966 S

Indexes

by Francesco Borghero and Francesco Salvestrini

Personal names

Place names